To Josephine –
Merry Christmas 1976
with love,
Suzie Shea

THE PSYCHIC WORLD OF CALIFORNIA

Books by David St. Clair

Child of the Dark
Safari
The Mighty, Mighty Amazon
Drum & Candle
The Psychic World of California

THE PSYCHIC WORLD
OF CALIFORNIA

David St. Clair

Doubleday & Company, Inc.

Garden City, New York

1972

For
Lee St. Clair
 —my father,
who won't agree with anything here
but will be proud that I've written it.

Acknowledgments

No one ever writes a book alone, especially this type of book. There are many people I want to thank. First, all those included in the text who gave me their valuable time and rearranged their busy schedules so I could interview them. Secondly, a number of people went out of their way to help me and to make sure I remained on the right track. With my deepest gratitude, they are: Wally and Yvonne Purtell, James Bolen of *Psychic* magazine and his secretary Valerie Leavick, Catherine Motta, Maggie and Gene Anthony, Jean Basile, the ladies at the California Historical Association Library in San Francisco, Isel de Carvalho, Rita Brown, Marcia Warzek, Norma Dart, Jerry Quintero, Doris Doane, Wanda Sue Parrott, Mike Elley, Jim and Brenda Crenshaw, Gordon Parks, Suzanne Crayson, Marjorie Kern of the Southern California Society for Psychical Research, Robert Betts and Bill Giandoni of Copley News Service, Jan Washburn, Priscilla Badger of *Time* magazine in New York, Dana M. Bailey, Jr., and Louise Kensy Tschugunov of Warren, Ohio, my agent Jim Brown, my editor Lee Barker and his wonderful secretary Jane Carvill.

And a special thank-you to Alberto Aguas, who bore it all uncomplainingly.

A Very Short Preface

Most people consider a preface superfluous, so I'll keep this one short. I only want to say that this book took one year, July 1970 to June 1971, to research and write. I traveled hundreds of miles around California from Mt. Shasta in the north to El Centro in the south, finding, evaluating and interviewing psychics, mediums, metaphysicians and the just plain bizarre.

There will be those who will say I've included some that don't belong and others who will cry I've excluded some that do belong. In an area this large with as many members of the occult as it has, there are bound to be questions raised over the contents of this book. Fine.

The first part deals with the fascinating occult history of California. At least I think it's fascinating. Those who find history a bore or who want to immediately meet the Psychic State's cast of characters are advised to turn to page 47, where the 1970's begin.

Each person selected for these pages was recommended to me by at least three different people whose judgment and knowledge of the field I respect. Occasionally after I met and interviewed a person I wound up scrapping him altogether, for reasons of my own. The feelings were mine. The judgment was mine. The final selection is mine.

I have not tried to "expose" anybody. To printedly denounce a psychic never was my intent. The frauds were always discovered in time. My purpose was to show these members of the Psychic State as human beings first and psychics second. My purpose was to find out what they did, how they did it and—most importantly—how the reader of this book could use this information in his own arduous search for psychic development.

This book was not written for the professional, for the skeptic, for the know-it-all. It was written for the man in America today who feels there is "something" somewhere. If I can help him find that "something," then this work will have served its purpose.

Contents

What Has Gone Before

In the beginning God created heaven and earth.
And California.
The Lemurians populated it.
And a black goddess gave it her name.

California, America's most psychic, occult and mystic state. California, the strangest state in the nation. Everyone admits it. No one disputes it. The forces of good and evil are at work in California. This is nothing new. The occult has been a way of life there since time immemorial.

Scientists continue to discover that there was human life in what is today known as California long before there was anybody anywhere else in the United States. Anthropologists have calculated that man walked the North American continent only 20,000 years ago, yet 1970 discoveries in the Mojave Desert of Southern California led Dr. Louis S. B. Leakey to declare that man lived in the Mojave Desert as early as 50,000 years ago "and more probably 100,000 years ago." Stone chips have been tested that "may date back as far as 120,000 years."

California mystics (and some historians) were not surprised by the discoveries, for they believe that California is nothing else but the remnants of the fabled continent of Lemuria.

California is different, even materialistic geologists admit it. The entire West Coast, from Vancouver to Lower California, holds distinctive and uniform differences in soil, plant life, minerals and fossils unlike anything else found in the rest of the United States. This land, lying between the eastern foothills of the Sierra Nevada to the Pacific Ocean shore, is markedly different from the land that is east of the Sierra Nevada or the foothills of the Cascade Range. Here things grow more prolifically than anywhere else. Here also are the oldest living objects on the North American continent: the giant redwood trees.

It was on this narrow strip of land—about three hundred miles in width and several thousand miles long—that the last survivors of the sinking continent of Lemuria took refuge. Theirs had been a mighty civilization, but it was coming to an end. Ending not because of wars and famines, but because Nature was changing and was slowly destroying what had taken thousands of years to construct.

Lemuria, according to mystics, mediums and the Rosicrucians (in a book written by Wishar S. Cervé in 1931), was once a gigantic continent bigger than both North and South America combined. Its western coast fitted in exactly with the present-day coast of China, down under and across most of India, most of Africa and over to the eastern coast of South America. Its western border stretched all the way across the Pacific Ocean as far as eighty degrees longitude. This vast land mass was the only surface of the world that was above water. Areas we know today as the Americas, Europe, North Africa, Russia, China and Greenland were either completely submerged or just marshy swamplands.

Here, on Lemuria, man and all the other creatures were born. Here, on Lemuria, was the Garden of Eden.

The Lemurians were a strong and proud white race who were left to develop over thousands of years into industrious, adventurous and highly psychic individuals. Granted, they had to start out as primitives but they had hundreds of thousands of years in which to progress. They had (say ancient manuscripts) stones that repelled water. They would tie two or three of these stones onto a raft and be pushed forward across the oceans. They build things to last, making their temples of marble and granite and decorating them with symbols so future generations would know who had gone before. They also had a lump in the middle of their foreheads. This was not a "third eye" but a gland that tuned them in to others at a distance much as we tune in a radio receiver. Where we will "stop and think" about something, the Lemurians would "stop and tune in" on something. Thus they were able to communicate with one another anywhere in their civilization. Also, they believed in reincarnation and picked their own time to die. They would dig their graves, say good-by to their families and friends and lie down. Three days later the family would pour strong acids over their bodies and fill in the grave.

The Lemurians were great travelers and colonists. They had to be, for they knew that their continent was sinking into the sea and they needed to find new places to dwell, places that were high and permanent. For as long as any Lemurian could recall there had been rumblings and volcanic explosions as chunks of their land fell into the water. Their continent was drifting just as the other swampy areas of the globe were drifting. The idea of a "continental drift," so new to us today was old hat to the Lemurians.

The first drastic changes in their land came about a hundred thousand years ago. The earth under Europe and Asia began to rise. Mountains formed and rivers cut through newly dried areas. This movement made the waters around relatively flat Lemuria rise and its western portion fell and was inundated. Magnetic waves, about eighty-two thousand years ago, caused portions of Lemuria connected with Africa and Asia to fall off or sink, leaving a series of islands and the continent of Australia. As Europe rose higher, more waters inundated Lemuria until it was about half its former size and isolated in the Pacific. Then about seventy-five thousand years ago the continents began to drift more and more. Africa separated from South America and Europe. Europe pulled away from North America while Greenland separated from Canada and northern Europe. The oceans' waters again ate away at lowland Lemuria while pushing it closer and closer to the American continent.

Now the Lemurians knew it was time to re-establish their culture in other places. Colonists went westward into the higher and drier areas of Europe. Others chose the fertile valley of the Nile and still others took the high land of Alaska. Then a new cataclysm occurred that pushed a land mass up between North America and Europe. This (probably) was Atlantis. As it rose it pushed other areas, especially in South America, to new heights. Where marshy lands had been enclosed by higher lands, deep lakes and streams were formed. It is possible that Hudson Bay was once a great sea connected with the St. Lawrence River and the Great Lakes. The Mississippi Valley had a great river that connected with an inland sea in the Colorado Valley. Utah's Salt Lake is a present-day remnant of an extensive Lemurian-era sea. Another sea was formed in South America in what is now the Amazon Valley. (Geologists have found coal, petroleum, fossils of mountain animals and oceanic fish in the Amazon soil.) The Lemurians used the "Amazon Sea," which met the Pacific at Ecuador and ran into the Atlantic, to sail to and colonize Atlantis. For generations they sought higher lands, abandoning their own sinking continent for the mountains of Central and South America and the western end of Atlantis (where the Gulf of Mexico is today). There was also emigration to Africa. Those who remained in isolated areas like the highlands of Australia, the Pacific atolls and the mountains of Japan slowly evolved their own ideas, languages and customs. It was at this time that the various races began to appear, for scientists have proven that the sun, the climate and food will, over a long period, change human skin pigmentation and body characteristics. And all this began, let us not forget, some seventy thousand years ago.

And there is something else we must not forget: the face of our earth is still changing. In just the past few years, earthquakes have eroded the coastline of Chile, volcanos have suddenly appeared in Mexico and Asia, tidal waves have washed away hunks of Pakistan and rivers have changed their courses to devour new lands. The United States has had to resurvey its borders with Mexico because of a river's erratic motion. The town of Carauari was built on the *right* bank of the Juruá River in Brazil. After a few years the river cut through it making it half on firm ground and half on an island. Today it sits on the *left* bank of the river, placed there by the waters themselves. In other words, it does not take a very great cataclysm to make changes in the earth's surface. Navy scientists claim that if there was an undersea movement that would raise the surface of the earth just four thousand feet *all* the continents would be connected by land above water.

The catastrophe that hit Atlantis was swift and sudden. It happened about fifteen thousand years ago, say the mystics, and millions of lives were lost. It sank into the Atlantic ocean, pulling down mountains and cities. The waters rushed in, forming the Gulf of Mexico. The islands of Cuba, Puerto Rico and the West Indies were too high to submerge completely. The majority of the people who called themselves Mayans were taken to a watery grave. Only their westernmost temples and cities were spared. The survivors abandoned them, seeking higher lands, and were absorbed by those whose homes in the Andes were untouched. In other words, the Indians are descendants of Lemurian colonies.

When Atlantis sank, North America rose. The eastern end of Lemuria was now flush up against this continent and the last true Lemurians clung for dear life to the mountains and forests of the only remnant of their once great land mass. They carved caves in the hills and tried to salvage as much of their knowledge as they could. They were isolated from the other humans and much of their technical knowledge had been lost. Their heritage had helped the Aztecs, Mayans, Incas, Chinese and Egyptians to chart the heavens, work out a calendar and to fly gigantic rocks through the air to build their temples and pyramids. Like all dying cultures these last Lemurians were more concerned with philosophy and tradition than science and manual skills. Those who had elected to remain on the last vestige of their continent were teachers and wise men, rather than workers and builders. It was their duty to preserve knowledge, not preserve buildings. They were considered (by faraway colonists who remembered) as the Fathers of Wisdom. This now sacred strip of land would someday be called California.

Archeologists and students of the occult claim the Lemurian wise men settled four major areas: on the sites of the present-day cities of San Jose and Santa Barbara, near the town of Carmel and inside magnificent snowcapped Mt. Shasta.

More stories and legends surround Mt. Shasta than any place in

California. It sits incredibly large and capped with pure white snow rising 14,380 feet above sea level. A tiny town, called Mt. Shasta, sits at its feet. Villagers talk little about the legends. It's almost as if the community wants to keep the mountain from outsiders.

It is said that several hundred direct descendants of the Lemurian race *still live* inside this mountain. They have buildings of marble and onyx with domes plated in gold. Strange lights have been seen soaring into the black night. Fires have been reported to glow with a "white intense luminescence," and in 1929 (long before flying saucers came into vogue) a group of golfers reported seeing a silver vessel rise into the air, float across the mountaintop and vanish. They said it made no noise and was unlike anything any of them had ever seen. Others have gone into the forests around Mt. Shasta and have been met by "a gigantic shaggy human" who picked them up in his arms and turned them around, giving them the idea that they were to get out fast. People have driven into the area, only to have a white light suddenly flash in front of them that "stopped the power of my car. I couldn't do anything to get it started again. Only after I pushed it back a few yards and turned the wheels toward the main highway did the motor kick over and move the car." Old-timers tell of "strange Indians" who used to come out of the mountain to shop in local stores. They wore a simple headdress that went down to the bridge of their nose, thus covering up any chance of seeing an existing "thinking gland" in their foreheads. The strange men would pay for their purchases with gold nuggets and refuse any change, as if gold was so plentiful it was almost worthless to them. Early settlers found inscriptions on rocks that local Indians could not decipher, but, since then, archeologists have compared them and found symbols identical to those of the *Druids*. Early settlers also found out that when they asked local Indians why a place was called by a certain name, the Indians couldn't answer. Many times the Indians themselves didn't know the meaning of the place names, as these words were not in their vocabulary. Ethnologists learned that tribesmen called an area "the Valley of Knowledge" because legend said it was a meeting place for ancient wise men. Linguists came up with the idea that the local Indian name of "Walla-Was-Skeeny" was really the *Latin "Vallis Scientia,"* which means "valley of knowledge." The Indians called the lily *wocus*. The Latin word for it is *lotus*. The ruins of a supposedly Lemurian-built edifice on top of a mountain was called *moynia* by the local Indians, yet the Latin word for any walled in place is *moenia*. In 1913 Professor Edgar Larkin, the director of Mt. Lowe Observatory in Southern California was in this region testing a new telescope. By accident he trained it on the sides of Mt. Shasta and saw "the gold tinted dome of some Oriental building." Soon he could see three domes in the sunlight and a fourth building of marble. Dr. Larkin was positive no such buildings existed in that part of the state and left the telescope trained on the site to see what nightfall would bring. To his amazement (and later public derision) he reported white lights illuminating these buildings even though there was no moon. He saw smoke rising from the forest. In 1932 a skeptical reporter from the Los Angeles *Times* went to Mt. Shasta to debunk the myths once and for all. His conclusion surprised even himself: "It is not, therefore, incredible that the last sons of lost Lemuria are nestled at the foot of Mt. Shasta's volcano. The real incredible thing is that these staunch descendants of that vanished race have succeeded in secluding themselves in the midst of our teeming state."

While it was the Lemurians that populated the state, it was a black goddess called Califia that gave it her name. (Both Women's Lib and Black Militants please note.) In 1510 Spanish novelist García Ordoñez de Montalvo published the revamped version of a story that had been known in Europe since the Crusades. He called his novel *Las Sergas de Esplandian* (The Exploits of Esplandian). It was about a mythical island "to the right of the Indies, very near the quarter of the terrestrial paradise and where there is a great abundance of gold and precious stones." The island was populated exclusively by women. Men were taken there for breeding purposes and sent away when the warrior ladies became pregnant. Any man there illegally was hunted down by packs of griffins wearing gem-encrusted harnesses. The island was called California after its ruler, the mighty (and beautiful) Black Queen Califia.

This legend was foremost in the minds of the Spanish when they came into Mexico. They heard, from the Aztecs and others, that there was a land to the north that was tropical and abundant with gold. When they wrote home they referred to this unknown country as "California." The name stuck.

De Montalvo had based his novel on old legends and the fact that he called it "the terrestrial paradise" ties in closely with ancient ideas that Lemuria was the original Garden of Eden. The amounts of gold, the climate and the richness of the soil make one wonder if his novel was not based upon tales of prehistoric expeditions to the last remaining segment of Lemuria.

The man Spain chose to conquer this mystic state was a mystic himself. Father Junípero Serra was a Franciscan who believed not only in the power of the Lord but the power of the mind. His faith tamed Indians, placated the military and healed his own body.

Father Juniper was born Miguel José Serra on the island of Majorca in 1713. Like all boys of his age he thrilled to the stories of his Spanish countrymen who had discovered such romantic places as the Philippines, the Amazon, Peru and Mexico. He grew up with two ambitions: to be a priest and to see the New World. At fifteen he entered a seminary, took on the robes of St. Francis and the new name of Junípero. He studied hard and even though in frail health and suffering from all sorts of ailments, he was ordained a priest at twenty-three. That same year he was asked to teach philosophy at the Lullian University, his Franciscan college. For thirteen years he read and taught and gained honors in the religious community; then one day he told his superiors that he wanted to go to Mexico. They argued that he was almost thirty-six years old and had a comfortable position. Also, they pointed out, his health was bad. Juniper countered with his own arguments and three days after Easter of 1749 he set sail for New Spain.

The voyage was dreadful. It lasted ninety-nine days. Food was scarce and water was rationed to a half cup daily. While the sailors complained, Juniper never seemed to mind. Once the captain asked him, "Are you not thirsty?" His reply: "I have found a good remedy against thirst. That is to eat little, to talk less and to save my saliva."

When they landed in Vera Cruz, the priest refused the horses the Viceroy had sent to carry him to Mexico City and insisted on walking the hundreds of miles over rough country. Again the captain asked: "How can you possibly make such a journey, alone and on foot? How can you carry enough food?"

"The Lord will provide," he answered, and set out with another friar wearing nothing but a cloth robe, sandals and a crucifix. He took no provisions, yet (and this is considered the first of his many "miracles") he was fed and given a dry place to sleep each night. One evening an insect bit his foot. He scratched it and the next morning his foot and leg were swollen and infected. These infections never healed but remained a kind of New World stigmata, causing him pain and suffering as long as he lived.

He spent a few months in Mexico City and then was given the task of converting some fierce villagers in the Sierra Gorda mountains. He worked there for nine years, founding a church and finally taking over as administrator of all the missions in that area. His foot and leg pained him badly, but he still spent six months of each year walking from village to village and mission to mission.

At this time the King of Spain was beginning to worry about the Russians and the English. News came that the British had defeated the French in Quebec and would probably move across the waters to New Spain. (They still thought the land they called California was an island.) The Russians had taken hold in Alaska and were trapping animals and sending hides to European markets. Spain was afraid the Russians would start trapping in California as well. There were Jesuit missions in Baja California and as far north as Sonora, but Upper California was unmapped, unprotected and unknown. Padre Juniper, on the basis of his work in Mexico, was chosen to establish new missions.

He arrived in Baja California and met the tough soldier who was to command the military part of the expedition: José Gálvez. He had a map, drawn a hundred years earlier, of what the coast of upper California looked like, and with Padre Serra, made a plan to set up mission-forts at strategic places northward. The first was to be at San Diego de Alcala, the second, in honor of San Carlos, at Monterey and the third, in honor of San Buenaventura, at the Santa Barbara Channel.

"Don José," Padre Juniper said, "you have named a mission for

San Diego, another for San Carlos and another for San Buenaventura. But is there to be no mission in honor of our father San Francisco?"

"If St. Francis desires a mission," replied the soldier, "let him show us his harbor."

They left, the soldiers in two ships and Padre Serra on foot. He was fifty-six years old.

At San Diego, after a torturous walk (where he met a muleteer who rubbed some homemade salve on his foot and leg that "miraculously" let him continue his journey), he found the soldiers who had gone before him dying of scurvy and the plague. Supplies of food and medicine had run out and the captain wanted to return to Mexico. Serra refused to leave, praying fervently to God for another "miracle." He knew that the missions would never be founded if they pulled out now. He also wanted to see as a reality the buildings, schools and farms he had created in his imagination. Each sunrise he and the army leader, Portolá, climbed to the top of a hill and searched the horizon for a miracle ship, and each night Serra had to convince the man to "put his trust in God" for just one more day.

On March 19, the feast day of St. Joseph, patron saint of California, Padre Serra finished celebrating a High Mass and listened to the sounds of preparations being made to return the next day to Mexico. Sadly he climbed the hill and looked through the mists. Suddenly the fog parted and there was a ship. She was on her way northward when anchor trouble made the captain put into the port of San Diego. There were provisions and medicines for everyone ashore. The "Sacred Expedition" to secure California was saved. Father Serra had done it. A soldier wrote to his family: "When Padre Serra prays for miracles they happen!"

Next on the list, once the San Diego mission was functioning, was Monterey. Serra loved the area because it reminded him of his native Majorca and also because the mapping expedition of a hundred years earlier had planted a cross under an oak tree on the beach. Serra's expedition found the cross and they also saw pieces of meat, fish and gifts that the Indians had placed at its base, in obvious reverence to its spiritual power. A Royal Chapel was built alongside a Royal Presidio, thus establishing Monterey as the civil and spiritual headquarters of the Spanish Kingdom in Upper California.

California had been conquered by the Spaniards. Never had there been a conquest equal to it. A land larger than the British Isles had been taken, peacefully, by sixty-four soldiers and a determined priest.

In 1769 a Spanish ship headed north sailed, by accident, into the narrow entrance of a choppy bay. The ship's padre reported back to the officers at Monterey: "I think that if it could be well settled like Europe, there would not be anything more beautiful in all the world, for it has the best advantages for founding in it a most beautiful city . . . with that harbour so remarkable and so spacious, in which may be established shipyards, docks, and anything that might be wished."

"You remember," Padre Serra chided the military, "if St. Francis wanted a mission he would show you a harbor? Well, he has shown it."

The ageing and ailing priest kept walking and establishing missions in places where no white man had ever gone before. By 1784 he had set up—and saw running—nine separate mission stations. Most of them administering and converting the local Indian population, were a stopover for colonists coming up from Mexico and outposts for the military. Then he returned to Monterey. "I have come home to die." He waited until his old friends could come and see him and until he had given his last instructions to the directors of the various missions. He gave the carpenter measurements for his coffin and knelt at the altar while the last rites were administered. Then he lay down on a rough wooden bed, clasped the crucifix he had carried with him from Majorca, said "Now I shall rest," and died.

Word spread quickly as hundreds of settlers and Indians came to pay their last respects. A guard had to be put around his body as everyone wanted to "touch the saint for the last time." The roses that covered him were stolen and kept as amulets. Pieces of his robe were snipped off as relics and sailors cut off locks of his white hair as a safeguard against shipwrecks.

Legends and "miracles" grew up quickly around his name. When he died, the bells at Monterey pealed all by themselves. Angels' hands had rung them, it was said. It was recalled that he walked for hundreds of miles never carrying a bit of food or water. "The Lord will provide," he had always said.

His always open wounds, which gave him so much trouble, were never looked at by any doctor. When the pains became unbearable he would calmly sit down, concentrate on his body, and pray that the pains would go away. They always did.

Once Serra and a companion became lost at sundown in an area with only cactus and thorn bushes. After praying for guidance they noticed a small adobe house with a burro tethered to three cottonwood trees in front. When they entered the hut they saw a beautiful woman with a fair-haired child sitting at her feet. The little boy was playing with a baby lamb. There was an old man there who invited them to share their simple meal. Padre Serra was enchanted with the beauty of the little boy and when the priest blessed the child before he went to bed, the lad raised his hand and made the sign of the cross.

The next day, when Serra arrived at his destination, he told about the hospitable family, only to be informed by permanent residents at the mission that there was no home like that anywhere in the area. To prove that he was right he led a group back the very way he had come. He found the three cottonwood trees, the only ones to be seen in the region, but the house was gone. There was no sign of any humans having been there. Serra was perplexed for a minute, then knelt and prayed, certain that he had visited with the Holy Family. He considered it a sign of heaven's blessing on his work.

The most famous legend around Serra concerns the swallows who return to the mission of Capistrano. For more than 150 years, on St. Joseph's Day, March 19, a flock of swallows has winged in from the ocean. They settle down for the summer in mud nests amid the ruined arches. Then, as if on schedule, on St. John's Day, October 3, they fly away.

Citizens of the Psychic State are well aware of their debt to Padre Serra and plaques and statues abound to him. In 1933 the people of California designated him as one of the two greatest men from their state to be placed in National Statuary Hall in Washington, D.C. His name is being considered by the Vatican for canonization.

The missions continued to thrive under Serra's successors until Mexico declared her independence from Spain. Then the revolutionaries who took over the government took over the religious outposts in Upper California as well. Secular administrators arrived like Spanish-speaking carpetbaggers to exploit the Indians and rob the missions. In 1844 the Mexican government, in order to get funds to fight the United States, sold the mission lands and whatever was left of the buildings to private individuals. The priests and the devout Indians had long been gone. In 1848 the U.S. took California from Mexico by the Treaty of Guadalupe Hidalgo. The "Psychic State" was now part of the United States, but the missions were used as army storage depots and flophouses for deserters and vagabonds. It was then that the spirits made James Marshall bend over and pick up a glittering heavy stone at a place called Sutter's Mill.

On January 24, 1848, Marshall went out as usual to superintend the men who were working for him. They were constructing a millrace by tossing out the heavier stones and using the natural force of water to wash away the remaining stones, gravel and sand. He stood that morning at the lower end of the race and glanced at the mass of debris that had been washed down. "I don't know what made me notice it," he often said later to friends and reporters, "but my eye was attracted to a glitter some six inches below the water. There are those who say it was Divine Providence that pointed that gold nugget out to me. There are others who say it was the Devil."

No matter from which end of the spirit world the impulse came, the fact is that gold was discovered in California. James Marshall's life was never to be the same. The news broke and workmen at the mill left their jobs to grab shovels, dishpans and sluice boxes. Workers from neighboring farms and ranches poured onto the property and started digging. Land around Sutter's place was invaded with frantic, hungry men. After they had marked off claims to land that wasn't theirs the men turned on Marshall. They were sure that he knew where other gold fields lay. They reasoned that if he had been shown the first strike by "the spirits," then the entities would probably have shown him where other veins were. Mobs followed him everywhere. If he went out of town he was followed by crowds who were sure he was on his way to secret diggings. If he remained at home he was watched as if he were under house arrest. Once a mob, brave on liquor and gold fever, grabbed Marshall and carried him to a nearby tree, threatening him with hanging if he didn't ask his "spirit helpers" where the rest of the gold was buried. A friend managed to snatch him away and send him riding out of town on a fast horse. He died a heartsick and poverty-stricken man. If his life had been vastly changed by his discovery of that nugget, so had the life of the "Psychic State."

The world poured into California. It came across the prairies from the eastern states. It went down around South America and up the other side. It came across the Gulf of Mexico and up. It came from Europe. It came from Australia. It came from the Orient. And it came hopeful, impoverished, ignorant, avaricious, arrogant, proud, pious and superstitious.

San Francisco got it all at once, like a meat pie full in the face. Sutter's Mill was in the northern part of the state, near San Francisco. There was a fine, beautiful port in San Francisco, perfect for boats bringing in the miners. It was easily reached straight across the plains and over the mountains. Padre Serra's religious outpost turned into the roughest, toughest, bawdiest town in the world.

Life wasn't worth a cent but eggs and medicines were worth dollars. Miners spent months in the forests to bring back a sack of gold they spent in days. Merchants, especially Chinese, Jewish and Italian, made easy fortunes from those who were sure just one more sift of the sand would bring them theirs. Clapboard buildings sprang up around the main square and straggled out in wiggly streets up the steep hills. Hotels and boardinghouses with nothing but mattresses on the floor were everywhere. Saloons and whorehouses were conveniently located right downtown. The busiest place was the Post Office, as miners, adventurers and juvenile runaways stood in line for hours to see if they had any news (or money) from home.

One resident was appalled over the number of immigrants and miners who were unable to cope with this rough existence and went mad. There were no insane asylums in town. "Maniacs were fastened with chains to trees or posts in the stables and the harmless lunatics were locked up in deserted ships in the harbor."

As money started flowing in regularly, wives and sweethearts came to San Francisco to join their husbands. Other women came looking for a rich catch. Wrote another resident: "Someone has remarked that in Eastern cities the prostitutes tried to imitate in the manner and dress the fashionable respectable ladies, but in San Francisco the rule is reversed—the latter copying after the former."

There were fires almost every day and some of them burned over half the city each time. But the early settlers were tough people in a tough place and they cleared the debris and rebuilt their clapboard structures.

Los Angeles felt almost none of the gold pressure. It was too far south, there was no way to get there except over the mountains or by choppy coastal steamer and when you did get there there was nothing to see. In 1875, when San Francisco was swinging from crystal chandeliers and quaffing imported champagne, Los Angeles had only 7,000 people, three banks, three hotels, one streetcar line and "the sewage was dumped on the corner of Tenth and Main to be used as fertilizer. But when evening breezes blew . . ."

The miners' very existence was based on luck and several were killed for the rabbit's foot, coin or amulet that had made them lucky. Charlatans moved through the camps selling magic gold dowsing rods, potions that if taken at bedtime would reveal gold in dreams and printed prayers and rituals to make the believer wealthy.

Then the mediums, astrologers and psychics came in and set up shop. Some had made good money forecasting events in the mining camps but others found it too risky. A New Orleans Negro who went into the northern camps working voodoo spells was captured and put into a rustic cage. For three months the miners bombarded him with questions about gold sites and their own futures. Finally the psychic became ill and the men let him go when they saw his powers wane.

The San Francisco City Directory listed 2,500 names in 1850. In 1852 there were 9,000 names. By 1856 the book had almost doubled in size and carried a list of business and professional men. This was the first year that readers of the occult were given official recognition. Under "medium" were the forerunners of the thousands of psychics that have settled in this "Psychic State." Their names will probably, someday, be engraved on a bronze plaque:

> Madame Ann De Cassins. 381 Stockton Street
> Mrs. La Domus. 92 Broadway
> Madame Lucretia. Virginia and Washington Streets

Unfortunately nothing is known about these three occult pioneers today. They fail to appear in any other records and newspaper reporters ignored them. Two years later Mmes. La Domus and Lucretia were gone from the directory but Madame De Cassins (who seemed to have a new address each year and listed herself later as "fortune teller") kept showing up in the lists until 1866. The first male medium to be listed was Samuel Cohen in 1860. He changed his name to Simon in 1862 (either that or the directory had given him the wrong name at first).

In the classified section under "Astrology" of the San Francisco *Call* for November 29, 1873, he advertised:

> Dr. Cohen. The only living Astrologer: he tells the events of your whole life: gives advice so as to be benefited. Over 42,000 consultations given here in San Francisco: it is not necessary to give your age. Fees, $2: by letter, $3. Dr. Cohen is a Physician: has been very successful in curing all diseases. Office. No. 405 Kearny Street, near Pine. Guarantees satisfaction.

It is a credit to Dr. Cohen that he managed to stay in business until 1885, because being a medium in a small town means you have to call a lot of right shots. Apparently he did, and for twenty-five successful years.

While Dr. Cohen claimed to be "the only living Astrologer" in San Francisco, other mediums claimed to be other things. A sample of the San Francisco *Call*'s classifieds reveal:

> Madame Clara Antonia, M.D. Medical and Business Clairvoyant, Physician and Trance Medium. Consultation in English, French, or German. Correct Diagnosis of all diseases. Clairvoyant Examination of Minerals, Ores, Mines, Locks of Hair,

etc. Office 323 Kearney street, between Bush and Pine. Office hours from 10 A.M. to 6 P.M., and 7 to 10 P.M.

And:

Dr. John Roll, the most wonderful Fortune Teller in the world, can be found at No. 835 Pacific street, between Stockton and Powell. He uses all kinds of witchcraft, cures all diseases and spells, causes love, returns anything that is lost, stolen or run away and cures drunkards from drinking. He will give love and luck to all that want it. Don't forget to call and see him.

A Mrs. Hubbard announced that she was "very successful in the examination of minerals," while Professor Castillo explained "the past, present and future." An exotic touch was given by Madame Exodius, an "Egyptian Fortune Teller."

A Madame Clair announced that she had moved her office and that aside from being a "Doctress, Clairvoyant and Fortune Teller" she also had "a beautiful Enameling for the Face, sold at her office cheap." Madame Mary Schworer had the nerve to advertise herself as "the only reliable and first established Business and Medical Seeing Medium on this coast." Her address was at a certain corner "above the fruit store."

So impressed were San Franciscans by psychics and their powers that by 1880 the City Directory listed three astrologers, five mediums and twenty-one clairvoyants. The world of the occult had come to stay.

When Mammy Pleasant arrived in California in 1853 people were just beginning to talk about mediums and the occult. She considered it a rough but safe place, for she was evading the police even then.

Mary Ellen Pleasant was one of the strangest and most unforget-table characters of the Psychic State's early history. She was born a slave but through her powers and her incredible scheming she managed to dominate the city of San Francisco for almost half a century.

Her father was a white gentleman and her mother a light-skinned quadroon from the island of Hispaniola. Mary had her father's fine features and her mother's coloring. She also had her mother's cunning, for the Dominican slave (just before she was taken away from Mary and sold to another plantation) told her she was descended from a long line of island voodoo queens. "Be full of pride for your background," she told the child, "but don't be foolish to let others know your true feelings."

Mary was purchased by a Missouri businessman, who sent her to a convent in New Orleans to learn to read and write. Learn she did but she also managed to learn voodoo curses and rituals. When her schooling was over she was sent to a family in Cincinnati, Ohio, who foisted her off as a bondwoman to a wealthy lady in Nantucket. The woman furthered her education by teaching her how to manage a prosperous yard goods store, how to buy low and sell high, to make wine, to cook and to cater to the tastes of the wealthy. When Mary Ellen was twenty-four the old lady died and the shop burned down. She was free of her bondage. The first thing she did was marry a rich Cuban tobacco grower from Charles Town, West Virginia.

He had a plantation and lots of money and his beautiful wife (who straightened her hair, put lightener on her already fair skin and passed as white) spent his money on fine clothes and helping runaway slaves. She knew the plight of slavery firsthand and had seen the Underground Railroad in operation during her years in Cincinnati. Her husband wanted her to "just be pretty and stay away from Blacks," so the first time he got a serious cold, she took care of him herself. She was a wealthy widow at twenty-eight.

Immediately she took up with the plantation supervisor, a freed, almost white Negro from Richmond named John Plaissance. His father had been the bastard son of the Haitian dictator Henri Christophe and his favorite white mistress. Mary Ellen was fascinated by him even though he refused to marry her.

She was also fascinated by helping runaways get to the Canadian border but after eight years of it slave owners discovered what she was doing. She and Plaissance hid out in New Orleans. He married her (partly because he was overwhelmed by her physical attraction and partly because she had $20,000 in gold coin) and changed his name to Pleasants to suit her. (She later dropped the "s" to suit herself.) Then she insisted on meeting Marie Laveau.

Books have been written about Marie Laveau and her name still sends shivers down spines in New Orleans today. She was the most powerful voodoo queen of them all, making a fortune from strange orgiastic rites and by having spies in every prominent white home in the city. Marie and Mary Ellen hit it off at once. The only thing she did not admire about Marie was the coldness in which she murdered newborn babies. She had seen three dried bodies hanging in the voodoo queen's cupboard that were "rich white women's unwanted children." The whites paid Marie Laveau to do a little bit of everything, then they had to pay her not to tell.

When local authorities discovered Mary Ellen's slave-freeing background, they tried to arrest her. She got her husband on a ship for California, then blackened her face and took a job as cook on a wealthy plantation. Like everything she did, she did it too well; when her fame spread as a culinary artist people took notice of her, and that was when one of them recognized her. Soon she was slipping out of town on a boat bound for California. The route in those days was down the coast of South America, around the tip end and up the Pacific Coast. When they reached Valparaiso, Chile, there had been a revolution and several new passengers were taken aboard. One of these was a Scotchman named Thomas Bell. He was a bookkeeper, he told her, and had lost his job in a local bank. He hoped that San Francisco would treat him better. He never dreamed how much better.

When the ship finally docked in San Francisco word had somehow reached the newly rich townsmen that "the best damned cook in New Orleans" was aboard. Young bachelors waved money in her face and begged her to come work for them. She listened to all the offers, then accepted one that wanted her just to be overseeing housekeeper at five hundred dollars a month. She took it.

Thus began her rise to the top. The house was a plush boardinghouse for bachelors. The young men were wealthy businessmen and mine owners but the lack of wives (or any place decent to house them) forced them to room together. Mary Ellen cooked the best foods and served the best wines. She decorated the clapboard building with lace curtains and window plants. The men liked her sense of humor and her sharp mind and gave her gifts of money and gold dust. She took the money and invested it in the stocks, bonds and mining companies she heard them discussing.

The men of importance in early San Francisco all knew about Mammy Pleasant. It was a small world and for those who used their heads, it was a rich world. Mammy kept up a correspondence with friends back East and soon runaway slaves began to seek her out. She sweet-talked store owners and offices to give her Negro friends menial jobs. Soon the town took on an air of respectability as wealth built fine homes and brought fine women out to live in them. Mammy placed her Black friends in the best houses. The Negroes were indebted to her for finding them a good position, the wealthy white families were indebted to her for finding them good help. Soon Mammy had a network of Black informers all over town. It's always been difficult to keep family troubles and gossip from servants and when any juicy news item came down the back stairs, it was reported immediately to Mammy.

She had the nerve to approach rich white girls and offer to get rid of their illegitimate unborn babies. She gave women cures for their husbands' impotency, sold amulets and powders to make a faithless wife stay home and convinced politicians they needed her spy network to discover what their enemies were up to. Everything worked beautifully and Mammy became the owner of three laundries, a first-class livery stable, two boardinghouses and empty lots all across town. She built a huge home, where she held weekly voodoo ceremonies. The rituals were twofold. One, to keep her Black informants in awe of her, and two, to put on a show for the whites that ended in dancing, whiskey and sex.

Mammy had few scruples and much of her time was spent grooming desperate young ladies to become attractive mistresses and wives. She got $100,000 from a love-stricken banker when she presented him with a blond blue-eyed wife she had found in a cheap saloon. Once, hearing of an attractive girl who had been widowed on an incoming wagon train, Mammy was at the city limits to welcome her. With some new clothes and some of Mammy's own jewels, the girl became the mistress of San Francisco's richest businessman. Of course both of them paid her handsomely.

Then one day Mammy ran into her shipboard companion, Thomas

Bell. He was working as a clerk in a large investment company. He said he hoped to advance, because the firm was well connected with the Rothschilds of London and it had large sums of money to loan on mining claims and other speculative ventures. Mammy investigated his company and one day called on him. Eyebrows raised as the lowly clerk conversed with the well-known woman. She told him how much money she had and how she wanted him to invest it. When he tried to change her mind about certain companies her voice rose. She knew what she was doing and if he wanted her business, he would do things *exactly* as she said. The investments were made and soon showed a profit. Percentages of these profits swelled the company coffers and Bell was promoted. Mammy introduced him into her world of society and business friends and they began to come to him for investment advice. In those days, when being a millionaire was nothing, Bell quickly made his own fortune, but always with Mammy Pleasant coaching from the sidelines.

Accounts differ as to their actual relationship. Bell remained a bachelor but it was whispered that he and Mammy Pleasant were lovers. Mammy had managed to get rid of John Pleasant by shipping him off as a cook on a coastal steamer. She never lacked for bedmates and was able to excite men even into her late sixties.

Mammy had taken on a beautiful doxy called Teresa and prepared her for eventual marriage to Bell. Teresa had a past and Mammy discovered the past was a jealous husband who was looking for her right in San Francisco. She bought a revolver for Teresa and taught her how to use it. One night, when Teresa was having a dinner for two important local bachelors at Mammy's place, the husband suddenly appeared. Whether Mammy had tipped him off or not is a debatable point, but nervous Teresa pulled her pistol and sent a bullet through the man's forehead. Mammy had a casket and flowers waiting, the body was buried without the police knowing about it and Teresa was forever in Mammy's power.

In 1876 Mammy bought half a city block of property in the finest residential area of San Francisco. It was bound by Bush, Octavia and Sutter streets and separated from the rest of the block by an intersecting alley at the back. There she built her mansion. There were thirty rooms, Roman fluted columns, stained-glass windows, stone steps and wrought-iron filigree. There was a separate coach house, a cast-iron fence, wooden sidewalks and twenty evenly spaced blue gum trees. The interior was hung with bronze and crystal chandeliers, the ceilings were gold and bronze paneled. The walls were decorated in frescoes, simulating French tapestry, by famed Italians Moretti and Trezzini. The furniture, nine-foot mirrors, drapery and rugs were all imported from Europe. There was a secret passageway right through the center of the house. It led from Mammy's room to listening holes in each of the bedrooms. There was also a secret voodoo temple in the basement.

Mammy moved in with Teresa and soon after convinced Bell to move in with them. One night Teresa got Bell drunk and had a preacher in the next room. When the millionaire banker awoke he was a married man. Mammy wanted him in her control, for he was in on almost every business deal of any importance in the state. Her guidance had made him one of the most respected financiers on the West Coast and her skill at amassing a fortune had given him undreamed (and undeserved) power. He was one of the original founders of the Bank of California. He was called "King of Quicksilver" because she had made him buy huge shares in the New Almaden and New Idria quicksilver mines. He owned two mines on the Mother Lode and had interests in many of the mines on the Comstock Lode as well as in Nevada and Mexico. He owned a railroad in Guatemala and was one of the founders of the California and Oregon Railroad. Naturally, successful society gravitated toward him and, without realizing it, into Mammy's hands. Once when Hawaii's King Kalakaua visited San Francisco, Mammy was introduced to him at a reception at the Palace Hotel. The King was so charmed by her "faintly dusky, aristocratic face" that he dined alone with her that evening. She told him that her father had been a Hawaiian. "Get me mad," she said, "and see how it raises my Kanaka blood."

As Mammy got older, she got greedier and used her voodoo powers to frighten, buy off and even steal from others. When someone got in her way, she didn't hesitate to kill them. Most of Mammy's property was in Teresa's name. Mammy didn't want anything in her own name in case she fell into debt or one of her voodoo-inspired schemes got her placed in prison. The beautiful Mrs. Bell, a virtual prisoner inside the mansion and a wife in name only, began studying books on magic. She needed a weapon against Mammy's domination. She learned to light a candle by merely passing her hand over the wick. This force frightened Mammy. Then she began to tell the old woman that she had "flown out of her body" while she was asleep and had looked into the past. She related some of Mammy's more horrendous crimes and Mammy was sure Teresa had acquired psychic powers "by her close living with me."

Bell became senile and refused to take Mammy's investment advice or even to give her any money. His money was in his name even though it belonged to Mammy. Finally, after she found out the terms of his will, she pushed him down the magnificent front staircase. Frightened servants came rushing to investigate the noise and found Mammy kneeling over his unconscious form, "using her long fingers to pull the protruding brains from a hole in the top of his head."

Teresa got everything after his death but her power of attorney was in Mammy's hands. When the last of the men who had been present when Teresa shot her husband had died, Teresa searched Mammy's secret passageway and found the power of attorney. She burned it. Thus, freed from the past and the voodoo woman's domination, she ordered Mammy from the house.

The old lady hung on until the police were called in. Mammy, still strong-willed but frail and ailing at eighty-three, was driven out of her own home. She died in complete poverty at eighty-eight. The night she left the mansion Teresa wrote in her diary: "She has told several that I would get rid of her if I could, but that I could not; and yet she had her choice to go or be ejected. It is funny, but so many people believe she is a veritable 'Voodoo,' and brings bad luck to anybody she has anything to do with. I believe so too, but it comes in a regular matter-of-fact way through her evil acts and the evil influence she exerts. Misfortune is the natural sequence to anyone who trusts her because she will turn every effort of her mind to bring misfortune upon them."

In Hydesville, New York, noises coming out of nowhere changed the entire occult picture of far-off California. In 1848 the sisters

Fox heard strange knocking sounds in their bedroom. They called Mama, and she too heard the sharp tapping. Once the fear subsided and curiosity set in, the girls worked out a method of making sense from the noises. One rap for "no," two for "yes," etc. Thus they were able to communicate with a ghost who said he was the spirit of a man who had been murdered in their house (before the Fox family had moved in) and whose body was buried in the cellar.

The story, once it hit the newspapers, brought the girls immediate fame. It also brought them an immediate bank account, for they began to tour the United States holding séances, rapping out questions to the dead and translating their answers. For the new nation of America, looking for its own roots and something of its own to believe in, the idea of "spirit communication" was ideal. The spirits talked of Christ but not that He was the *only* son of God. They belittled the Catholic Church and other organized religions, saying that "all of them were on the right path, yet none of them were on the true path." Groups were formed, hands were held and the spirits came through. The entities brought messages from friends who had "passed into the beyond," gave solutions to individual legal and moral problems, chastised those who refused to believe and healed those who did. In those days people didn't turn immediately to science and investigate everything—they turned to religion for the answers. Thus a new religion was born: the religion of Spiritualism.

Nowhere did it dig in as deeply as in the Psychic State. In fact, Spiritualists who were persecuted in other places found refuge in California. The state didn't care what you believed in, where you came from or how you made your money. In its rough and tumble, sunshine and muddy street way, it was a factual working *democracy*.

Of the literally thousands of Spiritualists that eventually made their way to California, it was a small-boned little lady from Maine who started things rolling for the Spiritualists on the West Coast.

Mrs. M. J. Upham's four-year-old daughter Florence had died and, even though she had done everything possible to save the child, she blamed herself for the death. She cried often and wished that she too would die. Then in 1847 (one year before the Fox Sisters) little Florence suddenly materialized in front of her distraught mother. "Mama, don't you cry any more; it was all right; it was to be. I am happy—don't cry!" The ghost-child repeated this several times. Mrs. Upham's mind was at peace. It was the beginning of her belief that one could communicate with the deceased.

Two years later she and her husband, Mr. Upham (in those days newspapers and magazines never gave people's first names, it was always Mr. Aldridge or Mrs. Sutton; rarely was it Philip Aldridge or Ruth Sutton), were awakened to see their bedroom glowing with light. His father stood before them and said, "I died tonight at twelve o'clock!" The apparition repeated this twice, then vanished. The room returned to darkness. Mr. Upham noted the time and the date. Later a letter arrived with the information that his father really had died, on that day and at midnight.

The Uphams came to California in 1858. They had belonged to a Spiritualist Church group back East but found none in the rough-and-tumble town of Sacramento. They tried to form their own group, but people were leery of ghosts. One night in a hotel dining room she heard guests snickering at her from another table. Sacramento was a small town and her "religion" was under discussion. Mrs. Upham rose in righteous indignation and reached their table. Suddenly her body was seized by a strange force and she lost her voice. She began to beat on the tabletop and make deep guttural sounds. Then she placed her hands, palms down, on the tabletop. The table (described as a heavy large center table) began to vibrate. It rocked and tilted, then traveled quickly around the room with a mute and possessed Mrs. Upham clinging to it. The dining room cleared. Mrs. Upham's fame was made.

For ten years she held services in Sacramento, talking to the spirits and receiving their powers. She vividly described death scenes. She "took on the diseases of others and healed them," scribbled prescriptions for medicines and cured by the laying of hands. She claimed that the spirit doctors wrote "in large letters on the walls" and she merely read their instructions. She was always amazed that others couldn't see the huge writings the way she could.

Mrs. Upham worked with a "spirit control" named Hickicum. He came to her after she moved to San Francisco in 1868. He said he had been a Mohawk chieftain some fifty years before and was now a medicine man in his spirit life. He had been sent to work through her. With Hickicum beside her she treated patients who were considered hopeless by local doctors. Her touch erased a growth on a man's heart artery that doctors said would kill him. A woman, dying from the amount of blood that was filling her stomach, was cured when Mrs. Upham placed her hands on her. Another woman had given birth and was in terrible pain. Her doctor couldn't find the problem. Mrs. Upham was called in, and, "placing her hands on the patient's side, pulled with such force as to throw her on her knees, causing the patient to scream a little. The cure had been effected—the placenta had grown to her side, and was, by this means, removed. The lady quickly recovered." So great did Mrs. Upham's fame become that people would have her look at their loved ones right in hospital wards and in front of the furious physicians. There were no laws in those days to regulate faith healers.

Mr. Upham died and she soon married a Mr. Hendee, taking on both names. One afternoon in San Francisco she was sitting in meditation when, "I felt impelled to write, and I was requested to sit one hour each day, and the spirits would write their experiences in the spirit life. This request was signed, 'Geo. Washington.' " Mrs. Upham Hendee wrote a long manuscript about George Washington's experiences after his death and had it published. Then she made contact with Martha and Mary Washington and had those spirit memoirs published too.

Perhaps her most amazing feat (aside from the cures and precognitions) occurred during a séance that was attended by more than twenty witnesses. It is a remarkable parallel to the psychics of our own day who claim that they had predicted the assassination of President John Kennedy. In Mrs. Upham Hendee's own words:

"While residing at Napa City one Sunday evening, and during my control at a Seance, I saw a funeral procession, which seemed to come in at one door and pass through the room and out at another door; the men walked with their heads bowed, and dressed in black, with black and white crape on their arms. There soon followed a band with muffled drums; the others on horseback. The black horses wore white plumes and the white horses black plumes. Then carriages of state, then foreigners; then the catafalque came in and was set down, and I was made to go forward and look into the casket. There I saw the face of Abraham Lincoln. Then it was taken away, and foreign ambassadors followed in carriages, with horses highly caparisoned, all passing on in the train. Then I heard the 'Battle Cry of Freedom' played and I looked and saw the Union troops, with flags lowered and draped in black and white. They marched on out of sight. I then came to myself when I heard them say, 'I am afraid it is Lincoln.' I had given a full description as they passed. This was on Sunday evening, at Captain West's, at Napa; and, on the next Saturday noon, news came that Seward and Lincoln were assassinated. I said I did not see but one, and, as Seward lived, there was but one; and I had seen the real procession that was to be. By this and many others testimonies, regarding Lincoln's death, it certainly seems established that the spirit world is often conscious of many things before they transpire on earth, and that it was to be his fate. It was so arranged in the realms above, for some wise and good purpose."

John Brown had been raised in Missouri and came across the plains to California when he was thirty-two. His spirit teacher guided him and a small group of pioneers, letting them see weather conditions, disasters and Indian attacks well in advance. John had had no schooling and had been orphaned at an early age. The family that took him to raise didn't want to hear any tales about spirits and made him go without supper when he tried to tell them the things he had seen. Finally, "I learned to keep such things secret."

One day when he was seven years old: "I was in the field alone when I suddenly became aware of the presence of a large number of people. As I did not see them *come* from anywhere, I was somewhat startled. Most of them were children; they talked to me, and wanted to play with me; but seeing some of them disappear suddenly, and then appear again close to me, I became frightened, although they seemed as natural as any children, and were friendly. The family I lived with were absent, but in my fright I ran into the log cabin and hastily closed and locked the door. It soon opened and a pleasant-looking man, bearing in his hands a staff about two feet in length, entered and said he had come to remove all fear of my strange visitors. He requested to take in my hands the staff he carried. I did so, and at once felt at ease with him. The staff, he said, was the symbol of truth. After a brief conversation, in which he assured me he would watch over and protect me and be my teacher and friend, he took the staff, bade me 'good-bye', and walked out. I ran to the door to call him back, but found it locked. On opening it no one could be seen. The spirit has ever since been my near and dear friend; my guardian angel, my teacher and guide."

Brown, with his thin frame and long white beard looking like the *other* John Brown of Harpers Ferry fame, never tried to use his psychic powers for personal gain or to build a group around him. Once, when some travelers bet on whether his predictions would come true or not, he lost his gift of prophecy for several years.

He arrived in California in 1849 and spent his first few months at the Mission of San Juan near Monterey. One night his guide told him there would be a steamer come to port the next day with the news that California had been admitted to the Union. Brown awoke and told the fact to several men who were staying at the mission. All of them scoffed. There wasn't to be a steamer for at least two weeks. Yet, the very next day, a special boat called and gave the news of California's statehood.

Brown worked awhile in the mines, then settled in San Bernardino. His gift of seeing into the future grew stronger, as did a new ability to cure by the laying of his hands. Once he helped the sheriff find the murdered body of a young miner, giving the exact description of a place forty miles outside of town. Once, when a man lay wounded in Los Angeles, he was asked to go there and instruct the doctors in the best way to operate. Brown stared at the patient while his spirit guide showed him a strip of cotton cloth and two pieces of bone that were in the man's body. The spirit made him draw the shape of the cloth and told him exactly where the incision should be made. The doctors refused to attempt the operation. Then the man's friends put him aboard a coastal steamer and took him to a physician in San Francisco, who operated just as Brown's spirit guide had instructed. Two pieces of bone were removed as well as a piece of cloth. They were in the exact size, shape and location that Brown had said they would be. And this, please remember, was in the days before there were any X-ray machines.

In 1883 Dr. Louis Schlesinger and his wife, Julia, thought that the local Spiritualist groups should get more publicity than the San Francisco *Chronicle* and *Call* were giving. There were many news items that went astray without being circulated among the hundreds of Spiritualists in the Northern California region. Dr. Schlesinger was a medium and quite clever in reading sealed letters and receiving impressions of people by holding one of their personal objects. His wife Julia, while being a firm believer in spirit communication was also a fiery believer in Women's Suffrage. They began to write and publish their own Spiritualist newspaper, a four-page monthly news sheet "devoted to Spiritualism and Reform." They called it *The Carrier Dove*.

The response suprised even the "psychic" Schlesingers. In just three years it grew to a twenty-six-page illustrated magazine with readers across the nation, into Canada, Mexico and Great Britain. It carried advertisements of mediums, furniture stores, piano teachers and medicines for tapeworm. It gave highly critical book reviews, passed judgment on what "scurrilous" mediums were up to and railed out at laws "aimed at keeping the female in abject submission." In 1889 they went weekly. They closed with the issue of June 1893. For ten years—*the* ten years of West Coast Spiritualism—the *Dove* dominated the religious psychic scene.

There were national publications like *The Banner of Light* in Boston, *The Better Way* in Cincinnati or *The Watchman* in Chicago, but none of them had the coverage or the intensiveness of *The Carrier Dove*. They would discuss Christianity versus Spiritualism in one issue and Theosophy versus their beliefs in another. They sponsored a "home for old mediums" in San Diego and tried to get people to celebrate "spirit births" (the day of a loved one's passing over to the other side) rather than lament the anniversary of a death. They published in-depth interviews with noted psychics and encouraged a series of West Coast camp meetings, where they set up tents for "lessons in metaphysics, psalm singing and mediumistic sessions." They even had a Children's Department, where supposedly true stories of "little angels coming to converse with wee Willy and Maud" were printed in basic English. They were delighted when Mrs. S. F. Breed (an unusual medium who divined the most unexpected things by listening to the spirits rapping around her) held a special children's séance in 1886. "She placed the little stand into the center of the room and took her seat beside it, then called the children, six at a time to come and put their hands upon it, while it danced to the time of a lively music. Then came the raps, and each child received some little message. It was indeed a beautiful picture to see the sweet, animated faces of the little ones as they heard for the first time the signals from spirit land."

If *The Carrier Dove* did anything at all, it was to acquaint the public with the legitimate mediums of the day. The West Coast was overrun with charlatans who were out for an easy buck. The *Dove* accredited those mediums they had investigated and found honest, something no metaphysical publication dares do today. They told of Evans, a young man who bound two slates together, threw them on the floor away from anyone's reach and commanded them to answer questions. Witnesses swore they heard scratchings from inside the slates. When they were untied, a chalked message could be read by all. They endorsed a Dr. Stansbury of San Jose, who received names of his clients' deceased relatives by "the remarkable phenomenon of stigmata." At a session an editor asked a question and then the doctor "pushed up his sleeve, and there, in bright red letters was my Mother's name, the writing extended down upon the hand." They endorsed a Mrs. Dr. Beighle, who had a team of spirit doctors working through her "Magic Right Hand." The editors watched her treat some of the 1,500 patients who came to her fifth-floor Market Street clinic. They recorded what they saw and what the clients reported feeling as this healing hand touched them. It is an impressive list: "1) Soft, pleasant and soothing. 2) Dry, rough and husky. 3) Damp and chilly. 4) Dry, heating and and prickling. 5) Damp with penetrating heat. 6) Scratching and irritating sensations like the operation of a fine-toothed curry comb. 7) Sticky, mucilaginous matter with an irritating sensation, exhaling an odor sometimes pleasant and at others the very opposite. 8) Raising blisters from an eighth of an inch to three inches in diameter. 9) Producing reddish lines along the spine and scarlet spots over the deranged parts, and other phenomena too numerous and mixed to be easily particularized." The only diseases that this squat, portly woman could not cure were "cancers, humors, eczema or eruptive diseases of the skin, which exceptions have been established by the doctor's spirit guides solely for her protection from contagion."

A physical manifestation of nebulous spirit matter is always good to show scoffers and when spirit photographers started to appear, California Spiritualists were delighted. Here at last was solid proof that there was a life after death.

In 1862, a Mr. Mumler, an engraver in Boston, Massachusetts, took some photographs of his friends. When he developed the plates he saw other faces on them aside from those he recognized. When he showed the plates to his friends many of them immediately cried out in shock or joy; for the faces unknown to Mumler were those of friends or relatives of the sitters who had long since died. (Mumler once took a picture of a plain, chubby woman whom he had never seen before. When her plate was developed there was an image of a tall man with a beard standing behind her, his hands resting gently on her shoulders. Mumler remarked that the spirit looked a great deal like the late President Lincoln. "Yes it does," replied the woman. "I am his widow.") As Mumler's fame spread, other "spirit photographers" opened salons across the nation.

In Petaluma, California, young George Ross was a non-believing photographer who kept having strange faces appearing in his work. He accused his supplier of selling him used plates. It took a San Francisco Spiritualist to convince Ross that the plates were ordinary, but *he* was a medium. Ross soon had to turn away clients, each of whom wanted a picture taken with their dead mother or departed husband. He was mercilessly investigated by the unbelievers of the day. They made him use plates that they themselves had purchased, made him put the plates into cameras they had brought and made him develop the plates in other photographers' laboratories. Still the images appeared.

What was unusual about these as well as similar photographs was that some of the faces that appeared had been dead long before photography ever came into vogue. There was no way for a person who died before 1839 to have had a photograph taken. The art of photography didn't begin until that year. Yet people dead for dozens of years before were recognized by their friends and relatives.

Spiritualist churches added cameras and darkrooms to their paraphernalia of spirit trumpets, sealed cabinets, slates and planchettes. They would hold hands, pray for the spirits to enter, then seat a member in a chair, point a camera at him and ask him to think of those dead friends he wished to have around him. The photographer would click the shutter as another medium placed his hand on the camera. (Sometimes they did without a camera, merely holding a sealed pack of photographic plates to their foreheads and concentrating on certain dead souls. These didn't come out as well, however.)

A highly respected gentleman named Chester P. Hatch sat for one of these portraits and when he saw the print he declared in writing: "The faces of my loved ones are fully recognized, but the faces on my knees and at my feet I do not recognise; still they may belong to the Hatch family in olden times. The Indian is one of my band [i.e., his spirit guide group]. I recognize the face at the left as that of my mother, Betsy P. Hatch; the face of the young man over my head is that of my son, Chester P. Hatch. At my left, and nearest me, is my first wife, Mary A. Hatch. The face beneath my wife I recognize as that of my grandfather, Samuel Hatch."

Mrs. H. C. Wilson, of San Francisco, had a daughter named Nellie Pearl, who showed signs of great spiritualist development. She died, age three. Then another child was born to Mrs. Wilson, a boy she named Llewellyn Burt. He also showed great interest in things spiritual and so when it came time to take his picture his mother asked the celebrated medium Mrs. Carter to place her hand on the camera. There was Llewellyn Burt sitting on an apple box atop a chair just as Mrs. Carter had placed him, but there was also dead little Nellie Pearl resting a ghostly arm in her brother's lap.

The majority of California's citizens did not accept Spiritualism (the way the majority doesn't accept the occult today) and did their damndest to discredit and belittle it. A Professor S. S. Baldwin made a good living giving a lecture called "Exposing Spiritualism." The professor would put a "spirit cabinet" on the stage and throw in a few musical instruments. Then he would get into the large box, be tied to a chair and the door would close. Then noises would be heard inside the box. Bells would ring and tambourines would rattle. Sometimes a guitar would rise out of the cabinet and float through the air. Bound slates would be opened and "spirit writing" found on them. At times even disembodied spirits would materialize right on stage.

After the phenomena was finished, Baldwin would invite members of the audience to come on stage to try to figure out how he did his stunts. The committee was cross-examined to see how many were Spiritualists, for he was willing to have half of them of the Spiritualist "religion" but not more. But the Spiritualists were so anxious to confront this man they often packed the committees and there were many onstage scuffles because of it. They said Baldwin was really a medium who refused to believe it. At times a Spiritualist would rise from the audience and denounce the professor as being in league with the devil and one night the police had to be called in when members of the committee interfered with his "manifestations." The newspaper reported that this "brought on a fist fight between Baldwin and an earnest believer; the professor was extremely handy with his hands, and put the believer into a real trance with a haymaker on the jaw."

The San Francisco *Daily Examiner* on December 19, 1887, had great fun reporting a story bannerlined: "Sealskins in heaven. Lady spirits with a taste for ulsters and diamonds. Clothes for the stars. A suit sent to Saturn seen on Kearney street. An amazed old gentleman." It appears that a Mrs. Patterson held séances at her boardinghouse at the corner of Mission and Third streets. She had two lodgers, Mr. Clifford and Mr. Wild, who helped her make contact with spirits that lived on the planet Saturn. An old carriage maker named McTavish was a constant client, getting business advice from the spirits and making plans to be taken to Saturn when the "next celestial rays were solid enough." McTavish gave money and gifts and was told that the medium had remitted his gifts on to the spirits. Then one day he saw an expensive tailor-made suit in front of him on Kearney Street. It was the very suit that the spirits had requested he make and send to them. They even told him the size and the color they wanted. When McTavish tapped the wearer of the suit on the shoulder, to his great surprise it was Mr. Wild! The *Examiner* gave the conversation word for word. "What does this mean, sir? These clothes are the same that I bought to be taken to Saturn." "Well, they've been sent to Saturn." "Sent to Saturn!" "Yes sir, they've been there more'n a week." "Then how the devil does it happen that you have them on your back?" "Mr. McTavish," said Mr. Wild in sorrow and pity, "you surprise me. It knocks me cold it does, to hear a man with your light talking like that. In one sense, this is the Saturn suit—in the same way that when you're dead your body will be you. Have *I* got to tell a man with *your* light that the speerits don't take to the speerit world the actyil things you give 'em, but only the essential semblance of 'em? How do you suppose they could pack a real suit of clothes through eighteen hundred million miles of space? Don't you see?" "It—it begins to break upon me," assented Mr. McTavish, mopping his brow in bewilderment. "I thought it would," said Mr. Wild encouragingly. "I saw your spirit guide dematerialize these here clothes with my own eyes in our rooms. She carried away the soul of these togs, an' the dross, the dead body of 'em, was left behind, and I took it. Wasn't that right? You wouldn't want me to throw the clothes away, would you, after the spirit guide had made 'em sacred like?" "No, no; certainly not," murmured Mr. McTavish. "I see it all now," and shaking Mr. Wild by the hand heartily, he departed on his way.

Of course the editors of *The Carrier Dove* were as indignant over these "brazen and heartless humbugs who have invaded and disgraced the ranks of mediumship in San Francisco" as the secular publications were, and would not hesitate to denounce anyone they felt was giving their beliefs a bad name. One of their more vehement denunciations was showered upon a projected city called "Summerland." It was to be an exclusive residential area only for Spiritualists, outside Santa Barbara. Their editor called the rows of twenty-five-by-sixty-foot lots "a huge swindle," and added, "When I beheld with my own eyes, what has been palmed off on the credulous Spiritualists of the country for a place to locate a town, I thought to myself the fools are not all dead yet. Some Spiritualists are very easily gulled; especially by anything coming through a medium, or purporting to come from a spirit or spirits."

If all this activity seems to be coming almost exclusively from the northern part of California, it's because the southern part was not the stronghold of money and psychics it is today. In 1891, when Spiritualism had already reached its peak, San Francisco had a population of 298,997 while Los Angeles had but 50,395. There was a First Society of Spiritualists who had their own hall and held weekly meetings. Dr. J. M. Temple was a well-known psychometrist and test medium who gave clients readings from the Winthrop House on Spring Street. Mrs. Florence Rich arrived from Boston and gave readings at the Albemarle and a trance medium named Mrs. M. White held readings at a place on the corner of Second and Los Angeles streets. Another psychic, Miss Susie M. Johnson, wrote about local conditions to a friend: "In all my mediumistic experience I have never encountered so hard an element for spiritual work as Southern California. Why, I cannot tell, unless it is because of the old Spanish Catholic influences so strongly entrenched here, and still a good deal of it in active expression. That California is destined to furnish conditions for a wonderful spiritual development, some day, I have no doubt; but, oh! the 'breaking up' that has first to be done!"

Oscar Wilde once wrote that "A map of the world that does not include Utopia is not worth even glancing at, for it leaves out the one country at which humanity is always landing." For countless nineteenth-century Americans (and quite a few foreigners), California was the fabled land of Utopia. The majority of them came for gold, but many of them came because it was "the place where Christ, Krishna and Man would understand one another."

There were several communities and colonies in the state that were dedicated to agriculture and the co-operative life. Sixty-eight socialists in 1884 founded a colony near San Francisco and posed proudly beneath the Karl Marx Tree. In 1876 a group arrived from Poland and set up a community farm near Anaheim. Being members of the Polish nobility they found plowing, weeding and cattle raising impossible tasks once the novelty wore off. One gentleman-farmer got disgusted with it all and decided to write a book. His name was Henryk Sienkiewicz and his book was *Quo Vadis?* A lady-farmer gave it all up to become one of America's most celebrated actresses. Her name was Madame Helena Modjeska.

The Mormons were the first to try to establish a religious colony in the Psychic State. They organized at San Bernardino in 1851. It was to be a welcoming place for new settlers arriving on the West Coast and the first link of a chain of settlements that led across the plains into "the land of Joseph" at Salt Lake City. The first settlers went deeply in debt to buy the land and worked hard to clear it, build homes, shops and a church. They also had to make their settlement into a fortress, because the Indians wanted them out of there.

As they grew in prosperity they grew in number and outsiders came to take advantage of the zealous work already done. In 1857 an elder from Utah visited the colony and wrote with shock that it was "a den of Apostates, thieves, gamblers, drunkards, Methodists and evry kind of foul Character." Soon after, the church leaders told the California settlers to sell their land and come immediately to Salt Lake. While the great majority loaded their wagons and took losses on their livestock, many others refused to accept these losses, renounced their faith and stayed on in California.

Hiram Butler came to Applegate, California, in 1887 to found the Esoteric Fraternity because the "spirit" told him to. He was a mystic and a prolific writer who believed that the sun influenced every phase of human biology and that immortality is "almost impossible, but it is possible." He also preached absolute chastity. He built a huge house and marked out a 460-acre farm that had, at one time, thirty "disciples" reading his fifteen books and practicing what he preached. By mid-1970 only three of the original members were left. Two brothers in their nineties and a widow in her eighties. The brothers are sure that they have found the key to everlasting life and in spite of the fact that no babies have ever been born there, they are confident that the sect will continue. "Immortality is there to he who truly understands," Butler wrote.

There are several tombstones in a graveyard behind the house. One of them reads: "Hiram Butler—July 29, 1841—Nov. 3, 1916."

By the time Thomas Lake Harris began building his religious mansion in the hills of Santa Rosa he had already tried to establish his utopian colony in Virginia, New York and Scotland. His ideas were based on Universalism, Socialism, Communism, Spiritualism and

Swedenborgianism. They were a collection of theories that made God and Jesus bisexual, praised hard work as a divine grace, advocated chastity and made him write poems about conjugal love. Harris was a mystic and a leader. Whether he was a roué and a charlatan has never been confirmed.

He was tall and thin, with a full white beard but a youthful face almost free of wrinkles. His voice was deep and soft. He could charm the birds out of their nests and his followers out of their bankrolls. His "little palace within itself" was built from the money his followers turned over to his Fountain Grove Colony and was as lavish as anything built by the gold barons of nearby San Francisco. It was two stories with an attic with a wide entry porch and huge sun rooms facing south. There were several sitting rooms, a paneled library, an immense dining room and kitchen, as well as several bedrooms both downstairs and up. Oriental carpets were on the floor and angels smiled from dozens of stained-glass windows. Harris lived in the mansion with his wife, his female secretary and his female friends. The married members and single men lived in a separate house across the road.

Money arrived from wealthy newcomers and from one of the first successful wineries in the state. His followers planted 1,700 acres in select grapes and in one good year pressed 70,000 gallons of cabernet, pinot noir and zinfandel that was quickly sold to San Franciscans.

In all fairness to the man, he probably was sincere in his beliefs even though as his fame grew the outside world began gossiping about the colony's living arrangements. They hinted that Harris had poisoned his baby daughter and that strange orgies went on in the disguise of religion. Harris denied it all, but what else could outsiders think when he published poems like this one:

> Girls, my girls, pure passion-roses,
> In you I have bled:
> In you all my life reposes,
> Bridal wreath and bed.

In 1891 a Miss Alzire Chevaillier, a professional agitator and pioneer of liberation, claimed that she had arrived at the Fountain

Grove Colony to "commune with the spirits and find salvation," only to find Harris sneaking into her bed. The white-bearded prophet already aged sixty-eight, heatedly denied the charges but Miss Chevaillier told her story to the press and in packed lecture halls around Northern California. The story of the "celibate monk who lured innocent maidens to his den" was front-page gossip for three months in Victorian San Francisco. Finally Harris left to eventually settle in New York City, living on the $40,000 he got from the colonists who bought him out.

As Thomas Harris left California, Katherine Augusta Westcott Tingley was planning on moving in. She was an organizer and a humanitarian. She was also wealthy and a follower of the mysterious Madame Blavatsky.

Helena Petrovna married seventy-year-old General Nikifor Blavatsky when she was in her teens. Then she left him and wandered around Europe. It was in Paris, in 1858, that she became a Spiritualist. The spirits seemed to do fantastic things for her, and she gave them much publicity. So much that by 1873, when she arrived in New York City, she was quite famous and accredited with "miraculous powers." She met a lawyer who was doing a series of articles on Spiritualism for the New York *Daily Graphic* and a great friendship bloomed. In 1875 she and her American friend, Henry Olcott, formed a group "to investigate the hidden mysteries of Nature and the psychical powers latent in man." They called this psychic study organization the Theosophical Society. The Madame could communicate directly with spirits, could read sealed envelopes and foretell the future. She wrote two massive tomes on her philosophy (*Isis Unveiled* and *The Secret Doctrine*), which declared that Spiritualism didn't have all the answers. In fact, she claimed, Spiritualism the way it was being practiced in the United States was all wrong. It should be a "culture of the spirits of the living, not a commerce with the souls of the dead."

Blavatsky and Olcott sailed off to India to enlarge their group of societies, leaving the North American groups under the control of William Judge. In India Madame received almost daily letters from some mysterious teachers in the snow-hidden Himalayas called the Mahatmas of the Great White Brotherhood. They had been reincarnated several times and were telling her all they knew. This information she passed on to the worldwide groups that eagerly awaited her instructions. Madame Blavatsky believed that reincarnation and the cleaning up of one's Karma (the evil committed during past lives) was an integral part of God's plan for humanity and the only way to eventually shuck off the mortal coils for "oneness with the Godhead." The letters from the Mahatmas substantiated her beliefs. Until the letters were declared fraudulent, that is. The London Society for Psychical Research (and one of her secretaries) said the Madame was writing these letters and lessons herself, pawning off a package of mystical philosophy that had been around since the fourteenth century. The Madame hurried to London but the damage was done. The societies argued among themselves, either denouncing or praising the clever Russian mystic. While she made a slight comeback, she never regained control of her groups and died in 1891.

Five years after she died William Judge died in America and passed the reins of the Theosophical Society to Katherine Tingley. She was, in some ways, as powerful a personality as Madame Blavatsky had been.

Mrs. Tingley was interested in charitable work before ever embracing Theosophy. She had founded clinics and welfare homes in Manhattan's poverty-ridden Lower East Side, as well as an orphanage on the Palisades of the Hudson River and another in Buffalo. She came to the conclusion that brotherhood was the answer to the world's problems and if that could be shown through Theosophy, so much the better.

She managed to get money to buy 330 acres of prime land at Point Loma, just outside the city of San Diego, and in 1897 sprinkled corn oil and wine on a cornerstone of a building destined to become the headquarters of the Universal Brotherhood and Theosophical Society. Flags waved, children sang and excerpts were read from the Upanishads, the Orphic Mysteries, the Bhagavad-Gita and the Bible. She promised that there would arise a city based on brotherhood "for the benefit of humanity and glory of the ancient sages." While she did not deny the occult side of her Theosophic-dictatorial plans, she minimized the importance of psychic phenomena and warned her followers to avoid their dangers.

The heyday of Point Loma came around 1907, when there were five hundred people living inside the colony in bungalows and tents and three large buildings with aquamarine and amethyst-glass domes. Forty-foot-wide avenues wound through the gardens and eucalyptus trees led to a Greek theater and a music school.

Mrs. Tingley had absolute power in her little town and did everything from supervising construction work to directing classic plays. She loved California and was certain that it was God's chosen land. "I have looked over the blue waters of the Pacific; and watched the sun rise above the mountains and listened to the mocking-birds singing; and the beauty of the awakening world grew marvelous for me with suggestions of the hidden harmonies of life. Then I thought of humanity and wondered what would happen could the veil of external things fall from before our eyes and reveal the glory of the spiritual laws of life."

Mrs. Tingley's management ran the value of the property up to $1,320,000, but the same management also put Point Loma deeply in debt. She sold pieces of land for as high as $5,000 an acre and floated a $400,000 bond issue to keep going. She died in 1929, aged seventy-nine. Her successor sought for a way out of her debts but that was the year the Great Depression hit. Costs were pared, schools were closed, permanent residents moved away. When World War II came, military installations and the demand for housing forced the Theosophists to sell the last of their property and move to a debt-free and quiet spot at Covina. They no longer thought of converting the world by showing them brotherhood in action. They were more interested in expanding lodges in other towns and in publishing books. Scholar Robert Hine has written that "Point Loma presented as good an example of a religious utopia as can be found in California history. . . ." even though Mrs. Tingley herself never thought of it as utopian but more as "a practical illustration of the possibility of developing a higher type of humanity."

The earthquake that hit San Francisco in 1906 did not do as much damage to the wood-structured city as the fire that followed. Water mains burst and firemen were helpless as the wind swirled the flames up one hill and down the other. The firefighters were demoralized from the very beginning, because the town's heroic fire chief was killed at the site of the first blaze. Citizens put it down to "acts of God and nature" but Spiritualist John Ball was positive that spirits from another world had destroyed the city. He even wrote a book about it (but had to publish it himself). He claimed that the spirits had been badgering him for over twenty years, telling him that unless the merchants of the city (especially the Jews) didn't change their attitude toward the working man, only death and destruction could come of it. Then when the earthquake struck, the forces of darkness moved in. "Evil spirits took advantage of the earthquake to destroy a good part of San Francisco. Spirits knew the water mains would be broken by the earthquake, and they also knew there was only one man who had formulated plans to check a conflagration under such conditions. This man was Fire Chief Sullivan whom they took good care to destroy before he could put his plan of salvation into action." Spiritualist Ball wrote that a few nights after the fire he was visited for the last time by the destructive entities. "I had just put out the light and got into bed when the walls of the room seemed to recede, and through the window a great multitude of spirits floated, or rather swam, for they had bodies about the size and shape of sharks. Their heads were monstrosities; they were bleary-eyed and besotted creatures, like the camp followers of an army left to gratify their degraded appetites and passions on the remnants of a destroyed and looted city." The leader was "a Jew, but he had one of the finest and most intellectual heads I have ever seen." Mr. Ball knew that it had been *his* prayers and exhortations that had defeated these spirit hordes and saved the city from total destruction. Now their leader had "brought his cohorts in to make a final attack." He waited, flat out in bed and staring them down, knowing that if he showed any fear they would grow in power. "My hair stood on end and my flesh crawled, but I knew they could not hurt me physically, and that I only had to stand my ground and in time they would retire as they had come." The brave man didn't budge and the evil spirits departed. He died feeling San Franciscans were ungrateful by not publically thanking him with a medal for his part in the earthquake aftermath.

In 1918 the city of Los Angeles put a rich young playboy named Harry New on trial for his life. He was accused of murdering his fiancée, Freda Lesser. The couple was well known in social circles and everyone was surprised when he broke their engagement. Miss Lesser tried often to convince him to reconsider but he would only get angry. Then one day she was seen entering his home. Neighbors heard a shot. The police were called and there was Freda on the floor; with a bullet in her heart. Powder burns showed the gun had been fired at close range. Tests showed the gun to have Harry's fingerprints on it. At the trial he claimed it was an accident, but there were no witnesses and no one came forward with evidence to prove him innocent. One afternoon the jury filed out to deliberate. The city waited for the decision.

That very evening a prominent Los Angeles lawyer attended a séance. He didn't believe in those things but was curious. The group sat around a table as the medium went into a trance. She groaned, then shook and as the witnesses watched spellbound, a white vaporous mist began to form before them. A face appeared clearly. A woman gasped: "It's Freda Lesser. I recognize her from the pictures in the paper!"

From the sleeping medium's throat came a strange voice—that belonging to a young woman. The voice moaned and then said: "I am a spirit unknown to you and must talk about a matter of life and death. My name is Freda Lesser. Please help me. They are going to condemn my fiancé, Harry New, for my murder. In just a few minutes they are going to find him guilty. But he is innocent; he did not kill me. I went to see him to try and persuade him to come back to me and when he refused I pulled out a gun and threatened to shoot myself. He grabbed the gun and tried to take it away from me and in the struggle it accidentally went off. I plead with you to do something to help him. Tell him that I always loved him and I always will."

The lawyer jumped up and, taking several members of the séance with him, drove quickly to the courthouse. He asked for an audience with the judge and told him the entire story. The judge recalled the astonished jury. After relating the experience at the séance he asked: "Do we know what it is that dies in the dead, or even that anything dies? There is no question that phenomena exist of which we know absolutely nothing. It should not be considered impossible that this dead girl could have communicated with us in this manner. We must weigh this curious evidence, but you must also be guided solely by your own beliefs, for there is no proof as to the truth of this phenomenon."

The jury went out again and came back within the hour. The verdict: Not guilty.

As Hollywood burst into activity it brought in new faces, new money and new ideas. Film stars swore by the heavenly stars and astrologers set up shops to chart their careers and solve their financial futures. The new permissive atmosphere brought renewed life to the Spiritualist movement as well as sudden appearances of Indian gurus and "spiritual masters" who founded sects, churches and colonies. Hollywood in the twenties and thirties was a mecca for all kinds who believed in the occult and the power of the psychic world.

Aimee Semple McPherson built a multimillion-dollar Angelus Temple and started the Foursquare Gospel denomination that counted 193,000 as among the faithful and with real estate valued at $59 million. For a quarter of a century she packed them in for her own brand of hellfire and brimstone and made no secret that she appreciated dollars for her efforts. "Folks," she would shout from the pulpit, "I am sorry to tell you that I have a disease, an incurable disease! It is aggravated by the clinking of metal. But the rustle of that green stuff soothes it." The congregation would laugh and pile the collection plates high with paper money. She was the one that coined the phrase: "I don't care what they say about me, so long as they spell my name right." Whatever she had (and people still hotly debate her psychic abilities) Aimee had it in abundance. So much so that when she swallowed too many sleeping pills and died in 1944 thousands of believers stormed her temple, sobbed at the pulpit and beat their heads against the ground.

Francis Grierson was another one whose occult talents drew him finally to the Psychic State. He was born in Ireland, raised in Missouri and went to Europe to seek his fortune in 1870 at the age of twenty-two. It was in Paris that he discovered he could play the piano by ear. He'd never taken lessons and couldn't read music, yet he would entertain his audience with quite intricate musical compositions. He claimed that he played "whatever came into my head."

One evening at a concert in Leipzig a critic complained that Grierson's original works were too reminiscent of Mozart and Rossini and that one piece was filled with the clichés of Chopin. After his annoyance subsided, Grierson came to the conclusion that he was a "spiritualistic musical medium" and that the dead composers were using his hands to play their most recent compositions. His fame spread (as this revelation spread) until one night he was asked to play for Her Royal Highness Princess Mathilde, the cousin of Emperor Napoleon the Third.

Grierson sat at the piano, stretched his fingers and his body suddenly became rigid. He tried to push his hands on the keyboard but he couldn't move them. Then the audience heard him speak in perfect French and without his usual atrocious American accent: "This piano is toned too low for me and it is necessary to tune it for the proper pitch to suit the piece I am going to play for you."

The royal guests snickered until they realized that Grierson was in a trance. Then the piano began to sound chords and trills, but Grierson's hands were rigid at his side. The keys went down but it was someone else's hands that pushed them. From Grierson's mouth came another French sentence: "I am Hector Berlioz. I shall play you an unperformed composition of mine, a set of heavenly impressions. . . ." The spirit of the grouchy old composer played as he had never played in real life.

No sooner was it over than he announced he was Sigismund Thalberg and played a fantasia for four hands. Grierson's hands played one set while ghostly fingers played the other. After that it was Franz Liszt who played a four-handed rhapsody, then Chopin played a duet and Mozart ended the séance with a few light-hearted pieces. Grierson arose, exhausted, and went to bed.

His fame called him back to the United States, where he played ghostly piano, held séances, joined the Rosicrucians, studied astrology and Numerology and wrote two books. One of them, *The Valley of the Shadows,* dealt with the early life of Abraham Lincoln and won high praise from critics, even from the Lincoln specialist Carl Sandburg.

Grierson was surrounded by admirers, who built him a magnificent stained-glass and paneled wood mansion at K and Twentieth streets in San Diego, California. To the Villa Montezeuma came Governor Downey, Mark Twain, Madame Modjeska and literary lights from all over the world. Grierson would go into a trance, wearing robes and jewels that were supposed to be "impregnated with the occult force of magnetism," and the spirit of Goethe would speak his poetry in perfect German. Isaiah would recite in Hebrew and Leopardi read his Italian blank verse while complaining that he was wandering in the heavens just as he wandered on earth.

Grierson went back to England but it wasn't the same to him and so he returned to California, settling this time in Los Angeles. One evening, now seventy-nine years old, he gave a piano concert where an unnamed oriental composer played exquisitely for hours. He finished a difficult piece and sat there, his hands resting lightly on the keyboard. His audience thought he was about to come out of his trance, but when he did not move after several minutes, a friend stepped forward and touched him on the shoulder. He fell forward, his fingers contorted in the position of the last ghostly chord he ever played.

The forties brought the war and war industries to California. As plants and factories, shipyards and munitions works went into gear, psychic things were forgotten as outsiders inundated the state in the brand new "gold rush." Midwesterners and Southerners were not impressed with spirits, astrologers or spiritualists. They wanted to earn a buck and get rid of their Depression memories. Metaphysical groups disbanded or dwindled into almost nothing. Mediums got jobs in factories. True, there were still more psychics living in the Psychic State than any of the other states, but materialism not mysticism was the order of the day.

Reverend Florence Becker was the last of the old-fashioned Spiritualists. She bridged the gap between the Age of Victoria and the Age of Aquarius. She was hated as much as she was loved, feared as much as she was respected. Ask anyone who has been around the Bay Area for a few years to name the greatest medium of them all—and they will almost always answer, Florence Becker.

They called her "Ma" Becker because she seemed ageless and was huge and motherly. She would sit on the platform in front of her congregation at the Golden Gate Spiritualist Church like an enormous female Buddha, singing hymns, glaring at latecomers and smiling at old friends. There was almost nothing she couldn't do with the spirit world. She saw your past, told your future, diagnosed your ailments, advised on your profession, helped your love problems and cured your ailing body. Her public forte was billet reading. While an assistant medium double blindfolded her, those in the congregation wishing information wrote messages on slips of paper and sealed them in envelopes. Collected into a large basket, they were placed on a table in front of her. The plump hand would dip into the basket and pull out one missive. Holding it a second she would identify the sender: "Is there a Louise here?"

"Yes, Reverend Becker," a timid voice replies from the back of the congregation.

"You are concerned about a man named Henry."

"Yes, Reverend Becker."

"He is very ill and probably will not last out the year. But you know that, don't you?"

"Yes, Reverend Becker."

"But he has taken care of you. Your troubles will be solved when he passes into the next world. Don't worry, Emma can't do a thing. Do you feel better now?"

"Yes, Reverend Becker."

(A bystander later questions Louise. She had been concerned about her Aunt Emma taking all Uncle Henry's money when he died. She had written on the billet: "Will I get my rightful inheritance?")

The hand dipped again. A man's name is called. "I don't like Chicago any more than you do," Mrs. Becker's voice booms out, "but it will only be for a short while. Then you can come back to San Francisco. Go with confidence. Does this answer your question?"

"Yes, thank you, Reverend Becker." (He had been offered a job in Chicago but his wife and children preferred to live in San Francisco. The money and advancement, however, were too good to pass up. He had written on his billet: "Should I accept this new position?")

Her church was crowded every Sunday morning and every Wednesday night. She was assisted by two licensed ministers and six "certified mediums." Her interests flowed over into such things as a church Pot Luck Supper, the Golden Glow Guild Meetings, a Craftsman Club, a Talent Show and babies being christened. Every January she would pack them in to where they were standing in the aisles as she made her prophecies for the coming year. Newspapers reported her predictions and other mediums squirmed with dismay when most of them came true.

Ma Becker never liked the press and rarely granted interviews, consequently stories grew up around her. She became that rare individual: a legend in her own lifetime.

It was said that one day, back in the thirties, she died. Her family notified her friends and the undertaker was called. Yet she returned to life, saying that she had talked with various spirits close to God who asked her to continue her work on earth.

It was also said that she was called to Washington several times when F.D.R. was President. Secret Service men escorted her to the White House with the greatest secrecy as she looked into the future and (supposedly) helped shape America's foreign policy. She saw him dying that April day but didn't have the heart to tell him. When Harry Truman came into office, she was also called a few times to consult with him. Neither President ever admitted it nor denied it. When Mrs. Becker would be asked about it, she would just smile.

At the age of eighty-three she died. It was a brief illness and her passing into the spirit world was effortless. Citizens of San Francisco, from all levels, paid homage to her in the press and at her graveside. "Many people can sing," said one medium, famous in his own right in the Bay Area, "but there are few Carusos or Flagstads. Mrs. Becker was a Flagstad."

She died in 1970, just as the new decade was opening, the decade that promises to be the most exciting one of all for citizens of the Psychic State.

Northern California

I thought that California was just California, the way that Ohio is only Ohio or Georgia just Georgia. I had traveled around the United States and been all over Mexico, Central and South America plus several of the islands in the Caribbean. I had never been to California and was unaware of the state's impressive diversity.

I expected palm trees and blue skies in San Francisco. Thirty years of Hollywood movies has given me the wrong stereotype of the West Coast. I was astounded to find foggy days, cold rain and pine trees. The sweaters and woolen suits I'd left behind all had to be repurchased. My ignorance and wonderment was as real in San Francisco as the wonderment I'd noted on the faces of Midwesterners when they first saw Manhattan.

Over ten years of living and researching the occult in Brazil and South America had led me to believe that I knew all about it. I had seen spirit possession, ectoplasm materialization, table rapping, psychic surgery, automatic writing, mediums in trance and the curse of the evil eye. I was sure that California would have nothing to show me in the mystic line that I hadn't seen before. I was wrong. I was sure that those in California's psychic fields were all kooks. Again I was wrong. I was also sure that nothing would happen to affect me personally the way it had happened in Brazil. Again and again I was wrong.

I met Harold White just a few days after he got out of the hospital.

He had been losing his balance and falling. Disturbed, he'd gone to a doctor, who ordered an immediate operation on the jugular vein that ran up the left side of his neck. The passage was obstructed and the flow of blood to the brain was diminishing. He spent five days in the hospital after surgery and a week later was back in his bookshop. There was hardly a trace of scar. "Oh, I knew I'd be all right," he told me. "My spirit guide said I needed the operation and that it would go without a hitch. I wasn't afraid of dying. My guide says I'll live way into my nineties." Mr. White is already well into his eighties.

Harold White is an important man in the Psychic State because his Metaphysical Book Shop at 420 Sutter Street in San Francisco is the focal point for the majority of Northern California's mediums, astrologers, healers and the just plain curious. Two rooms are crammed with books on every occult subject imaginable. The volumes come from United States publishers as well as English, Indian, French, German and Brazilian printers. No musty shop *a la* Dickens this, but a well-lit, dust-free, tastefully decorated bookstore where people meet to browse, buy and learn. There are four rooms set aside as lecture halls and classrooms. Here the greatest names in California psychic circles tell what they know and give instructions to those who feel they have "psychic powers" but don't know how to develop them. In any month of the year, classes may be taken in various types of astrology, in reading the Tarot cards, in learning to see your previous lives, in reading your aura, in learning to cure by the laying of hands, in hypnotism, in Numerology, in palmistry, in yoga and *ad infinitum*. He even had a "Hallowe'en Mystic Fair" where he lined up forty mediums and sold tickets that gave a glass of champagne, book discounts and three readings. More than two thousand people crammed the bookshop halls.

Mr. White runs around with a watchful eye on everything, seeming to be in a dozen places at once. He doesn't need this bookshop, as he is a very wealthy man. He really isn't doing it for himself either, "but for my spirit guide White Eagle. He is actually the boss here, you know."

White Eagle has been dead at least three hundred years. He was a medicine man with the Blackfoot tribe in his last life on earth and first appeared to Mr. White twenty years ago during a session with the Ouija board. "He's very opinionated and very intelligent," says Mr. White. "One day long after I had retired from my antique business he came through and gave me an order. 'Look, I want to establish something here,' he told me. 'Get up off that couch and go back to work. I want you to set up a metaphysical bookshop. It will be the foundation for a psychic center later on. Don't argue with me; you can do it! I'll be here at your Ouija board every week to discuss business problems with you.' I forgot about it until one day I happened to wander into a tiny psychic bookshop that was only opened on Saturdays. It was owned by two little old ladies, who asked me immediately if I wanted to buy the place. I knew that White Eagle had sent me there."

Harold White and White Eagle got together only after hc'd been studying psychic phenomena for almost sixty years. When he was a boy in London, he went to see a medium for the first time. "She was a beautiful woman and she told me many things. Of course I didn't believe her until the things started to happen exactly as she said they would. Even ten years later the events occurred as she predicted." When he was nineteen, he began experimenting with automatic writing. He would place a pencil in one hand, put the point on a sheet of paper and look away, not thinking of anything in particular, not doing anything to move the pencil. Messages began coming to him from dead friends and his dead mother. "By the time I was twenty-one, it had become second nature to communicate with the spirit world."

There was very little he could do with his spirit talents in the London of the late 1890's. There was one shop on Victoria Street that dared sell occult books, and mediums were arrested when they tried to practice. "You see, the Spiritualists considered themselves as a religious group and this naturally brought repressions from the Church of England. I remember one medium who was arrested and brought to trial and in order to prove her powers she asked to be allowed to go into trance. The judge and the prosecuting counsel forbid it. Strangely enough both judge and the counsel were dead within a month. Both of them."

His father made things difficult for him, introducing him as "my weird son," and when prospective employers discovered that he believed in spirits they refused to give him a job. So he emigrated to Vancouver, British Columbia, and got a job in a bank, was appointed at twenty-seven to be Trade Commissioner for British Columbia in South America, became Peruvian consul in Vancouver, married, fathered several children, ran for Canadian Parliament (and lost) and eventually came to San Francisco, where he ran a chic and successful antique shop for thirty years.

As soon as he arrived in San Francisco he got in with the local Spiritualists and eventually became president of the Spiritualist Church. Every chance he had he would consult his Ouija board. This board is not the ordinary one seen today, but a small well-worn piece of brown wood with the alphabet and "ready," "yes," "no," "doubtful," "try again" and "good night" painted on it. The planchette is small and squeeks on ivory wheels along a groove at the foot of the board. Mr. White has had this board for sixty years. "It's got my personal vibrations all over it. It is more 'me' than anything else I own.

"I've had about fifty different communicators, you know. Some have come from Venus, some were Aztecs or Incas and others were just old friends and relatives. My father comes through to me regularly now. He was converted to spiritualism after I left home. He still has his sense of humor and we get along very well. His biggest complaint is how badly the British Isles have deteriorated and he swears that his next reincarnation will be here in America. A young friend of mine who is recently deceased keeps trying to get through but he hasn't enough strength as yet. His inability to communicate with me upsets him greatly. I've also had some visits from the Yeti, you know, those people who are confused with the 'abominable snowmen.' There are some here in California. They were sighted near Sonora just a few days after we talked to one. Another regular visitor is Ankaton, an Egyptian who lived in Atlantis. He calls this new Age of Aquarius the 'New Egypt.' White Eagle, unfortunately, calls this new decade 'the sad seventies.'"

White Eagle is not optimistic about the future, because he sees an upcoming war with the United States and Russia united against China, in spite of President Nixon's overtures. Right after Marshall

Tito of Yugoslavia dies two other Iron Curtain countries are going to align themselves with Germany (probably Rumania and Hungary). While Russia will be involved in military problems in Egypt, China will start fighting for supremacy using her atomic bombs.

England and the United States will be drawn into the fight to help Russia. (Prince Charles, by then King Charles, will suggest that he abdicate and England become a Republic.) The final battle will be fought somewhere in Africa (the Middle East?) and "just as the United States is forced to its knees" a fleet of flying saucers will come out of the heavens "to create terror in the hearts of the Chinese and be on our side. Then we will see that saucers are real and that the beings in them are from other planets who have been watching us and don't want us to destroy ourselves and the pattern of the solar system. These people don't want to invade the world, they just want to save us from annihilation." Apparently the build-up to all this will be in the "sad seventies," with the final battle coming in the late 1980's.

White Eagle also predicts a man becoming President of the United States who will be "outside of both parties and a terrific surprise. He will be a beneficent dictator and everyone will fight him. The Church will fight him, big business will fight him, the students will fight him. But after a short time people will realize that he is working for their good and will let him have his way. He will bring in reforms that are needed today, but that no politician dares suggest."

White Eagle agrees with almost all the other mediums that there is a messiah coming to save the world. He also agrees that he will be here before the year 2000. He has already been born but contrary to what others say, however, he is an American and not from the East. "He will be the leader of the Sixth Race," says Mr. White, and will be golden in color.

The Sixth Race is the one that will take over from us, the almost extinct Fifth Race. "They will be called the Golden Race because they will not be white nor yellow, but instead a lighter almost Latin hue. The New World will be from California down to the coast of Chile. There will be great earth movements and Bolivia will be on the sea.

"There will be an earthquake here but it will not touch San

Francisco. It will hit Southern California instead. San Francisco is the chosen place for the Aquarian Age because it is the gateway to the Orient. Already, you see, San Francisco is called the 'Golden Gate' and the strange thing is that in the Atlantean days the main city of Atlantis was 'the city of the golden gate.' Which is a very extraordinary coincidence . . . if you can call it that.

"This new interest in the occult is the death pangs of this old race and the birth pangs of the other. Our young people have taken to this because they will be the parents of those who will come to take over. Old ideas must perish and make way for the new. If we are to have a new era, it must be *absolutely* new.

"The people who come into my bookshop almost always ask me, 'How can I develop my psychic ability?' They are on the right path providing they want these powers to help others and not just to entertain their friends or pick winners at the race track. Anyone who thinks he has the ability—and has love in his heart for mankind—can develop into a medium. The powers are dormant in all of us. It's time to take them out and examine them, not hide them and be ashamed of them because of what less-enlightened people might think.

"No matter what you do, you cannot change the world. There is a plan for us drawn up by masters far greater than we are. We are part of a giant whole. Yet like fleas on a dog or ants in a hill we cannot begin to understand the great intelligence that has mapped everything out for us so carefully. But why try to understand it? That's silly. All you have to do is try and fit into the plan that has been drawn up for you and be in harmony with it. That's all you can do."

While Mr. White's bookshop is the center of occult activity in Northern California, there are other shops in San Francisco that deal in psychic books and objects. Fritzi Armstrong has the Metaphysical Town Hall Bookshop on Mason Street. It has been in operation since 1943 and while Miss Armstrong is a noted astrologer, the store leans more toward the oriental philosophies and religions. It is decorated with wicker screens, Hindu paintings and cabalistic symbols. The air is heavy with incense and the smell of old books. One medium refers to it as "the spookery bookery," but customers do come in and lectures are given.

The first exclusively "astrological" shop to open in the United States was in San Francisco, at 1805 Polk Street. It's called the Solunar and its owner is a dynamic, charming psychic named Yvonne Purtell. Yvonne is in her forties, dresses stylishly and is a dead ringer for actress Ruth Roman. She began the shop in 1968 because she knew that astrology would be the coming thing. In order to stock her shelves with zodiac glasses, zodiac cards, zodiac jewelry, zodiac perfumes and just about everything else that would take a zodiac sign, she canvassed the nation's wholesalers and when she didn't find an item she wanted, she drew her own plans and had it produced. The shop is small, overcrowded and unpretentious. There is a minute back room that serves as storage space, bathroom path and consultation area where mystics give readings.

"I have psychic powers myself," she says, looking over her glasses, which are always pushed down to the tip of her nose, "but I feel my real purpose in this field is to point out the charlatans. When I hear that a new medium has set up practice, I go and have a reading. I do the same with new astrologers, Tarot readers, numerologists, all of them. I know my past lives and what has happened in this one and those that don't hit the nail right on the head get nowhere in my shop or with my clients. You might say I'm a kind of occult cop. Many distraught people pay good money to have their lives charted for them and to show them where they are going. At times clients are close to suicide or madness. They must have truthful readings or they'll be pushed off that thin line they are balancing. A false medium or an untrained astrologer can do more harm than good. I weed them 'out and, if necessary, expose them." Consequently, some of the best psychics in the business can be found at her tiny store.

Psychic powers are old hat in Yvonne's family. Her daughter Renée is on her way toward mediumship and her great-aunt Margaret was one of the strangest mediums in the Bay Area.

Aunt Margaret built a huge Victorian home in Palo Alto. It was constructed in 1904 with all the towers, cornices, stained glass and gingerbread of the era. No sooner did she move in than she discovered the place was haunted. "Something must have happened on the property before we built this place," she would say, "for ghosts don't jump right into a new house." (Aunt Margaret was long accustomed to taking strange manifestations for granted. When she was a little girl on her father's ranch in Scotts Valley, California, she and her sisters would place their hands on the top of a heavy old picnic table and move it around the yard. It was their form of entertainment.) By the time Yvonne was born Aunt Margaret was well known as a healer and a medium. The house was also well known for being haunted. Her first child mysteriously drowned in a few inches of water in a mop pail. Another went insane and still another was terribly crippled with arthritis. The neighbors walked quickly past the house and grocery stores refused to make deliveries. But still Aunt Margaret refused to leave her home.

As a child, when Yvonne would go and spend the night there, she would be so frightened of the noises she'd hear in the corners of her room that she would wet the bed rather than walk down the long dark corridor to the bathroom. One evening she was upstairs and remembered she had something to tell her great-aunt. "I ran downstairs and there was Aunt Margaret sitting in a chair in the dining room. Behind her was a strange figure. I didn't give it a thought but hurried over to touch it. My hand went right through it. I didn't see if it was a man or a woman but I could make out the shape of the shoulders, the arms and the fingers. It looked like it was made out of the same stuff you get when you turn on your television set in the morning before the station has come on the air. You know, gray and jumpy with white wavy lines. I called out: 'Aunt Margaret, there is somebody behind you!' and I touched her arm. It was ice cold. Then she looked at me and smiled. 'That's a positive thing,' she said, 'not negative. You must understand.' After a minute or so the thing slowly vanished. It was the first time I had ever seen a ghost."

But it wasn't to be the last. One day, years later, Aunt Margaret came to San Francisco to attend one of Mrs. Becker's Spiritualist sessions. She sat on the aisle and Yvonne sat to her left. As Mrs. Becker was reading her billets and answering questions while blindfolded, Yvonne noticed a woman standing in the aisle near her aunt. "I didn't think anything about it, because often members of the congregation would rush forward to consult with Mrs. Becker when she finished her billet readings. I thought this woman was there waiting for the medium to finish. But I also wished that she would sit down, because she was disturbing me. I could see, out of the corner of my eye, that she wore a full skirt and a beautiful brocaded shawl. I remember thinking what an expensive shawl it must have been. I was listening to every word Mrs. Becker was saying and so didn't turn to look the annoying figure in the face. When Mrs. Becker finished, she removed her blindfold and started to say something. Then she looked right at Aunt Margaret and said: 'Oh, your mother is standing beside you!' I turned and the vision vanished. Later Mrs. Becker gave a perfect description of my great-grandmother, who had died long before I was born and who had never been to see Mrs. Becker."

Aunt Margaret often complained that when she was home trying to read a book, "spirits would come through the doors to ask where they were." She would always carefully explain that they were dead and tell them how to get onto the astral plane they were looking for. A nephew, home from college, tried to live with his aunt but finally moved out. "It wasn't the noises at night that bothered me," he later told Yvonne, "but the heavy breathing in my face when I tried to sleep. It was as if there were people there who were trying to speak to me but didn't have the strength. I could feel their breath and hear their gasping. I never saw any of them, because I was too frightened to open my eyes."

The city finally condemned the old house and Yvonne and her mother went to move Aunt Margaret to an apartment. The woman was living in one downstairs room near the kitchen. The other rooms and floors had been closed off for years. "It was a chilly day," Yvonne recalls, "and she had a small heater going, so we kept the door to the corridor closed. As we were packing her books and things we heard a loud noise in the hall. It sounded like a crowd of people talking, laughing and moving about. I looked at my mother and she looked at me. I walked to the door and opened it. The hall was empty. Puzzled, I closed the door and went back to the packing. The noise came again, just like a crowded cocktail party in the hall. This time I waited, tiptoed to the door and yanked it open quickly. The hall was empty. Aunt Margaret looked at both of us and said, 'Don't be alarmed. It's just a few old friends from the spirit world who've come to tell me good-by.' You'd better believe that mother and I packed up and carried things to the car in a hurry, almost shouting the Lord's Prayer for protection as we walked through the house!"

As if that isn't enough, Yvonne has another aunt living with her now. The aunt came to stay when Yvonne's daughter Renée was born. She looks after the girl, gives her advice and fusses around the laundry room. She has been seen by everyone in the house (except Yvonne's husband Wally) and by several visitors. The family dog doesn't pay any attention to her anymore. Neither does the cat. Her name is Aunt Alida. She died in 1949.

While I have yet to be "convinced" by astrology, I must admit that it does have its merits. I must also admit that astrologists are the largest practicing "group" of psychics in California. There are more in the Los Angeles area than the northern part of the state, but some of those around San Francisco are considered powerful indeed.

Their dean is, unquestionably, a white-haired gentleman named Gavin Arthur. Mr. Arthur, aside from his claim to fame as an astrologer, bon vivant and member of San Francisco high society is also the grandson of U. S. President Chester Alan Arthur. He has been casting astrological charts for movie stars, politicians, authors, jet set members and hardened criminals since 1931. Alan Watts called him "the aristocrat of the Bohemians." Tallulah Bankhead called him "dahling" each time she was in town to have her stars read. Mr. Arthur, it is said, seasons his zodiac with enough theatrics to have made a good name as well as a good living for himself. He was asked by a top American magazine to draw Charles Manson's chart right after the Sharon Tate murders. His conclusion: Manson was fated to be a killer. He was also asked by Lady Bird Johnson to draw up Lyndon's chart. His conclusion (as published in *Playboy*): "Self-driving character, an executive eccentricity that is not queerness or unbalance but, rather, is *power*. A remarkable facility for intuition and insight which he is unable to use, because he does not trust spooky things. But a fine green line to Pluto keeps him constantly in touch with the people; and, a fine blue line to Uranus in the house of play makes him a superb showman. Yet his Jupiter in Leo makes it seem logical to shake the big stick, and this proved to be his downfall. He believed 'might makes right.' "

I did not seek out Mr. Arthur for an interview (those wishing to know more about his brand of astrology, especially as how the stars influence our sexual life, should read his delightful *The Circle of Sex*), but instead three others that I had personally seen practicing this ancient art. They know how to make the knowledge that the stars give them work for their clients, yet each of them approachs the material from separate angles. I discovered there is a difference between *tropical* astrology, *horary* astrology and *siderial* astrology. At times those differences can make all the difference in the world.

Sue Christeen Handley has been a tropical astrologist for only a short time, yet the charts she has drawn have delighted her clients more than any newcomer in the Bay Area. She lives in an old house in San Francisco with her two adopted sons, a couple of cats and assorted friends. Her manner is relaxed and informal. Her charm is formidable.

"I started studying astrology because I had a friend who was hung up on it. I was sure she was wrong so I read a few books to try and disprove it. Instead of ending up a scoffer, I ended up a believer. I've never been able to disprove it." She lit a cigarette and ran her hand through her short-cropped reddish hair. "Intellectually I find that I can't believe how a bunch of planets far far away are able to affect us. But intellectually I can't believe that two tons of metal is going to pick up and take me to Los Angeles either. I don't understand airplanes but they work. I don't believe in astrology, but it works.

"Astrology is valuable today because it is a pathway. We are all lost souls looking for something to guide us. That may be the reason so many people are turning to the occult, trying to find a pathway. The stars give us a pathway, actually it's more like a road map. It clearly points out the major highways and tells us where we will go if we stay on them. But if we want to experiment and take a side road we are warned about its conditions in advance.

"It's also good because it makes things easier for us. When we are going through a bad period—be it finance, romance or health —we can study the astrological chart and see the light at the end of the tunnel. It gives us courage to bear up under the most adverse conditions, because we can see that there is an end to them."

"Is there no way to avoid those dangers we see coming?" I asked.

"Sure there is. Using metaphysical techniques we can change anything. The old joke about staying in bed when your astrologer sees danger for you is not so funny in reality. Why flaunt trouble in the face? If you can avoid a bad situation by learning of it in advance, you'd be a fool to walk right into it. But there are also the laws of the Karmic to be considered. Many times you are forced to go through a certain situation for your own cosmic growth. Things happen that you don't like but you can't say it's good or bad, it's just something you have to go through—it's a learning process. I may not like what I learn but I know I have to have this information or experience as part of my Karma."

"Do you believe in Karma?"

"Most definitely."

"In reincarnation?"

"Absolutely."

Miss Handley's charts have attracted notice in San Francisco not only for the things she predicts but the way she predicts them. I asked her if she did it using psychic powers.

"I don't really feel I have psychic powers, particularly when I'm drawing up a chart. I follow a set of books and a set of rules and I figure out where the planets lie and their influence on each other. You don't have to be psychic to do that."

"But where do your interpretations come from? A rule book?"

"Oh, no. If I should see that certain aspects of a client's chart portend accidents, then I look closely and try to see what the other aspects portend. As I do this, suddenly I'll see a picture of what will happen. It's like being in a movie house and watching the accident take place on the screen. So I warn the client about this future event."

"And you don't call that being psychic?"

"Well, I have a retrograded Neptune and people with a retrograded Neptune tend to deny any psychic powers they have. I guess that makes me modest. But I did see a fairy once. Don't laugh, I mean a real fairy, one of those beings we used to call 'little people.' I was about ten years old and living on my parents' old farm near Indianapolis. I didn't have any playmates except a snake down by the creek. I used to go and talk to him when I was terribly lonely. Well, one day, when I was on my way to see him, I glanced down into a culvert and saw a tiny little lady with long golden hair and a little blue dress. I think I startled her, for she flew up and circled around me before she darted away. I wasn't frightened, just fascinated. When I came home and told my mother she gave me one of those looks she always did, and said, 'Yes, certainly. Now sit down and have lunch.' But I do remember her. She was so pretty. It was a warm summer day, but it wasn't *that* hot!"

Damon Runyon would have liked John Mazurek. He is big, rough, yet tender. His specialty is siderial astrology. He teaches it, draws up charts in it, and plays the horses in it.

"I always believed in astrology, but I used to be a tropicalist. You know, following just what the daily newspaper said and what the little old ladies drew up for me. In those days the business was full of little old ladies. I've got nothing against 'em, but whenever I wanted to use this knowledge to play the ponies and I went to one of them to see if it was my lucky day or not they would get all excited. They'd preach and say I was a sinner and try to instill the fear of Christ in me and all that blah-blah-blah. They said I wanted to use it for personal gain. Damned right

I did! I wanted to have the stars pick me a winner. What was so awful about that?

"So around 1945 I heard of an Irishman named Cyril Fagin who had discovered—no, rediscovered—the science of siderial astrology. The Orientals and the Hindus and all those eastern people had been using siderial for centuries, but somehow we Westerners got sidetracked to tropical. There's too much error in tropical. It's too vague."

Mazurek explained to me that siderial means measuring a star from a fixed point and using the constellations as guidelines and not the traditional birthdate zodiac time zones. "The little old ladies made astrology a religion. It's not a religion, it was orginally set up to be a timing device. It started in the valley of the Nile and was used by those old guys to tell the people when to expect the floods. They knew that when Ceres, the Dog Star, rose in the eastern horizon that the river was going to start to flood. So they got the hell up. They'd take their animals and household goods and get out of there. This was a yearly thing, timed in advance by the stars. It was a fixed thing. It was visual. It was siderial.

"Before all this mysticism, magic and crap got mixed up in it, it was an agricultural thing. It told people when to plant and sow. It was a practical thing so that the people could help themselves. They studied the stars to see how they would affect their daily living."

"In other words, what the majority of astrologers is using today is not the original astrology of the Egyptians. But what's wrong with that?" I asked.

"It's wrong because it's not exact. It's way off center. A lot of time has passed since the early ideas of the zodiac were laid down and the earth has moved slightly away from its position of some three thousand years ago. The signs have moved but the constellations have not. They are fixed. In other words, they are the points that should be charted today, because they are the same as they've always been. The zodiac signs have shifted because we have shifted."

"I'm not too sure I understand."

"Look. The constellations and the signs now overlap. The movements of the earth have made them overlap about twenty-four degrees. You will never be a hundred per cent correct today if you use the signs, because you have to take those twenty-four degrees into consideration. That's a lot of degree when you are trying to figure out something. What was valid several hundred years ago for a certain zodiac sign, just ain't so today. Take Cancer. Tropical astrologers will say that Cancers are home-loving people and all that sort of jazz, but these people—as least those in the first twenty-four degrees of the sign—are literary people per se. Their interests are creative, a far cry from what the tropicalists assign to them. I've had hundreds of people in the past few years come to me for a siderial chart because they simply couldn't identify with the pat personality traits the topicalists gave them. What's your sign?"

"I'm Libra," I replied. "The second of October."

"Okay, let's take you. The tropicalists say you should be interested in painting, want a home life, need partners and are good in business. Are you any of those things?"

"None of them," I admitted shamefacedly.

"There you are, but you are early enough in Libra to really be a Virgo in siderial astrology! You should be a writer, a loner and messed up as far as finances are concerned. Isn't that what you are?"

I just nodded.

"So there you are! You see? No wonder people don't understand astrology. The little old ladies have loused it all up!"

Mazurek claims that siderial astrology is the greatest predictive science known to man. He can figure out a person's lucky period down to the minute and advise them when to play the ponies and when to stay away from the track completely. He can tell you when to sign a contract, when to be interviewed for a job and when to ask for a raise. Not just the right day, but the right hour of that day. "This business of gamblers having a 'lucky streak' is true. Lady Luck smiles on you only at certain times. You don't have to know when a horse was born to know if he is going to win or not. You don't need to know when your boss was born in order to hit him for a few days off. What you do need to know is when the planets are favoring *you*. The hell with the horse and your boss. *Your* luck is influencing *them*.

"Siderial astrology, once you bring in those overlapping twenty-four degrees, can tell you anything you want to know. For instance, my lady friend and I breed purebred Arabian horses. We want fillies because they bring the most money and by using siderial astrology we can get a hundred per cent fillies. That's what we want and that's what we get. If we want a colt or two we get that also, because we can regulate the species by using the fixed zodiac without one margin of error. Our breeding technique is hooked up with the phases of the moon and it always comes out."

"Can people use this?" I asked. "If I was married and wanted a son, there would be a certain time for conception?"

"That's correct. If you wanted a boy and you did it on the exact moment, you'd get a boy. If you wanted a daughter and did it according to the phases of the moon, you'd get a girl. Screw around—if you'll excuse the expression—with tropical astrology and you'll get whatever they want to give you!"

Macielle Brown is very feminine. She is not the "little old lady" type that siderial astrologist Mazurek complains about, in spite of the fact that she is a grandmother. Her readings in horary astrology are known over most of the West Coast. She is gracious without being condescending. She can be frank without being unsettling. She is sure she was destined to be an astrologer.

"When I look at my own natal chart I see so many qualities pertaining to astrology. I'm Pisces with Virgo rising giving me the ability to be analytical about people and things. I've looked thoroughly into astrology and give the people who come to me the benefit of my research and experience. I believe in what I do and teach. If I would see another person with a chart like mine I'd say immediately: 'Hey, you're missing the boat if you're not doing professional astrology.'"

Mrs. Brown (who prefers to use the name Peggy K. Brown because of the better numerology vibrations attached to it) was an unwanted child passed among relatives until she came to California to be raised by total strangers, "who gave me love and a fierce pride in my adopted state." Her marriage has lasted twenty-five years mainly because her mother-in-law picked the wedding date by the stars. "She was my first introduction to astrology. She saw the latent abilities I had and was courageous enough, in those days, to insist I look into it. Our marriage has worked in spite of the fact that my husband is a double Leo and I'm a Pisces."

"Horary astrology is closely akin to tropical in that we use the familiar zodiac signs, but we use it to solve definite problems. It is the answering of a specific question at a time when the question has been expressed verbally or in thought to the point of knowing that this is exactly what you want to know. So often you will roll a question around in your mind, let's say, about moving. Should you move to L.A., for example. The job might be better, the climate be better, etc. As you mull this over and over in your mind, you can't make a decision and you can't place clearly the reason for making this move. As soon as the real reason behind the problem becomes apparent, i.e., for a better job, then you consult horary astrology and minutely examine the professional aspects of the stars' influences. The stellar pattern matches the vibrations of your Mercury or mind waves and your ability to accept the answer that is given at that time.

"There is another branch called 'mundane' astrology, which is quite deep and different in its interpretations. One needs many more things to do it successfully. In mundane it's necessary to set up charts for every month of the year and if you are doing it thoroughly you set them up for every country in the world. Then you are able to follow the trend of any nation's economy or politics. For instance, a good mundane astrologer would have seen De Gaulle's death. It could have been pinpointed to the very day."

(Still another astrological branch is taught in San Francisco by Daisy Jamison. She calls it 'spiritual' astrology and it has to do with reincarnation and your past lives. Her class, known as The Lotus Group, is one of the most exclusive and difficult astrology courses in the area.)

"You mentioned Mercury's vibrations," I said. "What about this word 'vibrations'? It seems to be used a lot in astrology and by the youth of today."

"The main idea behind the science of astrology is that of vibrations. We all know that the moon governs the waters of the earth. It's the pull and recession of the moon that allows the tides to go up and down. Human beings are seventy per cent water and deeply influenced by the moon because of this. Each planet has its own vibrations that, linked with the power of the moon, work on different parts of our bodies. For instance, the mind responds to Mercury, the muscles and circulation to Mars and Aquarius. The heart obeys Leo and each part of us responds to a different part of our universe. This makes us complete and in this way we are never separated from the universe. Just like a planet responds to different positions of the sun during the day, we too respond to the vibrations of the planets. Thus by studying their direction and knowing how to best gain and benefit from their vibrations, we can achieve the great potential that we were born with."

"But doesn't everyone feel the vibrations equally?"

"No. At the time of birth the stellar pattern is unique to the individual because of the place he was born and the exact time of the year, month and day. When we calculate this information it gives us an exact and completely different layout for each human life. Because the stars are in constant movement, often even twins who are born several minutes apart have widely varied personality differences. The interesting thing about astrology is that each one of us is a unique, original, individualistic person. The placement of our stars makes us different from everyone around us. Therefore our life chart is different. An astrologist makes a plan of where the stars were at birth and where the stars are during the lifetime. As they move reflecting and vibrating off of other stars, so do they vibrate differently onto us. When they are stronger we feel them stronger. When they are in conjunction with other planets we get the effect of the vibratory mixture.

"I like to refer to a person's life chart as the blueprint for the many mansions the Bible talks about. By knowing how to read this blueprint, by knowing where the strong points and the weak points are, by knowing when to walk softly across one section and use all your energies in another you know how to best live within this mansion which is your present life-span."

"That means we are all destined to a certain routine, doesn't it? Doesn't belief in astrology also make one a fatalist?"

She shook one manicured finger and scowled. "Oh no. Man is not 'doomed' to anything, because he has the choice of free will. As long as he tries to achieve the best that is within him, he will respond to the higher vibrations. But when he seeks to out-do another fellow or is careless or malicious, then he is deliberately not responding to the higher vibrations and he falls into negativity. He gets everything negative that planet has to offer. Through free will man has the ability to establish his own destiny using the very tools that his neighbor is using but creating a finer life. It isn't fatalistic. We all have a choice."

Reading the Tarot cards is, surprisingly, not as strong in the north of the state as it is in the south. Bookshops sell dozens of decks and instructions to go with them but serious "readers" seem hard to come by. Judy Mar is a novice with the old medieval paste-boards. She's given several readings and tuned into many thoughts and desires. She would like to tell others how she does it, but she doesn't know. "It just happens, that's all."

Judy Mar (she changed her last name from Morrow because it vibrated better in numerology) was at friend Sue Handley's apart-ment when someone brought out a deck of Tarot. She idly said, "Gee, I'd like to try those," and another person said, "Well, lay them for me." She did.

"It was just a joke," the thin and lovely brunette remembers, "but as I was saying the things that came into my mind as I looked at each card, everyone else was going 'ooohh' and 'wow!' Finally, I stopped and told them that if they were going to make fun of me I wouldn't continue. They said they weren't laughing, but were amazed, because the girl who was getting the reading had been read before by two other mediums and I was using the exact words they had used! It really bothered me, but I haven't let the cards out of my sight since."

Judy says that while she has never studied the Tarot cards or read any books about their meanings she knows immediately what they are saying. "One small corner of a card will suddenly become very important and I'll know that it is the message. For instance, one afternoon I was reading the cards for a woman and my attention was riveted onto the drawing of a tiny snail on one of the major arcana cards. I had never noticed that snail before. It had never been important before. Yet now it loomed larger than anything on the table. I told the woman that I saw her life going slowly, that she felt frustrated by time and the many problems she was carrying with her. She agreed that the slow passage of time was killing her. She wanted to move on because she hoped for a better future. I had been called by the snail and had interpreted it correctly. After that the reading went beautifully."

Sometimes she sees things and hesitates before she speaks, wondering if the person before her really wants to know. "Once a college boy came to me and I read in the cards that he was hiding something, something that was part of him yet something he was forcing into the background. He denied it. I looked closer and saw that he was contemplating suicide because of this. Again he denied it. Finally one of the cards almost shouted that the boy was a homosexual. When I told him he broke into tears. Then I explained that he wasn't alone in the world and that there were millions like himself who had accepted their 'difference' and were living healthy, productive lives. He went away thanking me, promising to stop thinking about suicide and start planning for a fuller life. I feel that people who come for a reading are really saying, 'All right, you can look deep inside me, but please don't wound.' When I do pull out the bad things I always do it in a way that says, 'Hey, you're being selfish and the only person it's hurting is you.'

"I feel my readings are more like tuning in a television set. I can't predict the future very well, but I can unlock hidden secrets and bring them into the open. Once they are aired, they can usually be solved. The biggest problem with this is that I can read people better and tune in on my friends' minds. Sometimes I'll tune in on things they want to keep secret. Often I'll want to contact Sue Handley, for example, and I'll just transmit a thought. It's easier than a telephone call and much faster. If I decide to come over for a visit, I'll send her a thought message and sure enough, when I walk in the door she has dinner ready and a bottle of wine already open.

"We are all born with the ability to communicate with one another, just like we are born with eyes to see one another, yet we use our eyes and deny our ESP. It's there, latent, inside us. Anybody can do what I do. It works better for me because I accept it, rather than fight it.

"But many of my friends don't like this ability and they've stopped coming to see me. It freaks them that I know when they are lying or being evasive. One friend bought a new stereo set and excitedly telephoned me. 'Guess what I just got!' she shouted. 'A new stereo,' I replied calmly. She was so furious she slammed the phone.

"To have this ability and to have the knowledge of what's going on in the mind of another person is a very lonely thing. You can't keep secrets from a good mind-reader. Also it plays havoc with your love life. Sue Handley says when she gets around to writing her autobiography she's going to call it *Witches Live Alone*.

In most of the United States palmistry is associated with gypsies, tents and pieces of silver, but in San Francisco those wanting their palm read head straight to a young man from New Delhi, a man with a soft voice, soft eyes and a great deal of clairvoyant power. His name: Joy Kapur.

One day back in India when he was in his early teens he decided to visit a local palmist. The man studied his hand and then proceeded to tell him everything about his life, how many brothers and sisters he had and what he hoped his future would be. "That did it," he says. "I figured if this humble man could read these things then there must be something to it."

He started studying all the palmistry books he could find and traveling for miles to consult other known palmists. The first reading he tried on his own, for a friend, shook him up. "I saw the line of suicide in there but I didn't want to tell him. He had been reading books on palmistry too and insisted that the line was there. I refused to admit what I saw but lied and said that he was going to have a long life. A few months later he killed himself. I wasn't surprised, because his tragic death had been clearly engraved in his palm."

"Then there is no escape from what is written in your hand?" I asked.

"No, I believe that 50% of your life is destiny and the other 50% you make yourself. Do you play poker? Good. Then you know that you may get very good cards and you may goof up. Another player may get bad cards, but he ends up by winning the game because of the clever way he played it. So destiny is before you. It is up to you how you play it."

"Are there any things in a life that cannot be seen in the palm?"

"I don't believe so, and if they are hidden, then I notice them in a strange way. Often I find my mouth saying things about a person that I really don't read in the hand."

"So you are not just a cold scientific reader of lines?"

He smiled. "When I try to be, it is of no avail. I seem to have quite a bit of intuition. Some people are born with it, others develop it. I just seem to have it. It is nothing so strange, however. Those who read the Tarot cards or the crystal ball or draw up astrology charts also have it. It is part of being a psychic."

"Do you do anything differently than the readers in India?"

"I don't think so, except that I read the right hand for men and the left hand for women. I consider men and women to be positive and negative poles, and they must be studied accordingly."

Kapur, who just turned thirty, always wanted to travel. He consulted a palmist in Bombay who told him he would go to the United States, live near the sea for seven years in a town whose name began with S. A bizarre series of incidents brought him to San Francisco. He feels happy there and doesn't plan to alter this part of his destiny.

"Why have you been so completely accepted in California?" I asked.

"Well, the mentality of those here on the West Coast seems to be different from other places in America. Here they are not afraid of new people and new ideas. It's almost as if they know that their old values—the values they fought so and worked so to obtain—are not really what they want. They are searching for something else. They think that maybe I have that something else.

"For instance, the other day I was talking to a prominent medical doctor and he said he didn't believe in palmistry. I asked him if he looked at a patient's nails when he gave them an examination. He admitted that he did, because he could tell about blood pressure from them. Then I told him of the things I have observed just by examining a person's nails. I told him what the half-moons can convey, what ridges in the nails of certain fingers can mean, what a square-shaped nail means and what kind of disease can be diagnosed from a wavy nail. He was fascinated with this 'new' material, yet these things that I told him go back centuries in my native land of India."

It was my turn to smile. "Many mystics," I said, "are predicting that in the final analysis it will be the wisdom of India that will eventually lead us Americans into the 'true' path of wisdom. Yet aren't India's mystical truths inadequate for our busy twentieth-century life? Won't we have to go into caves or sit along the banks of rivers to understand them?"

"Truths don't come just to those in caves, they come to anyone who stops long enough to meditate and listen. A great city is a marvelous place in which to live. But there are many temptations. There are no temptations in a cave. If you can remain aloof in a great city, that is wonderful. If you can avoid the poisons of your neighbors, the evil of fighting for what the other man possesses and be pure in heart toward your fellow worker, then you don't need a cave. Your mind is a cave, you can pull into it and still enjoy the advantages of a great city. To do both is quite beautiful."

"What other psychic sciences do you practice?"

"Well, I'm very interested in physiognomy. The features of a face can tell you a great deal about a person. So can the shape of his body. It is a more useful science than palmistry, because you cannot always ask to see someone's hand, yet you can freely read his face. This too, is an old Indian practice.

"How wonderful it would be if we could tell about a person just by looking at him. Think of the dishonest acts that could be stopped before they began. Think of the women who wouldn't be tricked by cheating men. Think of the salesclerks who would lose their jobs because they were discovered lying about the merchandise. A child's face shows what is in store for the man. We should use this information, it would save so much heartache and so many years of frustration in the wrong profession. A good face-reader could tell which child was best suited for teaching, which for politics, which for public relations, etc. Then the child could be trained in that field. How many years of tears it would save!

"I like to study the faces of the famous. President Nixon, for instance. His eyes are close set. That means he is stubborn and whatever he says he is going to do, he will do it. If he says he will pull out of Vietnam, then he will. But he will only pull out when *he* is ready, not before. No amount of persuasion or street rallies can move him. He has two vertical lines in the center of his forehead which gives him very good balance of judgment. The country will not be unsafe in his hands. He also has a square jaw and that shows he is very enterprising. People with a jaw like that are inventive and have great willpower."

"And Agnew?"

"Agnew's face surprised me. That nose means he should be prosperous. Someday he will be very rich. And those wavy lines in his forehead! That shows the man is a genius! He has to have a very high I.Q. You know," and he laughed, "I think Agnew knows much more than he pretends or shows. To know it and not tell it, ahh, that is the mark of a good politician!"

Vassily looked into his crystal ball for me in the back room of the Solunar Bookshop. He fussed with the overhead lighting, pulled himself under a dark cloth much like old-fashioned photographers used to do and I could almost hear his long, thin fingers caressing the smooth sphere. He knew nothing about me. Yvonne Purtell had only told him that I wanted a reading.

"Why do I get palm trees?" he asked, peering out from under the cloth. "Tropical shores and jungle valleys. Does that mean anything to you?" I told him I had just come back from almost fifteen years in South America. "Fine," he said. "That means I'm tuned in."

A few seconds more and, "I see mountains, tall difficult mountains.

You are trying to do something very difficult. You are attempting a project as overwhelming to some as trying to scale a mountain." I nodded. He looked again, then pulled the cover off completely and stared. "Are you writing a book? A non-fiction book about the occult?" I admitted I was. "You have talked to many people and you will talk to still more. Somewhere along the way you will hear the truth." He snorted and added, "I hate that terminology, 'the truth.' Anyway, there will be touches of greatness in it. Not because of anything you've done or written, but because of what others have let you know. There will be secrets revealed and many will benefit from the guidelines you will place on paper. You have psychic abilities yourself." I said that others had told me that, too. He added: "But don't get overly conceited, for while you will put it onto a page, you are not writing it alone. You are being guided." Again he peered out at me. "Do you believe that?" "Yes," I replied. "Good."

I believed it and I was delighted, for I had come across one of the few old-fashioned fortune-tellers still left in Northern California. Not that Vassily is an *old* man (he's in his thirties), but because of his grandiloquent manner, his carefully chosen words, his richly modulated voice and his ability to use all the psychic arts instead of specializing in only one.

I had heard that he not only read the crystal ball, he drew up astrology charts, read Tarot cards, calculated Numerology, psychometrized objects, read sealed billets and went into trance. I had also heard that he was temperamental, nervous and, at times, bitchy. I had been told that he hated interviews and would never consent to sit still for one of mine. I mentally thanked the spirits for bringing us together.

Vassily (he refused to give any more name than that) came from a large family in Massachusetts who were not impressed with his early psychic abilities and didn't try to understand him. They ignored him, left him alone and made him miserable. But, he admits, "I was a little trying on them. I think I gave them the heebie-jeebies."

He had his first psychic experience one afternoon when he was nine years old. The family had gone off on a picnic, leaving him all alone in the big empty house. "It was just a year after my mother had died, and I was very unhappy. I sat in the living room and tried to look out the window, but it was covered with a heavy gauze curtain and a screen to keep out the flies. Also a huge tree cut off most of the view. I began to cry because I was so unhappy and I remember saying to myself, 'I don't want to be here! I want to go back to where I came from!' Why I said that, I don't recall, for I had always lived in that house. All the time in this lifetime, anyway. Then through my tears I heard a voice. It told me to be calm. I looked to see where it was coming from and as I glanced at the window I saw the curtain was gone, the screen was gone and even the tree in front was missing. I had a clear view right across the street to the neighbor's weed-filled front yard. But the thing was that the weeds and junk were gone and there were beautiful flowers blooming there instead. The voice told me that I was looking at what was going to happen and that I had been given a gift. The flowers would be there next year, the voice said, and sure enough, next year the yard was cleaned up and the blossoms were there exactly as I had been shown."

"Weren't you frightened by this?" I asked.

"Not at all. As a matter of fact I felt more reassured than I had felt about anything I could see, feel or touch. Because I knew that even though there was something unusual about me, everything would be all right. I knew that this ability would take me out of this unhappy realm anytime I wished."

"Why did you come to California?"

He paused. "That's a very unique question. I came because I was led by my higher mind to come here. I recognized that there was nothing for me on the East Coast and that the furthering and development of my future was here. To come to this conclusion I went into meditation and later I attracted a very gifted seer who corroborated what I had already decided. It was just as well that I did come West, because my life with my family was becoming impossible. I would know what they were going to say before they said it. I was able to locate items that they had lost. I would jump for the phone just before it would ring. Normal people can only take so much of that."

"When did you start reading the crystal ball?"

"When I was twelve, but I've studied all the other methods as well.

I use the method that I consider best for the person who is having the reading. Some people have more faith in the Tarot, so I lay the cards. Others prefer psychometry. Some want me to read billets. I do whatever reassures them the most, but no matter what method I use, the end results are always the same."

I was curious about what had happened under that black cloth, the few times that he had lifted it I glanced at the crystal but couldn't see a thing. "What physically happens when you look into the crystal ball," I asked. "What do you see?"

"I use this ball to block out my thinking process. Images will appear and they will suggest a specific thing. They appear rapidly and I must instantly recognize their true meaning. The difficulty is not in seeing something, but in interpreting it comprehensibly for the person who is having the reading. Most readings will begin with some tangible fact, like the palm trees and tropical climate I saw for you. That shows me that I'm on the correct level and have made contact."

"When you saw that mountain, was it in color or black and white? Do the images stand still or move? Are they solid?"

He frowned, already getting tired of my questions. "The images are always in color. Not color as we know it, but in odd off-toned pastels. Sometimes they will move and at times they will disappear to be replaced instantly by something else. If the first time I see a symbol and don't understand it, I will look again and the ball will clear. Then another symbol, clearer and more detailed, will appear. I never really see *things*, just symbols that need interpreting."

"Some critics have claimed that all a seer really does is to go into self-hypnosis. Do you agree?"

He rose from his chair near the table. "It is a form of self-hypnosis, yes, but you must understand what the term really means. If one induces the hypnoidal state, they have a very subtle balance between the subconscious and the conscious mind. It is a trance state and, at times, can be a very heavy. On occasions I have lost control of my conscious self, but fortunately I've been training in this field for over twelve years and I know how to take myself in and out of these states without endangering myself."

I tried for one last question as he led me toward the door. "I have heard that there are some people who don't need a crystal ball, that they can do the same thing with a glass of water or a mirror-smooth surface. Is this true?"

A slight smile was on his lips. "Completely. The ancient Egyptians did their scrying with a highly polished reflective surface. I have used water in a bowl and even a doorknob. The quality needed is the reflective quality. You must be able to look within it and at the same time within nothingness." The pressure of his hand on my arm was pushing me firmly but gently from the room. "You see, a crystal ball is not needed if you have the ability. What I have is a mental ability and not a physical ability. Good day and thank you for coming."

I walked away whistling, delighted with the man and his interview.

I have found while talking to most mediums and practicing psychics, that they have been aware of their abilities since childhood. Almost every one of them recalls something that happened when they were small. It's almost as if each of us were born with psychic abilities, but our parents told us that there are no such things as ghosts, that the little man we played with really wasn't there and that we must believe only what we see. We took mother at her word for other things, therefore we took her word about the spirit world as well.

One such little boy who sees things and yet has a most understanding parent, is Kevin. His mother allowed me to interview him, but asked that I not use his last name . . . for obvious reasons. Kevin lives in a middle-class house in a middle-class San Francisco neighborhood. His mother is single. She never married and took Kevin to live with her, "because I felt almost compelled to have the child with me. Even before he was born I knew that he would be mine."

Kevin's mother was a prostitute who walked the honky-tonk neighborhood around Turk Street. His father was a professional Turk Street homosexual who created Kevin one night just to see if he could do it. The mother wanted to abort later, but was told it would kill her if she tried to kill the baby. As her time drew near she somehow made friends with a woman I'll call just "Miss S." Miss S. offered to pay the hospital expenses and raise the child, even though she had almost no income herself. The prostitute agreed, then after Miss S. had the baby boy for a few months, she returned and demanded a "cash payment" if the new mother wanted to keep him. Miss S. managed to scrape the money together and got a signed receipt.

Kevin was an ordinary little boy with huge brown eyes and straw-colored hair. His new mother took him everywhere and he began to walk and talk much sooner than the doctor books said he would. One afternoon after about two months of playing with words and trying to form sentences, he turned to his adopted parent and said— quite clearly—"I'm glad you're my mother in this life because you've been my mother in so many lives before."

Miss S. was dumbfounded, yet said nothing. As the months rolled on strange things would happen. Kevin would start to put away his toys and get the living room ready to receive guests. When Miss S. told him that no one was coming to visit, he would say, "Oh, yes, Sandy and her friend Marie are going to arrive for dinner." Miss S. hadn't invited them but no matter, Sandy and Marie would appear. Kevin would stop in the middle of a sentence and point toward the silent telephone. "You're going to get a call, Mom. It'll be Eddy." Then the phone would ring and Eddy would be on the other end. Kevin knows the day before what mail his mother is going to receive. He knows what's in a package before it is opened and often knows what gifts he is going to get before his mother buys them. He also watches his favorite TV programs in color—even though his set at home is in black and white. "I have done nothing to discourage this ability," Miss S. says, "but also I don't try to have him predict the future for me or to force himself. I figure that whatever will come, will come. I have no doubt that Kevin and I were together in previous lives. I am positive that it was meant for use to be together in this one. The fact that his real father and mother created a body for him in the way they did is immaterial. The important thing was that they gave his soul a dwelling place for this lifetime. I never believed in any of these things before, but when you live with it twenty-four hours a day, it's difficult to deny."

The death of Ma Becker in 1970 left a void in the ranks of Spiritualist healers that has yet to be filled. There are several pretenders, but none of them has the force that great old lady had. Probably, in time, Reverend Pearl Shannon will be *the* Spiritualist in the Bay Area. Her picture appears in the San Francisco *Chronicle* each week, on the religious news page, in a small advertisement for her Western Spiritual Science Church, Inc. It's on 44 Page Street in a building aptly named Druids Hall. There are two Sunday services (1:30 and 7:30 P.M.), a Wednesday evening service and a Friday service at two in the afternoon. The services are usually well attended. Many of the new faces lately have been those who used to go to Mrs. Becker. The reverend stands behind a podium that is draped in golden velvet. There are always flowers nearby. Her dark hair is tousled and falls pixieish over her high forehead. She has small features and is of average height. Her voice has a tremulous touch, belying the fact that she once studied to be an opera singer but switched goals when the Crash came in 1929 and nobody had money for opera.

Reverend Shannon is dedicated, devout and determined. She receives messages from the spirits but takes none of their nonsense. "An s.o.b. on earth will be an s.o.b. in spirit too," she once told a reporter from *San Francisco* magazine (in a rare interview), "but only for a while. Most spirits develop talent and understanding on the other side. They mature." In spite of her ability, she confesses that at times she has difficulty getting through to the spirit world. She claims that a medium is like a telephone, and she never knows if the call will go through, when it will go through, or whether she'll be able to find the person she wants. Yet she believes in what she preaches. "In orthodoxy you're told there is a heaven, but even the people who preach it don't seem too sure. Spiritualism says the continued existence of the spirit is a proven fact." She is not overawed by her powers either. "I was born mediumistic. I'm not like one of those women who feels a shiver run down her spine and says, 'Whoo, I'm a medium!' So I don't show off. I don't hold séances so that Joe can talk to Uncle Fred. I've seen many lives ruined by thoughtless communications. People start using the spirits as a crutch. They can't make a move without consulting spirits. When someone has a crutch like that, they can say, 'I did what the spirits said. They're to blame, not me.'"

Sometimes, in San Francisco, spirit help will come suddenly and unexpected. Take the time the youthful Mohawk Indian Richard Oakes was lying in the San Francisco General Hospital and there was nothing the staff of trained doctors could do to rouse him. Oakes had been a leader of the "invasion" of Alcatraz Island and one evening he got into a fight with a Samoan. The dusky stranger beat Oakes so badly with a pool cue he was taken to the hospital, where he remained unconscious for two weeks. Then one day three medicine men arrived. They had come from three different tribes to save the young man by ancient remedies. They gave him a herb potion and chanted over his silent form. Hospital authorities permitted them into his room because "in the eyes of the medical staff they were performing religious rites." Within a very short time (much to the surprise and consternation of the doctors) Oakes began to recover. He left the hospital on his own two feet. What did the Indian medicine men do? They refused to comment, but Oakes says, "I am convinced that it was their visit that really pulled me through."

Eastern religions and oriental occult practices have rooted firmly into California's psychic soil. Zen Buddhism, which took hold in the era of the Beat Generation and Jack Kerouac managed to survive the Hippie movement while at the same time weeding out the curious and leaving a hard core of adepts. They have a monastery near Big Sur, in the state's "Untrammeled Middle." Tibetan Buddhism, on its last legs according to the prophets and the Red Chinese, is making one last try for survival in Berkeley, just across the bridge from San Francisco. Its leader, the Incarnate Lama Tarthang Tulko, set up his Tibetan Nyingmapa Meditation Center and has university students, dropouts, adults and former addicts as disciples. Yoga, which seems to have spread across the continent in the disguise of health and reducing classes, is strong in San Francisco. There is a community center with daily classes in all the Yoga arts that caters to both occasional visitors as well as commune residents. There are also the followers of a mystic named Meher Baba, who believe that he was God and who swear his teachings are giving them a better life. And there is white-bearded, almost sixty "Father" Chiranjiva Roy. He once had twenty American hippies living with him in a non-drug commune outside Calcutta and he came to California to show the youth here how to turn into themselves and off of drugs. He has been credited with "helping 500 acid freaks become responsible human beings."

There is another movement that is little known but can be farther out than any of the others. It's called Subud and it's a combination of philosophy, mysticism and the Holy Rollers. Its founder is an Indonesian named Muhammad Subud but called "Bapak" (father) by his followers. Told that he was to die at the age of twenty-four he set out to soak up as much knowledge as he could, but instead of listening to the teachings of the great masters, they sat at his feet as pupils. Then one dark and moonless night a great ball of brilliant light was seen to float above him as he was walking and talking with some friends. After that the "new dispensation" process of *latihan* was shown to him. He determined to share it with the world.

Today his followers meet in a series of rooms in an old-fashioned downtown San Francisco office building. Newcomers are given written instructions and must wait three months before they are admitted to their first session. They are asked to sit out in the corridor and listen to the session going on behind closed doors. What they hear always unnerves them and sometimes sends them away for good. There is singing, shouting, chanting, screaming, loud talking, low whispering, shrieks, hysteria, thumping and moaning. It is like a movie sound track with scenes from a High Mass to a police raid. The vibrations outside are astounding. What is going on inside is even more so.

The leader (anyone who has been *opened* by the latihan) separates the men in one room and the women in another. Then after a few brief words about purity and self-involvement they stand and wait. Soon an arm will jerk, a face will twitch or a head will shake. A woman cries. A man sobs. A woman stretches her arms and begins to whirl. A man hugs his arms to himself and falls to his knees. Soon (hopefully) everyone in the rooms is being *opened* by the latihan. They are being shown the force of God. They are being "tuned in" to the cosmic vibrations. For most it is a fascinating and "enlightening" experience. For others it's "too heavy, man. I just got freaked out." Singers claim it has enabled them to hit higher and purer notes. Dancers swear it gives them greater balance and poise. Those with physical ailments claim to have been cured. Each session lasts a half-hour and then is suddenly over. There is no religious instruction with it, no candles, altars, statues or built-in hierarchy. One of its main purposes, "Bapak" has written, is to help people experience the power of God in the midst of many different external conditions. It prepares you for living and it prepares you for dying.

Basil Brummer experimented with Subud and found it "too intense, too disturbing. I had to quit because I thought it was making me lose my mind." Basil is an artist, complete with long black beard and professional credits. He was born in Texas, painted in Mexico, taught in Georgia, experimented with the occult in New Orleans and came to San Francisco because "it was a freer place where people were more tolerant of psychic abilities."

For five years he worked as arts and crafts director of the U. S. Navy Recreation Department at both Hunters Point and Treasure Island Naval Stations, yet he wasn't happy. There was something inside him that had to be expressed and it wasn't the same thing every other artist was searching for. Basil was convinced he had psychic powers—the problem was to search them out. He joined yoga groups (hatha, raja, mantra, bakti, purna), studied the Tarot, went into Subud, tried meditation, Spiritualism, astrology, Rosicrucianism, Scientology, Group Enlightenment, Zen (he stopped because he couldn't understand the English of the Japanese priest), Numerology, the I Ching ("good, but too much reading between the lines"), Dr. Rhine's ESP, and reincarnation. It was while he was studying "how to read past lives" with Dr. Patricia Diegel of Sacramento that he stumbled across the method that is currently bringing him recognition in California occult circles.

Somewhere along the way he had discovered that he could meditate better by tuning into the vibrations of certain types of music. He was asked by the Metaphysical Book Shop to give a few classes and show others. But the classes were poorly attended and one night only one girl showed up. Rather than give the long lecture he had carefully prepared he sat talking to the girl and then got the feeling that he could "paint her portrait with symbols rather than features." He had his ever present watercolors and asked her to pose. "I held her hands for a few minutes while we both meditated. Then I began to get a background color with a kind of feather-form imposed on it. I put what I had seen on paper. She liked it immediately and asked if she could have it. She showed it to her friends and that started it."

Basil now works on a commission basis for his "meta-psychic" portraits. He does not need to meet his client, just know a few things about him. Then he will sit down, meditate and "tune into my client's higher-self. I will get a full color image of what the higher-self is trying to realize. It is not a picture of this self but rather a diagram of the true personality and the goals this self has set. Then I put it on paper. I have discovered that the longer a client lives with this portrait and studies it and meditates upon it, the more knowledge he will have about his higher-self. Symbols, which are only designs to me, become meaning-filled statements for the client after a while. They are like psychic road maps or life charts showing the strong points, the danger areas and the beautiful places. I don't know why I will use a certain color or why I'll put in a certain symbol. It is not for me to know. I am only the instrument. The important thing is that the client knows what it means. People have told me that my paintings have helped them. No artist can ask for more."

If interests in things psychic can lead to happiness, it can also lead to confusion and tragedy. Most people look for the good in the occult, only a few search it out for its evil. Such a man is the "Zodiac," a ruthless killer and terrorizer in San Francisco.

The police claim they know who the Zodiac is. As of January 1971, he had killed thirteen people. His choice of victims is indiscriminate. He's killed students, teenage lovers, a waitress and a cabdriver. He sends letters and post cards to the San Francisco *Chronicle* bragging about his old crimes and prophesying his new ones. His spelling is atrocious and his memory poor, especially when he quotes from Gilbert & Sullivan. He signs his letters "Zodiac" and affixes a circle on a cross. Homicide inspectors have checked out and cleared "literally thousands of suspected Zodiacs, named by wives, mothers, acquaintances, friends, fellow workers, delivery men . . . not to mention police agencies throughout the world." In upstate Napa County nine hundred different tips have come in about the killer. With the police on his trail he was suspected, then sighted, then disappeared from a large gathering at the Metaphysical Book Shop's "Hallowe'en Mystic Fair." He had gone there to consult a medium. His first question to the psychic: "When am I going to die?"

Amid all the "positive" magic, "good" vibrations and "white" light of the San Francisco occult scene, stands Anton Szandor LaVey. He stands apart, laughing and stroking his pointed goatee. His bald head shines in the light from the flames of the black candles at his "black" magic ceremonies. He wears black robes and a priest's white collar. He is the self-styled "Black Pope" of the occult nether-world. Some talk of him with awe and great respect. Others never mention his name, refer to him quickly as "that man."

LaVey believes in the powers of the devil and says that it's time Satan was openly worshiped instead of being suppressed. He claims that if it wasn't for Satan there would be no need for the Christian church. "Satan has certainly been the best friend the church has ever had, and he has kept it in business all these years. Without a devil to point their fingers at, religionists of the right-hand path would have nothing with which to threaten their followers. For two thousand years man has done penance for something he never should have had to feel guilty about in the first place. We are tired of denying ourselves the pleasures of life which we deserve. Today, as always, man needs to enjoy himself here and now, instead of waiting for his rewards in heaven. So why not have a religion based on indulgence? Certainly it is consistent with the nature of the beast."

Anton LaVey's ancestors came from Georgian, Rumanian and Alsatian stock and a gypsy grandmother told him tales of vampires and werewolves. His first reading material was *Weird-Tales* magazine, *Frankenstein* and *Dracula*. In 1942, at age twelve, he decided that since guns and weapons could be bought in Europe easier than food and clothing that the Bible was wrong. The earth would not be inherited by the meek, but only by those who were strong enough to take it. He learned to play the oboe and the piano, joined the San Francisco Symphony Ballet Orchestra and then left high school and home to join the Clyde Beatty Circus. His job was simply to water and feed the lions and tigers, but Beatty saw his "natural ability to tame fierce beasts" and promoted him to assistant trainer. At eighteen he left Beatty for a carnival, where he assisted a magician, learned how to hypnotize and began to study the occult. He also began to study human beings. "On Saturday night I would see men lusting after half-naked girls dancing at the carnival, and on Sunday morning when I was playing the organ for the tent show evangelists I would see these same men sitting in the pews with their wives and children, asking God to forgive them and purge them of carnal desires. I knew then that the Christian Church thrives on hypocrisy, and that man's carnal nature will out!"

He married a lovely blonde named Diane, took a steady job with the San Francisco Police Department as a photographer, and studied criminology at City College. But what he saw in three years on the force only affirmed his ideas that Satan was the real ruler of the world. "I saw the bloodiest, grimiest side of human nature. People shot, knifed. Little kids splattered in the gutter by hit-and-run drivers. It was disgusting and depressing. I asked myself, 'Where is God?' I came to detest the sanctimonious attitude of people toward violence, always saying it's God's will."

He began dabbling in ritual magic and held weekly meetings at his home with a small group of friends. They studied the Black Mass and pagan ceremonies of such groups as the 14th-century Knights Templar and the 19th-century Golden Dawn Society. They read what the Aztecs and Egyptians had to say about Satan and as they worked these rituals and charms LaVey discovered he could conjure up parking places at the last minute in front of theaters, make business deals come his way and make two people marry even though one disliked the other. "I discovered an ability through magic to bring reversals to enemies and gain advantage for myself. I realized I had stumbled onto something."

So on April 31, 1966, at *Walpurgisnacht*—the most important festival in witchcraft—LaVey shaved his head and announced the formation of his Church of Satan. The temple was in a three-story silvery-black Victorian house on California Street. The rooms became crammed with books, tombstones, coffins and a skeleton. One room was set aside as the ritual chamber.

His church first attracted attention when he performed a marriage before a "living altar." The altar was a nude woman and the local press was invited. Shortly after that he performed his first funeral, where he consigned the soul of a young sailor to the devil. A U. S. Navy honor guard stood by.

From all across California the curious and the disturbed come for sessions. He bars no one, asks few questions. It is a church and open to the public. Some famous names have been there and admit it. Most of them prefer not to admit it. Public opinion is still one of negative suspicion.

Perhaps the most famed of his congregation was actress Jayne Mansfield. She attended several sessions and supposedly once stretched herself out naked as a Black Mass altar. Shortly after that she was decapitated in an automobile accident. One young man (who has asked to remain nameless) told me that he had seen Jayne at the Church of Satan many times and was there the night she "opened herself to the devil." He claims that on the night she was killed he and his family were at the church and the lights suddenly dimmed. He glanced at his watch and swears it was almost immediately to the minute the newspapers say the actress died. At home, later, his father was walking across the kitchen when he suddenly collapsed onto the floor. His eyes rolled back and his breathing was heavy. As the boy and his mother tried to revive the man he began to speak, but it wasn't his voice that came out "but Jayne's. She cried and said she didn't want to die. She asked us to tell LaVey that he had to do something. She blamed that Black Mass for her death." The man came out of the trance but never returned to the church. "It was too heavy," his son recalls. "Just too heavy to fool with."

LaVey has written his own book of rules and calls it *The Satanic Bible*. It was published in pocketbook form by Avon Books and runs 272 pages. Available at most metaphysical bookstores (some shops refuse to carry it), it has become a best seller. The Black Pope pulls no punches. This Bible graphically discusses sexual intercourse, encourages personal ambition and berates passivity. "Hate your enemies with a whole heart," he advises, "and if a man smite you on one cheek, SMASH him on the other!; smite him hip and thigh for self-preservation is the highest law!"

"Behold the crucifix; what does it symbolize? Pallid incompetence hanging on a tree."

"Blessed are the strong, for they shall possess the earth—Cursed are the weak, for they shall inherit the yoke!"

"There has never been a great 'love' movement in the history of the world that hasn't wound up killing countless numbers of people to prove how much they loved them! Every hypocrite who ever walked the earth has had pockets bulging with love!"

LaVey's Bible tells the novice how to set up his own ritualistic circle, how to dress (or undress), how and what to drink as an offering to Satan, what to ask for and how to work up enough emotion to cause whatever you wish to come true. He refers to this book as "a primer—a basic text on materialistic magic. It is a Santanic *McGuffey's Reader*."

Whether LaVey is putting on an act or not is a debatable question. His years as a carnival magician give him great theatrical flair, yet he seems convinced that his mission on earth is to be the Devil's high priest. His church "answers a need in this Godless society" and also brings him a good income. He is not concerned with scoffers, for "the victim of a hex or curse is much more prone to destruction if he DOES NOT believe in it! So long as man knows the meaning of fear, he will need the ways and means to defend himself against these fears. If religious faith and fervor can make bleeding wounds appear on the body in approximation to the wounds supposedly inflicted on Christ . . . why then should there be any doubt as to the *destructive* extremes of fear and terror? Therefore, never attempt to convince the skeptic upon whom you wish to place a curse. Allow him to scoff. To enlighten him would lessen your chance of success. Listen with benign assurance as he laughs at your magic, knowing his days are filled with turmoil all the while. If he is despicable enough, by Satan's grace, he might even die—laughing!"

THE BAY AREA

The small towns around San Francisco have their share of psychic humans and ghostly happenings as well. Many of the mediums working in the city live in the outlying area. Maggie Anthony, the self-styled "Tarot Queen of San Francisco," lives in Berkeley, in a house that has its own vaporous meandering spirit. The nebulous figure has been seen sitting on the staircase while Mrs. Anthony was giving readings in the living room. One of those who has seen this apparition is yours truly.

Berkeley has a branch of the California Society for Psychical Research. There is also the Tibetan Meditation Center, previously mentioned, as well as a beautiful Yoga Center near the university campus. Recently when a seminar on mind control was held at the Claremont Hotel the sponsors were amazed to see more adults than students. A Jesuit Catholic church called Neuman Hall has rock Mass and offers study groups in the occult. The traditional United Church of Christ holds a far-out Wednesday night service where the pews are removed, rugs are laid down and strobe lights illuminate the psychedelic posters hung on the wall. One Ash Wednesday the main worship room was darkened to represent the catacombs and on Easter a young girl portraying Jesus stumbled across its floor with the weight of a cross on her shoulders while sound effects simulated crucifixion nailing. Their Sunday services, however, are quite traditional. "The Wednesday night sessions are just like the old-fashioned camp meetings," one elderly lady commented, "but for worship, I come on Sunday."

The run-down hippie area near the university campus has more than its share of metaphysical bookshops, mediums and Eastern gurus. Haight Ashbury has thinned out to the place where only the hard-core hippie has remained to fight over tenement apartments with invading Blacks. The hippies who haven't changed (or don't have any other "bag") have all crossed the Bay Bridge to wander up and down Berkeley's Telegraph Avenue. Recently a local underground magazine made a survey and discovered (to no one's surprise) that 94% of the kids read magazine horoscopes and 68% scan newspaper astrology columns. However, only 6% believed that the predictions regularly came true. Three fourths of those questioned admitted to having participated in some sort of occult happening, and almost all of them said they believed in psychic phenomena. Over half believed in flying saucers, 65% thought they had extrasensory perception yet only 14% thought it was possible to communicate with the dead. Most of them believe in reincarnation and—quite importantly—85% believed that drugs were not the definitive answer to reaching psychic goals.

Berkeley's most famous occult character is Isaac Bonewitz. He hit the front pages in June of 1970, when he was the first student *ever* to graduate from an American university with a bachelor degree in "Arts in Magic." Isaac (his full name is Philip Emmons Isaac Bonewitz) is called "The Wizard of Mod" by his impressed fellow students and they ask him (sometimes even pay him) for love potions, hexes and cures. Thin, with Ben Franklin glasses perched on his long nose, he scoffs at old-fashioned ideas about the occult and tries to bring his friends up to date. "There is no precious distinction between Black and White magic," he says. "People who still believe in those concepts must be colorblind. Technicolor is where it's at."

Bonewitz came to Berkeley in the fall of 1967 after attending a junior college near his home in Laguna Beach. His original major was psychology but he felt that this was very limiting, especially for one who was interested in the occult arts and who was to "become a working member of the Aquarian Age." So he decided to try for a major in Magic. "Nobody said it couldn't be done, because nobody had ever tried it. I was the first person who had the guts to ask for an official major in Magic, and then it took me a year to find a professor who would agree to sponsor my major." When the letter of approval came from the dean of the College of Letters and Science it stated his course had been approved "as an individual group major in Magic (Thaumaturgy)."

Isaac then read, studied and reported upon such things as astrology, Tarot, hypnosis, the cabala and medieval witchcraft. No sooner had he received his degree than he was hounded by reporters, lecture tour managers and editors. He signed with Coward-McCann to write a book titled *Real Magic*. His plans are to start working for a Ph.D. in Magic, probably at Stanford University. After that the nation's only official wizard wants to write sections on alchemy for chemistry textbooks, add information on witchcraft for medical textbooks and try to introduce magic into sex education programs in elementary and high schools. "The kids of today need to know something about love potions," and he hints that they just might contain burdock root, mandico leaves and peppermint.

Students in the Bay Area are already being exposed to the occult. At Tamalpais High School problem students are being turned off drugs and turned onto psychic phenomena by week-long field trips to the mountains. "One of the things that amazed me," said the mother of one girl, "was that they came back talking less of drugs and more about the occult. Astrology under the stars is so much healthier than a needle in a dirty back room." At John Swett High School in sleepy Crockett, California, spectacled and over-fortyish English professor Robert Beck teaches an elective class entitled Supernatural Literature and Communication. Every student who takes the course has been enthusiastic, thus keeping it permanently on the administration's approved list. While Beck makes sure his students become acquainted with the short stories and novels dealing "with poltergeists, dreams, forms of ESP, predictive and analytical devices such as astrology, Tarot cards, and Numerology," he also makes sure they practice some of these devices. A typical hour will have a small group meditating in the yoga lotus position, a table of predictive card experimentation and another group adding up each other's numerological past. Beck has taken his students to the AMORC Rosicrucian

Museum in San Jose and the Metaphysical Book Shop in San Francisco. He's also had classroom demonstrations by professional mediums, water-witches and a palmist. "All these things are going to be important in their future. I'm trying to prepare them for the Aquarian Age they will inherit."

Tracy is a little town about forty miles due east of Oakland. A good highway connects them and this highway is haunted. Truck drivers, for several years now, have told of driving past Tracy on a rainy night and seeing the figure of a forlorn young woman trudging alone with a heavy suitcase. They've stopped and offered her a lift. She always accepts. The suitcase is put inside the cab and the woman, wearing a tan sweater and a brown skirt, gets up front with the driver. She says she is on her way to Oakland, she seems sad and doesn't talk much. After about a half hour of driving they approach a small diner. She asks if the trucker would stop so she could get something to eat. As he parks the vehicle she opens the door and walks toward the diner. That's the last she is seen. The suitcase always vanishes. Police have been called several times, yet the owner of the diner swears a girl with that description has never come in his place. She is discussed and forgotten until the next time. It's a rainy night, a trucker has just passed Tracy and a lone young woman trudges along the highway carrying a suitcase. . . .

In Los Altos Paul Ackley sees the human aura and instructs others to see it as well. A serious looking middle-aged gentleman with horn-rimmed glasses, Mr. Ackley is a member of the Stanford Parapsychological Research Group, the Northern California Association of Hypnotists and the director of the Institute for Human Development in Los Altos. He teaches such things as parapsychology, Tibetan Yoga, Polynesian Huna, the teachings of Gurdjieff, Ashvagosha (Awakening of Faith), past life perception, self-hypnosis, age regression, fountain of health and steps to higher consciousness. He says that when he teaches a truth, he will immediately follow through and teach the technique for applying that truth. "Man stands at a level in consciousness where he has the capability of taking over and accelerating his own evolutionary process." And in tiny, suburban Los Altos he packs 'em in.

In Sausalito a carved cedarwood statue of the Madonna cried real tears. In Napa Marceil Moore goes into a trance and gives messages from the other world. In Corte Madera Father Ewald of the Episcopalian Holy Innocence Church receives messages from the other astral planes and has been given the gift of "speaking in tongues."

BUT in Burlingame, Saratoga, Milpitas and Roseville mediums and psychics are personas non gratas. In fact Burlingame is so leery of having the occult practiced inside its city limits that it imposes a tax of $100 a *day* for anyone wishing to set up psychic shop.

One of the most amazing women in the Bay Area is Mrs. Betty Bethards. Amazing not for what she claims to do but for the things she really does. She has almost every one of the psychic gifts, has proven them over and over again, not just to individual clients but to crowds of people and exacting psychic investigators.

At first meeting, Betty Bethards appears to be a normal housewife. She's a little plump, dresses casually and is addicted to cigarettes and Coca-Cola. Born in 1934, she is married to a systems analyst named Chris and his two young sons, Chris Jr., and David. Her ranch-style home is in Novato, a small town tucked into the hills twenty-eight miles north of San Francisco. It was there that she had her first psychic experience.

"I was washing dishes when a friend suddenly stood beside me. I jumped because I had been to this friend's funeral and saw him buried just two days earlier! I was scared to death, and shouted, 'Go away, go away, you're dead!'"

But the friend insisted she help him. He wanted to give her information about some business affairs that his wife needed to know. Betty pushed aside her fear and agreed to help him. "It took me a week to get it all. We talked back and forth, him with telepathy and me out loud. No one else could see or hear him, and I only talked to him when no one was around. I thought I'd flipped. I was raised a Baptist and knew when you died you were buried and stayed in the ground until Judgment Day! But I mailed the notes to his wife and she told me they couldn't have come from anyone but him." The wife was grateful to Betty and Betty was grateful that the ghost went away.

For eleven years nothing similar happened. She would dream of course, and predict events before they took place or warn friends of upcoming accidents, but there were no more voices or spirits. Then one night she shook her husband awake and said, "I was floating over my body." He rolled over and said, "That's all right, honey, it'll be fine." He claims he really didn't know what else to say. The next morning she insisted on seeing a doctor, because when she had been out of her body she'd been told she had pneumonia. Her doctor told her she was in perfect health, so she insisted on seeing another one. He said she was fine, too, but after she insisted, he agreed to X-ray her chest. Sure enough, she did have pneumonia. They put her to bed and her temperature soared. So did her spirit and once again she found herself out of her body, across the room and looking at her own form stretched out between the sheets. A voice told her she didn't have to go back if she didn't want to. She was tempted. Peace and quiet for eternity. Then she thought of her husband and her two sons and immediately was back. She recovered quickly.

Three years later she started writing "automatically" and filled notebooks with messages from a spirit guide called Michael. Once the guide told her to lie on the floor and call her husband. Then, in a trance, Michael and Chris carried on an hour's conversation. But Betty became weary of Michael when many of the things he promised never came true. She told him to go away and prayed to be released from the responsibility of being a mediumistic channel. "But I prayed that if it was God's will for me to do this I would. I was still a real skeptic and found it hard to accept that there were spirits out there in space talking to my brain. I really wanted to quit it all and get back to my bowling."

It was then that her present spirit guide, Uvalla, appeared. He told her that in his last life he had been a Peruvian Indian about four hundred years ago. He also told her he had lived many times before and in life received his teachings directly from Jesus.

Betty uses Uvalla (or vice versa) to do good for anyone who wishes to try him. She has located lost children, discovered misplaced documents and cured those who were about to undergo the surgeon's knife. Her abilities have been tested by a team of experts from Sonoma State College and by the California Society for Psychical Research. Its vice-president, Lloyd Dunlap, not only believes in Betty but helped to organize a non-profit healing center called the Inner Light Foundation so Betty can continue her work. "I'm convinced this woman possesses powers far beyond those we consider normal. I've joined her foundation because Betty uses these powers exclusively to help others, and I feel privileged to be able to help her."

Her psychic abilities are increasing, and investigators say tapes of readings she gave just a year ago compared with those she gives today show a marked increase in her clairvoyance. Uvalla tells her that there is no race difference "on the other side" and is also quite upset about the way American society is heading. Uvalla predicts that there will be a revolution in the streets by 1973 unless enough people—including our nation's leaders—can be persuaded to change their hearts and their way of dealing with their fellow man.

"I used to think only God heard my thoughts," Betty said, "and I figured he had so much else to do he wouldn't pay much attention. But now that I know all those other people are listening, it makes me stop before I sent out any negative thoughts. So the next time you're washing dishes, glowering in your head about some spat with a neighbor or one of your kids, watch it! Dear, dead Aunt Hattie, and who knows how many other souls, may be tuning you in."

THE SAN JOSE AREA

San Jose is on its way to being another Los Angeles. It began as a military outpost in 1777 and today stretches out over 1,300 square miles of factories, homes, small farms, garish roadside eateries and shopping plazas. It has, probably, the best climate in the state and the largest number of trained but unemployed workers. It also has something else: it has some of the strongest and most honest psychics anywhere around.

I had heard about the Universal Receivers Prayer Group and dismissed it as one more "social club" where middle-class housewives got together to read books on the occult and to dissect the member that failed to show up. I figured that with a name that had word 'prayer' in it that it must be religious and antiquated. As I say, I dismissed it. I wasn't going to investigate it. I've been wrong before but this time I was really out in left field, for I discovered that the Universal Receivers are the most powerful psychic group operating in Northern California today. A group to be reckoned with. A group to respect.

It was formed in 1968 when Jerome (Jerry) Quintero attended a metaphysical lecture and met Marcia Warzek. Marcia was interested in psychic phenomena "for my own sake and nobody else's" and Jerry was sure that he had "some of the answers but needed someone to help him experiment with others." Marcia had a large home in a fashionable San Jose neighborhood. She was willing to invite a few of her friends and Jerry called some of his. The first evening eighteen people met to discuss the occult world and tried to put into words what they had been feeling about psychic phenomena.

Jerry was positive that prayer was important and they formed a circle around a tall white candle and a small closed box. The box contained requests about health, about finances, about love, etc. These requests, or petitions, were sealed into individual envelopes and placed inside the "prayer box." No one knew what the other person had written. No one prayed aloud. They just prayed that "God or the Higher Self or the Spirit world would hear us and listen to what we had to say."

"Much to our delight," recalls Jerry, "our prayers began to work. One woman was cured of a bleeding ulcer. A teen-age boy improved mentally and didn't have to be admitted to an institution and a man named Brown found his father after searching twenty-eight years for him. Found him within two weeks, and with a last name like *Brown!"*

So the group attracted attention. Friends told their friends and people started coming to the Friday evening sessions from as far away as Sacramento. In four months the eighteen original members grew to over eighty and they had to hire a hall in which to meet. Since then they have sponsored San Jose's First ESP Convention, renting the huge Civic Auditorium, held seminars and psychic demonstration lectures and have started to interest teachers and college graduates in the value of ESP in education.

They don't do this for money. Jerry holds a mundane job, Marcia works as a secretary to keep herself and her teen-age son. Norma Dart, the group's secretary, also holds down a job. Admission to the weekly session-meeting-experimentation is one dollar. This goes to pay the rent on the hall and buy coffee and doughnuts. It's a far cry from other mediums I'd met who charged $15 for a "reading," $35 for "past lives chart" or $75 for a "spiritual healing." I asked them if they would talk to me. They readily agreed and they also agreed that I could use my tape recorder. "We have nothing to hide," said Norma, "others do, but we don't."

Jerry Quintero is a big man with a big smile. He looks like the corner fruit-and-vegetables man. Marcia Warzek is plumpish, blond and attractive. She might be mistaken for your beauty parlor operator or the girl at the telephone switchboard. Norma Dart is short, has dark hair and a pixie face that's beginning to line. She talks softly, uses her hands constantly and enjoys life. These three "ordinary" people just may revolutionize the psychic part of the Psychic State. I turned on the tape.

MARCIA: What we do in the prayer group is to form a circle and join hands. Someone says a short prayer and then we have meditation for five minutes. After this we break up into groups and teach what we know. We are all teachers and we are all students. Our objective is to spread this knowledge as much as we can. We use everything to try and find the answers to our questions. As scientists use various pieces of equipment we use Numerology, psychometry, astrology, Tarot, trance mediumship, palmistry, meditation, breathing, anything we know a little about.

JERRY: We have people from all walks of life, yet when they come to our meeting they are all equal. It doesn't matter if a person is an M.D. or a factory owner, a housewife or a mechanic, they all start from the same point. In most cases these people have heard about psychic studies and psychic phenomena but they have never actually delved into it or participated in it in any way. Everybody has the equal opportunity to learn and advance as their own awareness allows them to. We have seen a lot of amazing things happen with people who thought they had no psychic abilities at all and after a little while with us they've started doing automatic writing, psychometry, they pick up vibrations, imagery, all this stuff.

NORMA: This is one of the main reasons the group has grown. People actually experience things and when they do they tell their friends and then their friends come. It's like opening a door to a new world. I remember one young man who came just because his girl friend was interested in the occult. The first meeting he waited for her out in the car. The second meeting he came in, but just sat around drinking coffee. After the third meeting she told him: "Look, either you open your eyes to see what's going on in part of the world that's not in your own narrow corridor, or we're through!" So that night, unknown to his girl, he tried to do automatic writing. The words came gushing out and he came running to the next meeting to show us pages of spirit messages. He insisted that everyone see what he had done. It was as if he had discovered the psychic world all by himself. Now this young man is one of the group's staunchest supporters and keeps telling us: "How could I have been so blind?"

JERRY: We don't send out announcements. We don't advertise or insist anyone gets an invitation. Even when we have a speaker we don't send out mail or get on the phone. People just come. Many professionals have started because of our group. It's amazing how mediums and clairvoyants have developed from those who had no knowledge of any gifts they had. This is our main objective: to share knowledge.

NORMA: And this is only the beginning. Several mediums have predicted the growth of this organization into a foundation, and this is where we are headed. It's going to be a training ground for future teachers, a kind of hub where information will be disseminated.

ME: Have any of you expanded your psychic powers during this time?

JERRY: Well, in February of 1969 we were sitting right here in Marcia's living room and I felt that someone else was in the room. He was very strong. Marcia had experimented with automatic writing and was giving readings with it, so I asked her if she could pick this spirit up with her writings. She took a paper and pencil and he came through, filling page after page with enormous scrawled words. He said his name was Matthew and that he was from a higher realm. He said he had been assigned to our prayer group as our protector and we would have protection in our group as well as in our private lives. We had much work to do and he would help us carry it out. There is a power he has and we can all feel it. When this man comes he won't let me ignore him. He never shows up unless he wants to say something important. He doesn't waste his time in playing little games. He has solved many of our problems and guided us through many difficult moments. I appreciate his presence. Because of him we developed five trance mediums in just four months.

MARCIA: Matthew will come through me a couple times an evening, especially if I'm giving heavy readings. People accept the spirit writings easier than they would accept the same information from me. Once I get tuned into them I know what they are thinking and I also see the resolution to their problems. But once I give them the answer, I never remember what it is. Yet there is another thing. In almost every reading there is something there for me, a bit of advice, an answer to a problem of my own, etc. The feeling of gratitude I sense is overwhelming. Sometimes I get so upset that I'll be crying and carrying on, with tears streaming down my face yet a great sense of peace inside me. The old human me just keeps getting in the way.

JERRY: She gives counseling through her automatic writings. She has helped people more than she ever expected.

MARCIA: I used to be only interested in myself, in Marcia and nobody else. I thought my problems were enough for me without taking on everyone else's as well. Now it's the most gratifying thing that's ever happened to me.

ME: Can anyone do this?

MARCIA: They can if they want to do it to gain knowledge and to help others. There are some people who want to learn these things for reasons other than good. There are people who would like to harm others if they could only find the way. But if you are basically a good person then you can do it. Just hold a pencil or a ball-point pen in one hand over a notebook or a sheet of paper. Hold your pen easily, don't strangle it to death and try to clear your mind of all thoughts and images. Let your hand and arm sit loosely on the table. Some people find it easier if they shut their eyes and look in the opposite direction. Others light a candle. It depends on what feels best. When the hand starts to move don't fight it, control it or think of anything. In the beginning you may only get squiggly lines or circles. You may also use up a lot of paper. But keep at it and soon words will form and messages will start to come through. Don't expect earth-shaking revelations, not at first, anyway. After a while the messages will be clearer and more profound. As you are testing the spirits, the spirits are also testing you.

ME: But isn't this dangerous? Can't you call down an "evil" spirit as well as a "good" one?

MARCIA: If you are protected the way we are with Matthew, it's not dangerous. I suggest that those who wish to try this never do it alone, that they always have someone around them or in the same house with them that understands and doesn't scoff. I also suggest that they do their writing after meditation or praying and asking to be surrounded by white protective light. Prayers and meditation attract the higher type of spirits.

ME: Norma, you said earlier this evening that everyone can do your specialty, psychometry. What is psychometry anyway?

NORMA: It's simple and easy and is nothing more than reading the vibrations coming from an object that a person has been wearing for a while. It works best with such things as watches, rings, keys and glasses. The vibrations of the human body have entered these objects and a psychic can tune into them just the way a radio tunes into air wave vibrations. The main thing to remember is that first impressions are the most important. The first vibrations you get are usually the correct ones. When you start analyzing them or calling on your conscious mind to explain them you confuse and lose them. If you see a color, say it. If the watch is hot or cold, heavy or light, say it. If you see a symbol, speak it aloud. If you see a picture, a scene, an image, then say it. Many times the view you get means nothing to you, but is quite meaningful to the person you are reading. I can see past lives sometimes. Sometimes I see things that happened in a person's childhood. Other times I see what the future will bring. And there are times when I see members of their family, because objects can pick up the vibrations of other people close to you as well. I've taught this to hundreds of people. It is like Marcia's automatic writing, it's tangible proof that "something" exists out there in the psychic world. When the newcomer sees for himself, he believes. It's better than a hundred books of theory.

ME: This gets to the question of *why* do people want to do these things. *Why* get involved in the occult?

NORMA: I think it's terribly important to understand your own motives and not play games with yourself. You may, on the surface, tell yourself that you want to help people when what you really want to do is take the center of the stage and get out there and show off. You may only want to impress people with your psychic abilities, to put everyone down and say, "Hey, look what I'm doing!"

MARCIA: I know people who say, "Oh, I want to help people" when all they really want is to find out what Mary Jane is doing with Joe. And these are the ones that get into trouble every time.

JERRY: About four years ago I got some instructions mentally on how to contact anybody's higher-self. How to contact anyone on this side and anyone on the other side. You *can* contact them. I kept this information for almost a year because I was afraid to use it. Then one night I told Marcia about it and asked her if she would be willing to try it with me. Norma was sleeping on the sofa, it had been an exhausting session, and we were able to tune into Norma's higher-self and get answers to our questions. When she awoke we told her what we had done and she confirmed the correctness of our answers. Then I tried this on my teenage son and the answers I got, I knew were the truth. Then we tried to contact others that we knew. We surprised ourselves with this power. But we've turned it off. We don't use it anymore. We don't have the right to invade people's private lives and innermost thoughts. We wanted to know if it worked, and we tested it. Now that we are sure it works, we won't use it.

ME: How did it work? Did Marcia go into a trance?

JERRY: No, she didn't have to go into trance, but as I asked the questions she received the answers. It was with emotions more than words. I wish I could tell you more but I promised Matthew that I wouldn't tell anyone. It is too powerful a tool. Or a weapon, depending on how you would use it.

ME: Let's get back to the original reason for the group. Why prayer? What does prayer have in this Age of Aquarius? What has prayer to do with machines, television, subways, skyscrapers, etc.? Isn't prayer a little old-fashioned for we "moderns" of today?

MARCIA: Can I answer that one? I was always interested in the psychic and not the religious. I'd had enough of that when I was a kid. I had been a Catholic all my life and it hadn't given me much of anything, so prayer was out and the psychic was in. But as I delved into the psychic I learned that you cannot leave yourself open to everything in the occult without asking for guidance and protection. Prayer is really asking for divine guidance, call it God, call it the Universal Mind or whatever.

JERRY: When the prayer group began we decided to put a box in the center of the circle and place in it all the requests for help. We say a short prayer aloud and then we each pray silently. This allows us to pray as we wish and for whatever we wish, because we don't all interpret this infinite mind of God, or whatever we call it, in the same way. We don't all have the same names for it. But as long as we have the same *feeling,* then we are united in thought. This unification is what gives us power and this is why we get results. In reality, prayers are not the words that you say, prayers are what you *feel* inside of you. You can say pretty words but if your thoughts aren't right, your words don't mean a thing. Now, when all these people are united in this common thought, in this common request for help from *their* God, things happen. I remember an old Spanish lady who came to the meetings twice. Her legs were so bad it took her forty-five minutes just to get out of bed in the morning. It took her ten minutes just to get out of a chair. She listened to our prayers and didn't understand anything we were saying because she can hardly speak English. But she *felt* what we were thinking. In two sessions she was cured. Her doctor can't explain it. *I* can't explain it. I just know that it happens.

MARCIA: One time a gal wanted a piano. She had studied to be a concert pianist but had to give it up when she got married. Now she had free time and wanted to go back to her studies but there was no money for a piano. I told her to put the request in the "prayer box." She said "Oh, no, it's selfish and you should put in only for spiritual things." So I told her, "No, you are an artist and you need something to create on. It would give joy and pleasure to everyone around you." Well, she put it in and within a week and a half someone moved from the city and asked her if she wanted their grand piano. Free.

NORMA: We also have a prayer chain. Once we heard about a little boy who drank kerosene and was rushed to the hospital without much chance to survive. So we immediately got on the phone and started calling the members. I would call one woman and she would call four, who in turn would call four more, etc., until we had almost a hundred people waiting to pray. We had agreed upon a certain time and we sat in our homes and offices and at the same time we began to pray for this little boy. His lungs were filled with fumes and his stomach was burned, but he was saved. His doctors called it a miracle.

JERRY: There have been many "miracles" of this kind. After you do this for a while you don't consider it a "miracle" but more as help you are giving others. There was a teen-age boy who had been under treatment with several psychiatrists but he got worse rather than better. Finally, the doctor told his parents that unless the boy showed a marked improvement by the next session he would have to be institutionalized. The parents asked us for a prayer chain. We prayed the day before his appointment. The next day the doctor was so impressed with the boy's reaction, his coherent answers and his personality change that he decreed the boy could stay home and continue treatment there. The parents, of course, were grateful because they knew that once their son had been committed they would probably never get him out again.

MARCIA: Remember those X-rays of Judy's? She had brain damage and there was a clot that had to be operated on. Well, they let her leave the hospital over the weekend and scheduled the operation for the following Monday. That Friday night we prayed for her and when she went in on Monday they took another set of X-rays to see if the clot had moved or not, and it was gone. It had been dissolved. And the doctor was *furious!* He told her she must be trying to pull some trick on them. He told her, "And another thing, you said you had a mastoidectomy and you lied to us!" "Well, I did," she said, and pulled back her hair that she kept purposely long in order to hide the mark of the operation and said, "See, here's the scar." The doctor turned purple. "There is no scar there!" he thundered. "You've lied to us!"

NORMA: We've never kept any kind of record on these cases, and we never investigate later to see if the prayer has been a success or not. People have told us when we have been of help. We've had requests for people even out of the state. All we ask is the name of the person we are saying the prayer for and all we ask while we're praying is that "perfection come into their life." That's all that's necessary, really. We don't have to know all the details, but the help gets there.

ME: Why, and this may be a silly question, why hasn't the medical profession come to the same conclusions that you have? What has stopped these college-educated, supposedly up-to-date men of science? The AMA is going to hate this book!

JERRY: Well, the AMA doesn't like a lot of the things they hear, but it's getting to the point where they can't just simply deny it. These psychic healings are happening all across the country, not just because of us but with other prayer groups as well. But you can't be too hard on them for this, as it's the only thing they know, and they have their functions. But what I think *is* wrong is that they try to convince (often by lobbying laws) everyone that their function is the only one that's workable. And that isn't so.

NORMA: But we've discovered that there are many more doctors today who are using their psychic powers to fight disease. There are teams of husband and wife, where the woman is a medium and her husband a licensed physician, who are combining their skills to cure. A good psychic or sensitive can tune in to the body's various psychic centers and spot a disease before it is advanced enough for a medical doctor to become aware of it. A good psychic can tell when this condition is starting—just beginning —to manifest.

ME: Do you think that most doctors are psychic to some degree but that their medical education has forced any intuition they might have into the background?

NORMA: I think that a good diagnostician is automatically psychic and intuitive, but he wouldn't want you to think that and wouldn't want to be called that.

ME: Can prayer and psychic healing be felt even by scoffers?

JERRY: Yes. But there is one thing that must be pointed out. You should never interfere in another person's Karma. You don't know why this person happens to have this suffering or this disease. Maybe it is something he must go through in order to pay off and clean up his Karma, so you don't meddle. You must go along with free will. You must wait until he requests a cure, until he asks for the lifting of this burden. When there is no request you are, in a sense, sticking your nose in because *you* want that person to get well. It's to suit you and not to suit them.

ME: My last question is similar to "how many angels can dance on the head of a pin." The question: what happens when you pray? What is the physical thing that happens to the prayer energy? Where does it go? What does it bounce off of?

(Jerry was about to answer when Marcia gave a short scream.

He and Norma turned to look at her as she grabbed for a note-book and a ball-point pen. "It's Matthew," Norma whispered, "and he's very insistent." The room was silent as the enormous letters filled both sides of the paper. The only thing I have on my tape is the sound of incredibly swift scratches across Marcia's notebook. When the spirit had finished, Marcia slumped for a few seconds, then tried to read the scrawl.)

MARCIA: Prayer contact with God [she read haltingly] we all know is direct contact. It is the only way to make direct contact. Wishing will not do it. Prayer is the only way. Real prayer is not words alone, but thought. Words alone, no. It is the thought behind the words. It is the feeling behind the thought. Collective thoughts are more powerful than one thought alone. This is why in a group the power is multiplied. The thoughts form together and go together to one source. They are not merely doubled or tripled, they are multiplied because they gather with other thought forms and go direct.

JERRY: What Matthew is saying is that prayer works because of the power and the intensity and the conviction. Rote prayers and chanting just won't do it. There must be conviction and meaning behind a prayer. Without it, it is worthless.

There are others in San Jose who are into occultism and psychic research. The Rosicrucians, of course, have their big Egyptian Museum with its plaster reproductions, its green and pink lotus columns and its souvenir stand. This branch of the Ancient Mystical Order of the Rosy Cross was founded by H. Spencer Lewis in 1915. He operated out of San Francisco, then Tampa, Florida, and finally San Jose. The AMORC (Ancient Mystical Order Rosae Crucis), as they call themselves, are in constant battle with a group in Quaker-town, Pennsylvania. This branch swears it is the "only true order" and is not as well known as AMORC because it "doesn't advertise but lets the initiate come to it" and also because they are "deeper" in their teachings. While AMORC teaches you "the mastery of life," the other group (who call themselves The Rosicrucian Fraternity) flatly states that they do "not now, nor never did, teach New Thought, Mental Science, Astrology, Numerology, Hypnotism, Spiritualism or the transmutation of base metals into gold." Their chief West Coast spokesman is a dynamic little man named J. Allen Gilbert, who gives Quakertown instruction to San Franciscans at his Altora Soul Science Academy on Polk Street. The name of his group has been deliberately changed because "of the bad association the word Rosicrucian has with many seekers of the truth." And, just to complicate the matter more, there is another separate "international headquarters" of the Rosicrucians in Oceanside, California.

In the practical and practicing psychic arts, a few names emerge from the dozens in San Jose as being qualified, top people. Ken White reads the Tarot cards, and does it well. Bob Ellis practices palmistry and uses his psychic talents to read both past and future. Jean Hartman, a graphologist from Seattle, breaks handwriting down on a "Cyclegram." It looks like a fusion of an astrological chart with a Rorschach Test. Eight syndromes and forty indicators pinpoint a personality so perfectly that San Jose doctors, psychiatrists and even the police have called her in on difficult cases. Lucille Ziegler is a thin black-haired lady who comes up with amazing things from an ordinary deck of cards. She would have been burned as a witch in Salem, but has to turn away clients in San Jose. Pat Wortman does finger painting while listening to her higher-self and her works have been purchased by both clients and collectors. Dennis Bolling is a young blond "white witch" who left San Jose for studies in England because "the revelations and researches that enlightened me all portend to complete cataclysmic pandemonium" at home. He ends his letters with, "Perfect love, Perfect Trust, Blessed Be, flag, flax, fodder, frigg."

In an air-conditioned, wood-paneled and Muzak-filled set of consultation rooms, Dr. Harley A. Talley granted me an interview. He is a licensed physician who uses both astrology and hypnosis to cure his patients. He is in his late forties, has graying hair and a soft voice. "I use a branch of astrology known as 'medical astrology.' It's a combination of tropical and siderial and when I draw a chart it's to diagnose an illness as well as to suggest a remedy. I do want to emphasize that because I'm well grounded in physical diagnosis I would never be so one-sided that I would depend on this method one hundred per cent with a patient."

ME: Is the basic premise that certain planets affect certain parts of the body?

DR. TALLEY: That's the premise, yes. In medical astrology the angle at which the ray strikes the earth is very important. For example, if there are planets in the 8th house of the sign that might be there, this would affect the loin area. If there were planets in the 7th this would affect the kidneys. In the 2nd house, regardless where Taurus is, it would tend to affect the neck.

ME: Could you work this out for a patient so he would know what illnesses to expect in the next month? As if between the twentieth and the twenty-second of next month I could have pains in my liver?

DR. TALLEY: "Yes, this could be done, maybe not that exact, but enough to warn you that during that time there would be a period of low energies and that you should protect your health and work for a positive approach. I had a patient a while back who came to me with a long history of multiple cerebral strokes. He would feel faint and fall down and his various doctors would put him to bed and tell him to keep calm. When he came to me, I checked him over physically and noted a certain skip of beats in the heart rhythm. So I did a chart on him and found there was a terrific amount of planetary afflictions or unfavorableness in the Leo area. From that I made a diagnosis of an incomplete heart lock. I started to exercise him rather strenuously and give him some breathing exercises. It was exactly the opposite of what other doctors had prescribed, but he was cured. He's had no more of those spells.

ME: You also use hypnotism. Why?

DR. TALLEY: I use it because through it I'm able to get into and influence certain parts of the body that only function when the conscious mind wishes it. I get through to the unconscious and the body opens up to my suggestions and my probings.

ME: Have you taken people into their past lives through hypnosis?

DR. TALLEY: Yes, but only when they've asked it. To me, reincarnation is a desirable belief and I accept it myself. But that doesn't say that one idea is all-inclusive. If I'm working with a person and she tells me she has knowledge that she was once Marie Antoinette, I have no way of saying yes or no. I can only agree that she feels there is some principle working within her which would also, from her point of view, be working with Marie Antoinette. I've known four persons who thought they were Marie Antoinette, so I can't deny one any more than the other. I feel that there might be some universal type of mass mind or mass consciousness to which we may be individually capable of tuning into a certain segment. If we are able to tune into *only* this segment, it becomes the only type of impression that we know. If four people tune into the Marie Antoinette type of consciousness, then these four people may all believe they were once Marie Antoinette.

ME: If a person came to you and said, "I think I was Marie Antoinette, would you hypnotize me and take me back to see?" would you do it?

DR. TALLEY: I would go along with them to a certain extent. As long as they have a burning desire to get behind something, I'll go along with them, yes.

ME: Do you think the medical profession is going to move with the Age of Aquarius the way the man in the street seems to be moving? Toward a greater awareness of the psychic?

DR. TALLEY: I think that the individual doctor will move along. He'll move along as fast as political medicine moves.

ME: Thank you, doctor.

DR. TALLEY: You're welcome.

He wears a black suit with a white turned collar. His hair is gray and full. His face is remarkably free of lines for his seventy years and his eyes are brighter than many of the young students at the San Jose boys' school where he teaches. He claims that his subject, hypnotism, is what has kept him young. "My memory is better now than in any time of my life," said the Reverend James E. Healey of the Society of Jesus. "By using self-hypnosis I'm able to bring my subconscious to the surface and remember names, faces and facts a hundred per cent faster than many young people I work with. Hypnotism keeps me away from the doctor's office, has made it possible for me to keep all my teeth and lets me relax and get a refreshing sleep after a busy day here at the school."

Jesuit priest Father Healey is known as *the* expert in the subject of hypnotism in Northern California. He makes it interesting (and workable) for hundreds of students as well as the thousands of adults who have attended his weekly Monday night lectures and demonstrations. He himself has been interested in it ever since he was a small boy back in Arizona sixty years ago. "It was a little town without much going on, but once a year a traveling hypnotist would come through and leave me pondering. I remember he hypnotized a man in the window of a general store. He put the man's head on the back of a chair and his feet stretched out on the back of another chair. The man stayed rigid like that all day. Then that night he placed a huge rock on the man's chest and invited some nut to swing a sledgehammer to try and crack the boulder. The hammer smashed twice against the stone but the hypnotized gentleman under it didn't even bend. I'll tell you, I lost many hours of sleep over that. It made me just a little bit afraid but it also made me very curious."

When he started studying for the priesthood he looked up the Church's position on hypnotism. "They were very restrictive, of course. They said you were not to deprive anyone of the use of their mind and if you do it you must have two witnesses and be competent, etc., etc. But the competence you need is that of an eight-year-old child! Children are the best subjects and the best hypnotists, because they can relax and will accept suggestion and repetition. There is a doctor near here who uses hypnosis to remove children's tonsils. He just tells them to close their eyes and think of their favorite television program. 'Can you see it?' he'll ask. When they reply that they can, he'll say: 'Now keep watching it. How long does it last? About an hour? Okay, keep watching it and when it's over tell me, because I want to give you an ice cream after it's over, but you've got to watch it for the entire hour. Just keep your mind on the show now. I've got a little work to do here and so you'll have to pay attention to the program and tell me what happened.' He does this all the time and it's amazing, because the tonsils come out and the children have felt nothing."

He says that it's very easy to use self-hypnosis and his instructions to his students are concise.

"I tell them the simplest possible method is to start counting mentally and on the odd numbers close your eyes. For instance, on one you close your eyes and dwell on this odd number. You say two and open your eyes immediately. Say three and close your eyes and think about that number. As you continue your subconscious figures out that what you want is relaxation and feels that you are conditioning it to respond to the odd numbers. The even numbers act as a signal to your subconscious that you want to relax on the next number. Then when you get to eight or nine, or maybe even to twenty or thirty, your eyes don't want to open. You could open them but they are so comfortably closed that you just keep on counting, but this time just use the *odd* numbers: thirty-one, thirty-three, thirty-five and so on. If you are saying this aloud, you can tell when your voice starts to slow down. There will be more space between the numbers. Your subconscious will be completely convinced by this time that what you want is relaxation. With much practice you can start and just get to one, two and your subconscious will know what you want and you can hypnotize yourself instantly. I can do it to myself now just by flicking my fingernail against my thumbnail. If I want to go deeper I flick my fingernail again, but usually I'm already so relaxed that's it's too much trouble to do it."

Father Healey says that once you have your subconscious mind ready you can give it a post-hypnotic suggestion. You may ask it for the answer to a particular puzzling problem. You may request more energy or a good night's sleep. You may ask that the right answers come up the next day during a final exam or a job interview. You may ask for better health, for pain to go away or to stop smoking.

"Normally you want your suggestion to start working immediately, but sometimes it takes a little time for your subconscious to get into gear. If your suggestion is about your own health, tell yourself that you are *feeling* better, *feeling* happier, *feeling* stronger. It's important to use the word *feeling* as much as possible because our reasoning and our will is in the conscious mind, but our feeling is in our subconscious. Our subconscious controls our nervous system, our vascular system, our digestive system, our temperature. It works twenty-four hours a day without tiring, while we can tire our conscious mind just by thinking. We can go into the garage and start thinking what we want to keep and what we want to throw away and by the time we've decided we're too tired to do any actual work. Yet your subconscious never gets tired. This efficient workman we have inside us is like a gigantic computer and self-hypnosis puts it into operation for an instant feedback. According to one scientist, by the time we are fifty years old we have seventy trillion bits of information all stored away. Each second we receive and file impressions and knowledge. Our minds are like a seesaw with our conscious up and our subconscious down. With hypnosis we can bring the subconscious up onto a level with the conscious and once they are on a horizontal plane they become mutually helpful. Hypnosis is the simplest possible way to attain the state of meditation. As you relax physically you relax mentally and emotionally, which means that your consciousness mind slows down. When that happens your mind is not so much on the defensive or so much inclined to criticize, quarrel or reject suggestions.

"Now you don't need any cue to come out of it. Anytime you want to, you open your eyes. You're really not *in* anything, you're just relaxed. It's not dangerous. The fact that stage hypnotists have been doing this for years and without any reported danger to anyone proves that the idea of it being 'dangerous' is just a lot of hogwash. It is one of the free gifts that God has given us. We should use it, but not abuse it."

Father Healey says that by telling your subconscious mind that you cannot lift a fork of food to your mouth or that you have no strength to open the refrigerator door, you can lose weight with self-hypnosis. He has helped a number of women have painless childbirths through hypnosis and once hypnotized a highly nervous woman just before she was married "so she wouldn't burst into tears or start to laugh hysterically" during the ceremony.

While a few of his fellow Jesuits think he's some kind of a "kook," others just ignore him. "John XXIII used self-hypnosis and he thought it was great. Of course he was way ahead of his time. Ten years ago a priest teaching people how to relax would have been a big problem, but now the Church has bigger problems to worry about."

Father Healey is sure that once the Age of Aquarius gets under way that hypnotism is going to be used much more than it is today. "It serves at the conference table when people can tell themselves they will relax and not fight. It serves in the classrooms where students listen better, understand better and retain more. Medical men say that hypnotism is effective sixty per cent of the time. That's quite a record, because if a new drug comes out and is forty-six per cent effective that's fine but if it's sixty-four per cent or over it's considered a miracle drug. Well, hypnotism belongs in that upper bracket."

"Once I heard a lecturer discussing this subject with a group of psychiatrists and physicians. When one of them asked him if it was true that a girl could be seduced under hypnosis he answered: 'Yes, but with martinis too, and a lot easier!' "

Rita Brown is another of the amazing psychics working in San Jose. She is in her mid-thirties, attractive and with a delightful sense of humor. Her auburn hair sits piled up cloudlike, yet she has her two feet planted firmly on the ground. In an area where "kooks" and charlatans run rampant, Rita Brown remains stable and scrupulously honest. In spite of the fact that her personal life has been messed up by three bad marriages, she is able to counsel others and give sound, practical advice. "A medium can never help herself," she says. "My Karma is heavy and I know it. My mission this time around is to help others. I'll worry about myself in the next lifetime."

Rita is quite sure that she was a little Negro slave girl in her past life. She has seen herself as being about twelve years old and very black. "I lived in a shack with my parents and a lot of other Black people. I remember there was a big white house near our place but we were forbidden to go into it. I must have been brought straight from Africa, because my face was covered with tribal scars. The first time I saw myself I thought they were disease scars, but now I know they were tribal markings. There were some white children living there too and they used to tease me about my scars and my black skin. I remember trying to pull the skin off my face, thinking that maybe it was just a covering that kept me from being white. I was so desperate that I killed myself. Don't ask me how, but I committed suicide. I saw my body lying in a wooden box inside the shack. There were candles at each end of the coffin. That's probably why, this time around, I have so much to do. Suicide is the worst thing you can do to your soul."

Rita always has a crowd around her. She's got that kind of personality. Psychics and others interested in the occult arts gravitate toward her. She gives them readings and friendship. She makes even the most up-tight visitor feel at home.

There is very little, in the psychic world, that Rita hasn't tried and very little that she can't do. She can see a person's past lives, she can draw up an astrology chart, read handwriting and communicate via ESP. She erases illnesses by pinching certain areas of the feet and has been used (while in trance) to convey messages from people on another planet. She has become known for two major talents: Numerology and reflexology.

Rita uses Numerology to find out your past and your future. She says that we all have the name we deserve because of the vibrations from the letters of the name. When we chose a family in which to be born (coming from the astral plane) we also influenced our parents to give us a name that would have the necessary vibrations for our life chart. This name, exactly as it appears on our birth certificates, is what Mrs. Brown uses. She takes each letter and adds its corresponding number, getting totals and subtotals that tell her all she needs to know about where you have been, who you are and what you will be. The mathematics of it are quite simple. "They would have to be," she admits, "for I *hated* arithmetic in school!" The breakdown looks like this:

$$1-2-3-4-5-6-7-8-9$$

A	B	C	D	E	F	G	H	I
J	K	L	M	N	O	P	Q	R
S	T	U	V	W	X	Y	Z	

I will admit that when I first heard about Numerology I was a scoffer. I couldn't see how your name had anything to do with your fate, unless that name happened to be Rockefeller of Kennedy or the like. Mrs. Brown took my name, added the new first name I adopted as a writer, and included my birthdate. Then she drew up a chart and showed it to me. It looked like nothing I'd ever seen before with the years all in a line and numbers under them like this:

$$\frac{1945}{6} \quad \frac{1946}{6} \quad \frac{1947}{5} \quad \frac{1948}{11} \text{ etc.}$$

Yet when she started to read this cryptic chart I sat back in bewilderment. "When you were seventeen you left home for good." I agreed. "Then between 1950 and 1955 you were living in a big city trying hard but accomplishing little." I gulped and agreed again. "In 1956 you broke the patterns of the previous years and started traveling." It was uncanny, but true. "You traveled until 1959, when you decided to take a permanent residence." Absolutely right. "You stayed in one place, were ill in 1962, made an important decision in 1965 and uprooted yourself once more in 1970."

"But how can you tell this?" I exclaimed. "It happened just as you said it did!"

"Of course it did. Numbers don't lie. Two and two makes four every time."

"But if you've hit everything perfectly in the past, without ever meeting me before, then you must be right about the future."

"Aha," she smiled, "that's exactly why I did your past. Now you will be convinced that what I say about the years to come is also correct." She then went on to tell me many (marvelous) things about my profession and my upcoming private life. Even though she did it on a broad yearly scale, some of it has already started happening.

"Married women take on the vibrations of their husband's name," she says. "That's why it's important to see that the name suits you before you get married. I have given counsel to many women about the added vibrations they were going to take on. I can see, just by adding up a couple's name, whether the marriage is going to work out or not. I'm very seldom wrong."

Mrs. Brown had advised actors, writers and those in the public eye on changing their names for better vibrations. "You can 'out-live' a baptismal name," she says, "and can influence your future by a different set of numbers. Don't ask me *why* it works, it just does."

Rita Brown has classes, in her home and at a San Jose community center, in vibrations that show colors that have healing powers. She believes that certain parts of the body have direct vibratory (or nerve) connections with other parts. Should your left shoulder ache, for example, by stimulating the pad of your left foot (just below the big toe) your shoulder can be healed. Your knees and hip can be treated by pinching the center of your heel pad. The second and third toes influence the eyes. The third and fourth toes, the ears. Your teeth can be influenced by pinching the fleshy part of your hand just below the fingers. The side of your thumb can control a nose cold, and your liver can be put to right by pressure on your forearm just above the elbow.

If all this sounds silly and far out, may I go on record as saying that I've watched her in action and been present when ailments have improved or gone away altogether when she started to squeeze, pinch and rub? There is one woman in San Jose who will be eternally grateful to Mrs. Brown. She lost the sight of her left eye years ago. Rita applied pressure a few times to the woman's foot and her sight has been restored.

"I don't work magic," Rita says. "I just work with facts that have been forgotten or misplaced over the centuries. That's what the psychic world is all about anyway, using nature's gifts to their fullest."

The "vibrations" of the city of San Jose has attracted some of the top people in the occult field. Gina Cerminara, whose best-selling books, *Many Mansions, The World Within* (about famed psychic Edgar Cayce) and *Many Lives, Many Loves* (a fascinating treatise on reincarnation), find the vibrations of San Jose better than any-place else. Marcel Vogel uses these vibrations to make plants grow or to test their reactions to fear and love. Working at IBM's Advanced Systems Development Division, he has become known as "San Jose's floral answer to Dr. Doolittle." He takes ordinary house plants and wires them to a machine that records electrical impulses. When he gives a command, the plant sends out a reaction.

Impossible? Well, not quite. One experiment Mr. Vogel used was to tell a plant he was going to burn it. The first time he said it, the plant didn't think he meant it and gave no reaction. Then when he really did mean it, in his own mind, the plant sent out strong reactions through the recorder. When he actually burned the plant, another reaction was set up.

He claims that plants and men could understand each other if they just tried. As a former male nurse he says it's extremely difficult to know what's going on in the mind of a mental patient, but if the doctor places a plant in the room with the patient, he can read the plant's reactions and therefore read what is going on in the sick man's mind. Vogel believes that each emotion has it's own electrical field, so the plant would be an accurate recorder. "If we can develop a sensitive measuring tool for the emotional responses of people, then we can come to grips with the basic problems which plague society now, namely a measure of the interaction between two humans, positive or negative, love and hate. All we really need is to discover the extrasensory perception (ESP) between plants and man." So if you have a garden, go out and talk it into growing better. If your trees have shallow roots tearing up the sidewalk, just tell them to grow deeper. You might even keep your neighbor's apple tree from dropping its fruit onto your back yard.

Heather Buckley lives in a mobile home in an enormous trailer park just outside San Jose. She is in her early fifties, has reddish hair and is well known in psychic circles for her book *Spirit Communications for the Millions*. She was married, at one time, to Dan Buckley, a gentleman with a soft voice and pleasant manner who is a trance medium. In fact, *Spirit Communications* is almost all about him. When Dan and Heather started getting messages from the "other world" they were just playing with their Ouija board until a message told them to attend a certain outdoor festival. Not knowing what it was they were going to see, they went off as if on a picnic.

"What we saw sobered us," remembers Heather. "It was a psychic seminar and we saw mediums practicing all kinds of phenomena that we had never heard of before. We knew that we had been told to go to this meeting because it would help us to understand what was going to happen to us." And happen it did. Dan started getting messages from various spirits via the Ouija board. Then one night, as his fingers started moving with the planchette, he stopped and became rigid. From out of his mouth came a strange voice. It was his first experience as a trance medium.

"For three months we had a series of teachers," recalls Heather. "One was a woman named Helen Murphy. She told us that she had died recently and now was attending a spirit school. It seems that spirits go to school for advancement and once they get enough knowledge then they become teachers and have to find a student. She said that there are more teachers than students because there are so few of us on this side ready to open ourselves and receive them. Whenever they find a receptive student, they move in quickly." Helen Murphy didn't teach them anything earthshaking, just that love, understanding and humility were the qualities humans should cultivate if they wished to evolve. Once Helen said that her husband was still alive and the Buckley's managed to get his name and address in Ireland. They wrote him a letter, "being very careful how we worded it," and put it in the mail. It came back. "When we asked Helen why the letter was returned, she said, 'Oh, you don't understand. He got the thought.' What she meant was that by our actual sitting down, concentrating and writing we used energy to send that letter. She had taken that energy and managed to commuicate her message to him. This taught us a lot about the workings of the spirit world."

Then one day the teachers changed. Gone were former humans and in their place were beings from other planets. They especially recall Sanoastra from Jupiter and Vannius from Venus. "They told us about their life on other planets, but their main concern was the situation of the world. They said our world was a powder keg and anything could blow us to pieces. This was just at the time of the Suez Canal troubles."

"In most cases when I'm in a trance," Dan says, "I don't know where I am. Sometimes I am like . . . over there . . . looking at myself. Sometimes I can hear, other times no. Mostly they just take over and it's like I'm under an anesthetic. I have no conception of me, as me, at all. I do nothing special to bring this on, I just sit and relax and if they want me they take me. I can be talking and suddenly: wham! Fortunately it's never happened when I've been walking down a street or driving my car. Sometimes I can see the entities even though others cannot. Whether this is exactly the way they are or it's my conception of them, I cannot say."

One of the first people who came through Dan was Heather's grandmother, an old lady who would never have been caught dead at a séance while she was alive. "She thought it was very funny that I couldn't see her," Heather says, "because she could see me and touch me. Her message was, 'Seek ye first the kingdom and its righteousness and then all of these things will be added unto you.'"

"We've done that since then," Dan adds, "always keeping our mind upon the spiritual side of these messages. That way many things have fallen easily into place for us, without having to mess around with a lot of other things we didn't need."

After Dan had been used as a trance medium for three years he developed an amazing gift: X-ray vision. He claims that he can look into a person's body, see what is wrong and at times give a correct diagnosis. He's tried this often, telling friends in advance what their X-rays will say, and according to Heather, "He's been one hundred per cent accurate."

Dorothy Vurnovas lives just three trailers down from Heather. They met a few years ago, when Dorothy's dog refused to go past Heather's place. Finally Dorothy decided to investigate and discovered she had a kindred friend in spiritualism living close by. Dorothy is fifty years old, yet she is so tiny and talks with such a wee voice that at first you mistake her for a child. She looks like one of the elves in *The Wizard of Oz*.

Her first psychic experience came when she was three years old. Her Indian grandfather chanted over her and removed a wart on her right thumb. She can easily recall the warm fireplace and his singsong ritual. Then when she was four, and living in Chicago, her father died of cancer. Her mother took her to the funeral parlor and held her up to peer into the casket. "I touched him and said to my mother, 'That's not daddy. That's just his shell. Daddy's sitting over there.'" On the day of the funeral she was on her aunt's lap and the woman was trying to explain to her why she would never see her father again. But Dorothy thought the aunt was joking with her. "I told her she was being silly because Daddy was sitting right there beside me. I could see him and sense him. Nobody else did, but I could." After that her father was with her almost constantly. He would sit on the windowsill while she took a bath, he'd warn her when it was going to rain or snow and would send little messages to his widow. Then Dorothy's mother died and the girl began living in a series of foster homes. "They were all good people but they refused to listen to me when I started telling them about my Daddy's visits. One woman used to beat me when she heard me talking to him in my bedroom. My own mother didn't think anything about it, because my grandmother, who lived in the South, used to bring illiterate little Black boys into her home, give them paper and pencil and have them do automatic writing."

When Dorothy was eighteen her father came for the last time. He told her that she was a big girl now and no longer needed his protection. "Then he went away. I miss him. He was the best friend I ever had."

Dorothy sat in on a few meditation and prayer groups in Heather's trailer until one night she too went into trance. She shook and shouted and then started talking. She had received the spirit of a hellfire and brimstone preacher who had never been able to "come through" before and was just as surprised as anyone in the room. After that a little boy named Marvin came through. He said he had just died in an ambulance. That he had a sister named Sandra and he had been staying with an aunt because his parents were on a trip to Europe. Heather, realizing what had happened, called upon the group to pray for this little boy. It was then that Dorothy saw two spirit guides, Samuel and Margarita, who came and took Marvin "to the other side."

From then on Dorothy only received the spirits of dead children

who were lost and confused. Children who failed to realize they
were dead. They would always ask, "What's this place?" or, "What
are all these people doing here?" One little boy said: "You must be
witches, it sure looks like some Rosemary's Baby stuff to me!" Another boy knew he had died and told Heather: "You sure are a
funny-looking St. Peter!"

Heather has all of Dorothy's trances on tape and it's amazing how
her voice changes as each child comes through to her searching for
the path to the spirit world. One child came through muffled and
hollow and only later did they realize that he had died suffocated
in an automobile trunk. A boy who had drowned came through
gasping and bubbly. Another had been crippled and the sounds
of his spirit twisting out of his bone-stiffened body is audible on the
tape.

"Doing this never depressed me," Dorothy says, "I would be
tired sometimes when I came out of the trances, but never depressed.
You see, these children weren't oriented to what we call the horrors
of death. By the time they came to me their suffering was over. They
were released, forever, from physical pain. How could I feel depressed about that?"

Neva Johnston Avery is a beautiful person. If the phrase seems
old-fashioned, maybe it's because there are few beautiful people left
in this modern mechanical world. She was born in Long Lake,
Minnesota, fifty years ago and is now living and preaching in
various Spiritualist churches in San Jose.

Mrs. Avery has studied the majority of the world's religions and
has read her Bible thoroughly. She's taken something from each one
and has come to the conclusion that no matter what we call Him, He
is still the One and Only God.

When she gets up to speak at church meetings she never knows
what her subject will be. She opens the Bible, reads a Scripture or
two and then waits as the "vibrations" start building up inside her.
Then she opens her mouth and her voice is heard. She's taken to
taping her sermons and has been consistently surprised by the statements and ideas she has expressed. "I've paid attention to these
things," she says, "and I've learned from them."

She started learning a few years ago, when she was rudely awakened at three in the morning by a group of children. They told her they were the spirits of youngsters who passed over to the "other side" and had chosen her to be their pupil. Being as they were enrolled in a school, they had to find a human on whom to practice teaching. "They would be so elementary about their ideas," she remembers with a laugh. "They would show me a symbol and ask me what it meant. When I gave the right answer they were pleased but when I was way off base, they delighted in explaining everything in detail to me. Then they gave me different sensations in my body and asked me to identify them. They made me feel love, fear, elation, happiness, worry, sorrow and others. Then they told me what each emotion signified in the spirit world. They also told me that while they were young, their Masters were very old and that they belonged to the School of Light. They said that all children who pass onto the other side are enrolled in this school. It's just like on this side, where they learn to grow and to adapt to their new status."

Then about two years ago her teachers permitted her to see and talk to young children. They appear to her at three in the morning, giving their first names and their ages. "All children know their names and most of them are very proud of the fact that they have 'so-many years' old. Sometimes they give me their last names and where they used to live. Other times they tell me how they passed over; if they don't tell me, I never ask. One little girl named Janie calls it 'happy land.' She is four years old and is the prettiest little thing! One of my last little girls appeared to me and said, 'Hi, I'm a phenomenal!' She means a 'phenomenon' but at nine years old those long words are difficult. She was the cutest little girl. Her name was Kirsten Jones and she said she was from New York. She came to me on November fourteenth, nineteen-seventy, so she must have passed over just a little time before. She wears tomboy clothes and has a husky voice, not girlishly high-pitched at all. She is a Negro girl but there is something about her skin that's not just right. It seems to be blotchy and spotted. I don't know if this is from pigmentation or from a disease. She has beautiful hair that is in short full curls all over her head. It's not kinky, but full and glossy. Her mother must have been very proud of that hair! She said that the one thing she always wanted was a pair of ice skates, well if her mother ever reads this book, I'd like her to know that Kirsten has her skates: beautiful white ones!"

Mrs. Avery has over two hundred spirit children who have come to her, talked to her and tried to make contact with their parents or family through her. They come and put their faces right up to hers and tell her how happy they are in their new schools. "There is one thing I want to stress, children need love and very, very, definitely need the help of their parents. The parents, whether they be Catholic, Jewish, Buddhist or Spiritualist, must teach them that when they are in trouble and cannot reach their parents that they are to call out for God or Jesus. Those names have certain vibrations that will bring older spirits to their aid and help them onto the other side. How many times have these little tykes told me that they left their bodies and then saw themselves lying there on a bed or in a casket. They saw their parents suffering and crying yet they couldn't get through to them to tell them that they were all right, that there was no need to cry. It's so hard on the children! If they would teach them to seek God or Jesus, then the children would be spared seeing all this suffering."

Mrs. Avery has one boy that used to make her cry whenever he came to her. His parents had beaten him to death, yet "he still felt love for his mother and father. He didn't hold their brutality against them. I cried because I pick up a child's grief. I think it is this sensitivity of mine that attracts the children to me."

Here is a partial list of some of the children that have come through to her in the latter part of 1970. Maybe your child or a friend's child is here, if so, it should be a consolation to know that the youngster is happy, adjusted, and studying hard in the astral School Of Light. (Please note that the spellings of the last names are, in most cases, the way Mrs. Avery thinks they sound. None of the littlest ones knew how to spell their names for her.)

Ruth Kulk. Eight years old when she died in 1969 or 1970.

Henry Hinkle, nineteen, was from the East Coast and loved cars and old airplanes.

Roy Webb, three years old.

Margaret Alvarez, Negro, approximately two years old and very independent. "She is a little doll. She came to me wearing a home-made knitted bonnet. It is white with popcorn stitch decoration and ties under her chin. I'm sure her mother or someone very close had knitted it for her. Margaret is progressing beautifully in the School!"

Mary Cristable and Sherry Delaney, both teen-agers and both arrived at the same time in Mrs. Avery's bedroom. They first appeared on January 13, 1970.

Johnny Sanford, "a young boy who is progressing beautifully."

Ralph Tillman, approximately seventeen years old, "very bright for his age."

Albert Miranda. He came to her in December 1969. "Albert is very proud of being 'almost four' years old."

Lillian and Edith Powers. Twins and possibly from Australia. "I keep getting a name that sounds like Axminister from them."

Crystal Martin, thirteen.

Alice Mahoney, three.

Timmy Bianca, four.

Marcia Klaag. She came to Mrs. Avery on February 3, 1970.

Jack Helman, three, from San Diego, California. He told her, "I coughed and coughed." She says he was one of the fortunate ones, because he had a cousin named Shawn who passed over in 1970 and even though the cousin was only two, she helped him get adjusted to the other side.

Ronnie James and his mother Thelma James passed over together early in 1970. Mrs. Avery thinks there was an accident involved. There was an eighteen-month-old boy Paul who suffered injuries from the same accident but didn't pass over until June or July of 1970. "Ronnie gets great help and guidance from his mother, and she is enrolled in a higher school."

Gino Gunnitz, nine.

Marilyn Winetta (or Wynetta), seven.

Vernon Harris, nine. "He came through to tell me that his father's name was George Harris, he thought I should have known it. Apparently to Vernon his father was an important and well-known man. Most fathers are to their children."

Mrs. Avery asks that when you pray for a loved one who has

passed on, give the person's name and at least the city where death occurred. "The spirit of a poor child who has no one to pray for him over here and no one waiting for him over there, can hover around this old earth for a year or even hundreds of years until he discovers the way into the astral plane. Usually they will stay around their home, because this is the only familiar surrounding for them. It's what we call 'earthbound' in Spiritualist circles but what others refer to as 'ghosts.'"

Sunnyvale is a little town about twenty miles northwest of San Jose. It's the place that artist-turned-guru Vernon Childs chose for his youth rehabilitation headquarters. Vernon is tall, thin and good-looking. He has a way with the ladies and is impressive on a speakers' platform. Now in his thirties, he's decided that his gifts, especially his varied psychic gifts, should be put to use for the "children of Aquarius."

Vernon dresses in "hippie-style" clothes and has grown a small beard. He wears the peace symbol and can say "right-on" or "far-out" with the best of them. Yet this is all a facade, to convince the youths of today that he is not "over thirty" in every sense. He tries to get through to them to help them get off drugs and onto the occult. While it has been rewarding, it hasn't been easy.

"My sessions are rehabilitation on the clinical level as well as the psychic level. What I am trying to do is reach out and make communication. I go into the communes and have stopped kids on the street, but being as many of them don't get mail or read a newspaper, my work has to be advertised by word of mouth. It usually happens that a youth will come to me and listen to what I have to say and then go back to his group and tell them, 'Vern doesn't have all the answers, but he seems honest and on the right track. Let's take him in the next time around.'"

The youths that visit his center vary in age from fourteen to twenty-four. While none of them are drug addicts, all have gone the drug route and found it lacking. Many have experienced strange things and have come to Vern to ask why. Often, during a talk session, one will say, "Well, gee, why should I spend hours in meditation and discipline when I can get it all through drugs? Why go through all this psychic stuff when I can open up immediately?"

His answer to that: "I explain to him that he has not opened up immediately; all he did was open up one small iota of his psychic awareness. He probably didn't even touch on his spiritual awareness. It's like learning to play the piano, and when we start we all begin with middle C. Drugs start you on your psychic middle C, but that note is not the ultimate note. It's just the beginning. Meditation could move him in rapid order right straight up the keyboard to high C. Then he could play all the music ever written."

Vernon does not deny that drugs do, in some cases, produce psychic effects. "But I also warn that it's a chemically produced psychic effect that might open up a door before you are ready. This is where the danger lies. If these subconscious traumas that have been buried from this or other lives are opened up before you are ready, anything might happen. Sometimes the mind moves into the lower realms of the astral plane and a 'bum trip' results. I don't recommend drugs for psychic awareness, but if they've been taken and some positive results have appeared, it is a step forward in convincing a young person that there is something to ourselves that is above flesh and desire."

A number of his "students" have shaken the drug habit and gone into yoga or the other Eastern teachings with very good results. "All I hope for really, is to take some of the kids off drugs and give them a substitute. If I can show them that through metaphysical studies they can get even *better* effects than they got through drugs, then I'm satisfied. They will see that they can take a psychic 'trip' whenever they wish and that it's absolutely free. No scraping or stealing for money to pay the pusher. They become their own 'pusher.' They will become more spiritual and, best of all, the 'trips' can be made without ruining their bodies. In fact, psychic development actually improves the health of the body!" Right on, Vern, right on!

David Waterman lives in the average town of Modesto. In April 1970, he went with a group of church young people his own age to spend a few days in the Sierra National Forest. Everything was going according to plans when Dave turned up missing. His friends and church leaders searched for him, then called in sheriff's deputies to help them look. When he showed up much later, on his own, he told a strange tale that was published in the Modesto *Bee*. He said he had been drawn away from his group by some "mystical" force. "I saw this purple bush and then I began to follow a number of them. Something was pulling me." He described the force as an "om, or a god conscience." He wandered for some time until he arrived at a power-generating dam. There he became aware that the vibrations of the generators were on his own wavelength. "I just laughed," he said. Young Dave Waterman does *not* take drugs.

THE SACRAMENTO AREA

Sacramento is the state capital and, to some, the future psychic capital of the world. They claim the vibrations are best there, that its position away from the earthquake fault is a "psychic blessing" and that San Francisco and Los Angeles are "burning themselves up psychically." The city does not strike me that way at all. It is more a government seat and factory town. It reminds me of Southern California with its neon, its garish doggy shoppes and its bewigged women.

Mrs. Patricia Diegel was the one who really brought the occult to town, at least the commercial aspects of it. She did life readings. She claimed she was able to look into your past lives and tell you who you were many times before. Her clients were varied, ranging from schoolgirls to respected businessmen. She would tune into them, tell they they'd been in Lemuria, Atlantis, Egypt, Greece, New York, Kansas City and Sheboygan, then charge them thirty-five dollars for the information. She was able to get a number of gifted people around her who read Tarot cards, drew up astrological charts and did psychometry. Her husband taught meditation in a special churchlike room. He, before he married her, was a Catholic priest.

Mrs. Diegel claimed, to intimates, that she first came to earth from the planet Mizar. In case you've never heard of it, it is the center star in the handle of the Big Dipper. She and a group of forty Mizarians built a spaceship and landed on a mountain in

Greece. The natives below saw the rocket and figured the hill was populated by gods and goddesses. They called the mountain Olympus and Mrs. Diegel was Diana the Huntress while her present husband was Poseidon, the King of the Sea.

It is her mission to find and bring together the forty original Mizarians, who have all reincarnated on earth in this lifetime. "I am supposed to remind them who they are and the abilities they had before and put them back on the path of what they came here for, which was to help the earthlings evolve." So far she's found the majority of them.

Mrs. Diegel is reluctant to talk about many of her psychic achievements, but I am indebted to Mrs. Maggie Anthony, the San Francisco Tarot reader, for the following story. It seems that a woman contacted Mrs. Diegel to see if she was also from Mizar. Mrs. Diegel met her in a hotel room and they pulled the curtains and meditated for a concrete sign that Mizar had been the right road for the woman. Suddenly there was a crashing of glass as a large, hot stone came flying through the window. It burned the draperies, flew across to Mrs. Diegel's lap, burned a hole in her dress and fell onto the floor, where it singed the carpet. The woman picked up the stone, held it and began to cry, for she sensed that she was close to a piece of her true home for the first time in dozens of incarnations.

The chain of Universal Truth Centers that Mrs. Diegel founded closed down the early part of 1971 and she made announcements that she was going to tour the United States and give psychic readings. Those who know her said the failure was just bad business management and that Mrs. Diegel tried to take on too much with too few trained people to help her. Almost everyone agrees that she is a gifted psychic as well as a good businesswoman. But rarely do the two ever mix.

The Reverend Frank Basile and his young wife Jean believe so much that Sacramento will be the metaphysical center of the nation that they packed up and moved there all the way across the country from New Jersey. He is now a driving force in the Pyramid Church of Truth & Light, where those "searching for a new approach to God and spiritual truth without feeling pressure to conform" can attend lectures and seminars on the occult. He founded the School of Metaphysical Inquiry (incorporated as a church), where classes in all the psychic sciences can be taken.

Reverend Basile's real love is outer space. When he was a boy in New Jersey he used to look up at the stars and "get homesick." When he started reading, his attention was drawn to the Adventures of Buck Rogers and now that he is a man, his favorite television program is "Star Trek." He is sure that in a recent past life he was a member of a spaceship searching the heavens for "life and new light."

When he was sixteen years old he and a group of buddies observed five flying saucers hovering on the horizon near Mitchel Air Force Base in Long Island. "We watched them move away in rapid speed, then stop and hover and then move on again." He and his cousin set up telescopes in their back yards and would phone the other whenever one spotted a saucer. He believes that flying saucers are real and that the United States Air Force "knows more about saucers than anyone else. It's significant that the Air Force has never carried out a twenty-year investigation of poltergeists, but they have done this with flying saucers. They must consider them to be more than just people's imaginations."

Reverend Basile was an Evangelical minister for ten years and knows his Bible thoroughly. He's convinced that this book is filled with references to spacemen and UFO's. The most important reference is found in Genesis 6:1, 2 and 4:

And it came to pass, when men began to multiply on the face of the earth, and daughters were born unto them, That the sons of God saw the daughters of men and they were fair: and they took them wives of all which they chose. There were giants in the earth in those days; and also after that, when the sons of God came in unto the daughters of men, and they bore children to them, the same became mighty men which were of old, men of renown.

"This indicates that spacemen did come from others planets and mate with the daughters of men to create a race of giants, not only in size but in intellect as well. What this means is that there was an attempt by space people to biologically enhance the physical characteristics of the humans on this planet. A renowned scientist named Max Flindt recently wrote a book called *On Tip Toe Beyond Darwin*. He is an engineer, a scientific researcher, he's worked on classified space projects for Lockheed Aircraft, he developed magnetic mercury for the Atomic Energy Commission and he's now doing biological studies and research at Stanford University. His theory is that mankind is a hybrid product of prehistoric unions between spacemen and the early primates and that the breeding was done to establish a future colony. A very important point to remember is this: man appeared very suddenly on the evolution scene. The best that Nature could do with the other animals was to produce three great ape families that took five hundred million years to develop to their present brain case, which is about a million neurons. At this rate, one neuron was developed over six months and man, who has *ten* billion neurons, should have taken about ten times as long as the apes in order to develop his tremendous brain. In other words, it should have taken man five billion years to develop this brain, yet man came into the evolutionary scheme in about two million years. It's also interesting that man has 312 distinct differences from the other primates, not only in his skeletal structure but even in the weight of his brain. It's quite obvious that man doesn't make any sense in the scheme of evolution. And what about the geniuses here among men, the Da Vincis, the Einsteins, the Shakespeares? Only man produces outstanding individuals. What is this, a throwback to the ancient superintelligent spacemen? A genius chimpanzee would be one that could sit with children of the third grade and read and write. Yet this never happens!"

And because of this early mating-game, the spacemen are observing us. "Look at it this way," he says, "if you had been here from another planet thousands of years ago and were responsible for the creation of the human races, wouldn't you be interested in the progress of your biological experiment? So here they are today, hovering over us like a mother hen with her brood, anxious that we don't kill ourselves off with atomic bombs or pollution yet still scientific enough to let us maintain our free will."

Reverend Basile keeps in constant contact with those who are contacted by UFO's (there is an amazingly growing number) and compiling data on the times and places and the messages. Gayne Meyers, of Grass Valley, California, gets constant communications from spacecraft. His latest is a shocker. The space people have discovered that there is a strange radiation coming from the sun which is responsible for the evil tendencies of mankind. Now they are working on a way to shield the world from these rays. If this happens, the negative vibrations will cease and those who are "out of harmony with God" will have their personalities altered and they won't be able to cope without expressing their "evil" tendencies. "The vibrations of this planet will then rise high, spiritually, and these people who are on the lower planes of vibration will crack up, go mad, commit suicide or drop dead because they won't be able to function. This is one of the theories about the Aquarian Age," reminds Rev. Basile, "that the vibrations of the planet will change drastically."

The reverend would not be at all surprised to find out that spaceships have been taking humans aboard, brainwashing and programming them and sending them back to earth to carry out their plans. "There are thousands of disappearances every year that can't be rationally explained, because of the strange circumstances. Maybe a space spirit comes into a body at a premature death or at a suicide. Maybe people die in an automobile accident, yet come back to life when a space soul takes over. I believe that this flying saucer enigma is so important that it necessitates we change our whole concept of our history of this planet, that we alter our concept of the evolution of man, rethink our theology, reinterpret the Bible, and seriously consider the vital importance of outer space communications. The survival of our planet depends upon our taking a new look into space."

Robert Elkins is a wicca. That's not the same as being a witch. The soft-spoken, rotund young man with the ancient blue eyes says that wiccacraft is the survival of Europe's oldest religion, whereas witchcraft is "a bastard offspring from a merging of wiccacraft and

Christianity during the late Middle Ages." The word itself is Old Anglo-Saxon and means "to know."

When Elkins was growing up in Hazard, Kentucky, he was trained in wiccacraft ways by his great-aunt. She, in turn, learned her spells, charms and cures from *her* great-aunt. The old lady told him that a wicca "was the product of his time," and should study the scientific facts of his era and never get out of tune with the truths of his age. "What a wicca knows, must fit with what is known and must not contradict a known fact. If we are to delve into the problems of today's modern world, then we must have a firm understanding of the world's knowledge. It's not enough to cast a spell. A true wicca must know about medicine, biology, social customs, religions, botany and, especially, the working of the mind."

Bob Elkins teaches wiccacraft in Sacramento and helps people draw up pentacles, star-shaped charts filled with symbols, that are guaranteed (if done correctly) to bring a person anything he wants.

I asked him why these charts work.

"Because wiccacraft studies the principles and laws that constitute our immediate and spiritual environment. Many people use witch-craft effectively to get what they want. They can cause things to happen, yet if you ask them the principles behind its workings, they couldn't tell you. They go through a very involved kind of ritual and they produce the results *because* they go through this. The secret to making 'magic' work is to emotionally swamp your ego. If you can induce an intense enough emotional state your ego will be tem-porarily out of commission. During this time you will actually merge with what is called the Oneness. When this oneness with the universe takes place you become *one* with God. That means you become as powerful as God. You have the same creative potential God has. So whatever you think, whatever you conceptualize, when you are in this state with the ego pushed aside, will be. People who practice witchcraft don't know they are doing this."

"Is this the same thing as going into trance, or going under hypnotism?" I asked.

"You could call it a kind of trance, yes. I'm sure such people who walk on fire have gone into a state in which the ego is out of the way completely and the only reason they are not even more remarkable is because of their expectations. The feats they accomplish are the ones they expected to accomplish before they merged. They set themselves a limit. If they had set themselves to levitate, they would have levitated. Certain saints in the past went into what we call ecstasy. It was so intense that the ego was completely out of the way and they levitated because they expected to levitate."

"But this is a very complicated mental process, isn't it?"

"Well, first of all, the important thing to learn is the concept of Oneness. You study this, intellectualize this and you learn to know that this is so. It's quite simple. You must understand that there is only one reality and that reality has a duality. The duality of that reality is that which is manifested and that which is unmanifested. That which is unmanifested is the source of all the universe. That which is unmanifested has endless power for becoming. Now there is only one being in existence, and that is what we call God. Everything that is manifested is an individualization of that one being. Every time there has been a great human feat or test of endurance, one thing has always been noted: that the ego was pushed aside. The man performed astounding acts or became all-creative because he merged—even if only for a moment or two—with the Oneness of God."

"But why do we have this blocking ego?"

"What you are doing is getting hung up on asking why an absolute being does anything. An absolute being does not do anything for a 'why.' It does things. It is. It has no one to answer to."

Before I met wicca Elkins, I had heard the story of the growth on his leg. It started slowly, then grew to where it looked as if two large marbles were together under the skin. He never goes to a doctor, just uses his wicca power on his body. Within a short time the growth vanished completely. How? Easy! "When I merge into the Oneness, anything I tell my subconscious, it does. So I told it that my body would start getting rid of the tumor. I got a book on how it had begun and learned the various steps it had taken to grow. So I told my body to start creating a lot of white blood cells and to send them to the site of the tumor and take it apart in the reverse action that it had grown. I told it to flush out the dead cells through the body's natural functions. Then I forgot about it. A few weeks later, when I was taking a bath, I looked to see how it was coming along. It had disappeared. This proves what my great-aunt said, because without a knowledge of biology I could not have given my subconscious the exact instructions to dismantle that growth."

Because of this concept of Oneness, he does not believe in reincarnation or Karma as is conventionally known. "Where will you go when you die?" I asked him.

"I won't go anywhere, I will always be."

Less than fifty miles east of Sacramento, on a good highway, is the town of Placerville. There is nothing there that is particularly psychic but several mediums claim that it's what's going on *above* Placerville that is important.

A number of messages have come through purporting to be from flying saucer spacemen. They tell of a great city that's being built in the air (or astral plane) directly over Placerville. This city is being constructed by beings from other planets and they're working feverishly to finish it in time. When the earth becomes so polluted with waste or atomic radiation and man cannot live on it any longer, the space beings are going to reach down and pick up "those humans who have the best vibrations and are closest to goodness and spirituality." Then these humans will be placed in a state of suspended animation, or hibernation, for twenty or thirty years until the earth's atmosphere has been cleared and the pollutants have gone. They will be taken out of this suspended state and sent back to earth to become the nucleus "for a new and better civilization. This would be a civilization, obviously, of people who are in tune with the spiritual, intellectual and psychic things of life."

The City Of Jesus is rising slowly, but *surely,* on five mountainous acres twenty-five miles north of Oroville, which is ninety-three miles north of Sacramento. As the houses go up, the well is dug and the first families arrive, Brother Jim Grinolds sees a decade-old dream coming true.

The Reverend James W. Grinolds (who prefers to be called just Brother Jim) was discharged from the service in 1954 and settled in California. He married a lady from Missouri named Bonnie and worked during the week as a draftsman and on Sunday as a Church of Christ minister. The main thing that bothered him about the new California society was that there was no place for the spiritual down-and-outer. Not the drug addict, or the unwed mother or the prison convict, but "the man who has all the outside things but remains empty inside." He noted that it usually wasn't the poor man or the diseased man that committed suicide, but rather "the man who has no spiritual side." He thought it would be wonderful to build a city where these people could come and "recharge their batteries, help pay for their room and board by manual labor and find out that others love them even if their friends and family don't seem to." Brother Jim had the plans in his head and even the name, but there was no money with which to start.

Then one evening, after he and his wife had moved to San Jose, where he was employed by IBM, he got the tremendous urge to take in a meeting of the Universal Receivers Prayer Group. They had attended once, thought it was interesting but also thought that "our particular thing was Jesus, not the psychic and the occult." But the urge was great and so they went. The evening went by quickly and nothing of any importance occurred until one woman asked him if she could give him a reading. He reluctantly agreed, as he was just about to start for home. The woman told him several things, yet kept saying, "You have something to tell me." He tried to think and drew a blank. Then as he had his coat on, the idea came to him, "Maybe she wants to hear about my city." He asked her if that was what she meant. "She let out a scream and rose about a foot off the ground," he recalls. "Where have you people been?" she demanded. "We've been waiting for you for two years." It seems, unknown to Brother Jim, that the plans and details of his proposed City Of Jesus had already been received and recorded by various mediums in the group. Another woman brought out a crystal ball and described the land. She saw it as being in the mountains, as having a view of twin peaks. She also saw a house trailer and a lean-to on the land and a stream running along one edge. They got a newspaper and looked in the want ads. There was a piece of land available outside Oroville for just ninety dollars down. Brother Jim had only ninety dollars, so everyone thought this must be the promised site.

That Sunday afternoon Brother Jim and a small group drove up to the property. He was all in favor of it, because he wanted to get started, but his wife wouldn't even get out of the car. "This is not the place," she kept saying. The others agreed. The "vibrations" just weren't right. In order not to have wasted the entire day, they decided to drive over and look at a nearby dam. As they stood there, the woman with the crystal ball gave a scream: "There," she cried. "There are the twin peaks, and down there is the valley I saw. Your piece of land is in that direction."

So next Sunday an even larger group went up and drove to the area near the twin peaks. The land was beautiful and fenced in. There were no "for sale" signs and by the end of the afternoon they were more discouraged than ever. While Jim went off to explore a far corner, the others sat down on a tree trunk, held hands and began to pray. Two non-believers, along just for the outing, became frightened when "a noise like whispering began to grow louder and louder from the tops of the pine trees."

No sooner did the prayer end than a battered pickup truck appeared from over the hill. A man stopped, got out and asked: "Are you people looking to buy some land? I've got a piece up the road that's for sale."

They called for Jim and, over his protests that he didn't have enough money, piled into the back of the truck and let the stranger show them his land. "As we turned the corner," remembers his wife Bonnie, "we stopped talking and got goose bumps. For there, on this property sat a house trailer and a lean-to. And in order to get there we had to ford a stream. It was exactly like the scene in the crystal ball."

"As if that wasn't enough of a sign," says Jim, "the owner's wife had been painting with oil paints. Most of them were those fill-in-the-colors ready-made things, but one picture sat alone against two gas drums. It was a painting of Our Lord standing on that very hill and looking down into the valley. That did it! I knew that this was the place."

The problem now was one of money. He calculated that he

might be able to get a thousand dollars for a down payment, but certainly couldn't afford more than fifty or sixty dollars a month after that. The land was nicely cleared, had a tool shed and a generator on it. He knew the owner wouldn't sell it for what he could afford. "But I decided that since things had gone this far, I might as well go for broke. 'How much do you want for the land?' I asked."

The man thought for a moment and then said, "As soon as I can sell it, I can get back to Michigan and take a job that's waiting for me. I don't want to be difficult. How about a thousand dollars down and sixty dollars a month?"

After the deal was completed they asked him how he knew they wanted to buy his land. "Well, it was the strangest thing," he said, "I was sitting up here wondering how I could get to Michigan when a loud noise came through the pine trees. It turned into a voice that told me to go down and talk to the people who were on the lower road. I didn't know you were there and when I saw you I didn't know how to start the conversation. I would have felt like a fool telling you I'd heard voices!"

The City Of Jesus is rising there now. They are building a meditation center and a few cabins. There is a lot of work to be done but faith has taken it this far, and will take it to completion. Anyone who wishes may go there. It's free and no questions are asked. You can study, meditate, write or just live. Brother Jim will even pick you up and take you there if you don't have transportation. The city needs everything, clothes, food, hardware and building supplies, yet it already has much more than other Californian cities. "It has love," says Brother Jim, "and that's just the greatest thing going!"

MT. SHASTA

Funny, but I wasn't going to go to Mt. Shasta. I went as far north as Redding to interview an Indian medicine man who didn't exist and found I had an afternoon free. If you've ever been in Redding, then you know there is no better way to spend an afternoon than *out* of Redding. I decided to go and look at the mountain. I wasn't sorry.

It sits there, enormous, longer than I had imagined and sharper at the top. It was half covered in snow, that November day, and the sky was so clear it looked unreal—like a Japanese painting.

The mountain dominates everything. Especially the little town of Mt. Shasta at its feet. The houses, the few two-story buildings, the trees, the people, everything is overshadowed and overawed by this magnificent hunk of stone and ice. Rather than being frightening in its size and power, it's almost comforting: as if it's protecting the area. I had *heard* a lot about "vibrations." Well, Mt. Shasta made me *feel* them.

The local Chamber of Commerce gave me a mimeographed sheet that stated the town had 2,500 people, that it used to be a logging town but now gets just as much money from tourists. "The air is pure and the water is the best in the world; there are few places as beautiful."

Then it went on to say: "It has been generally accepted that the name Shasta came from the Shasta Indians who lived in this area. Shasta means white. These Indians were a white tribe of a highly devotional nature and had seven points in this area where they held devotional ceremonies. There are many legends concerning the white man and the Indian here."

One of the legends the Chamber of Commerce tells concerns great incredible bells. It seems that there are two cities lying *beneath* Mt. Shasta. They are Iletheleme and Yaktayvia and form the Secret Commonwealth of Mt. Shasta. The Yaktayvians are the ones who make the bells. By ringing the bells they were able to hollow out great masses from the center of the mountain. The vibrations of the bells worked on a high frequency that the human ear could not hear. They sliced and burrowed like the laser beam. Tunnels, corridors and homes were carved from the rock this way. The vibrations even illuminate these underground cities, by "vibrating the atoms of ether in such a way as to produce light." Apparently on one slope, where no man has ever stepped, there is an enormous but *transparent* bell. It's invisible until you get within eighteen inches of it. When the wind strikes this bell it gives off a peculiar vibration that "repels any curious would-be trespassers on the holy ground that surrounds the entrance to the Secret Commonwealth." This is why, according to the legend, your car will stall when you get close to the mountain.

This is why "on various stretches of the highway you can hear a great booming bell-like sound; sometimes it's a rumbling, clashing sound like many chimes."

(This has nothing to do with California but when I was in Peru and in Mexico I talked with many experts about Inca and Aztec civilization. I contended that the Indians must have had some other way of transporting enormous boulders across mountainous terrain and then cutting them so exactly that no mortar was needed (in Cuzco) and a knife blade still cannot be placed between them. I contended that there just weren't enough Indians in the Andes or in early Mexico to do all this the way that Cecil B. De Mille had us believing the Egyptian pyramids were built. That's when I heard the theory that the Indians had some kind of "musical instrument that made a high-pitched sound." So high that it could make a stone float in the air and could be focused down to a thin cutting edge. If a violin can shatter a crystal, why then couldn't another kind of instrument slice rock? Now again, but in California, I heard almost the same kind of tale.)

And it was in Mt. Shasta that I met Nola Van Valer. They pointed out her house to me. It was on a main street, rather bleak and forbidding and in need of paint. It was set apart from the other houses by its huge front lawn and an iron picket fence. The people of the town whispered she was a witch. Others said she was one of God's chosen. I knocked at the door, a dog barked and was taken away, then the door was opened.

Mrs. Van Valer sat in a wheelchair. She was eighty-three years old, white-haired and blue-eyed. She had fallen and broken her hip, she apologized, and was unable to move her legs. Her hands were palsied and shaking. Yet at the same time there was a great strength in this woman. A physical and mental force that transcended her age and her infirmities. Her voice was clear and her conversation was lucid. I hadn't been with her five minutes when I began to get those "goose bumps" that I always get when I'm in the presence of a powerful medium.

Mrs. Van Valer, along with Kenneth Wheeler, is the Radiant School. It is not a cult, or a creed or a religion, even though it has been chartered in the state of California as a non-profit organization. Their simple mimeographed brochure sums up what they do this way: "To you looking for a path to a higher state of understanding, these courses of instruction may present a challenge to Mind—a gold mine, to open hearts—an end to a long search for an expansion of consciousness. The lessons cannot be passed over lightly. The contents of these lessons cannot be claimed as new revelations. Some of the teachings pre-date the birth of Christ. However, each age requires words suitable for its particular time, place and society. For that reason these lessons are in plain English words. At first they may seem too simple. Remember the words of Christ were often scorned as being too common."

Mrs. Van Valer wrote the lessons. Where did she get them? From the Masters, who came and taught her their wisdom on the slopes of Mt. Shasta.

It's quite a story. She and her husband, in June 1930, went with some friends to spend a week on Mt. Shasta. They lived in San Jose and he worked as an electrician while she attended meetings of the Christian Science Church and practiced healing. They chose Mt. Shasta for their vacation because it was cheap. The Depression was on and they didn't have money for hotel rooms. They took a tent and some cooking utensils and climbed the mountain.

"Then suddenly there was a strange man in front of us. He smiled and we smiled. He was dressed in a long robe but looked so pure. He said he had been watching us and that there were many things he wanted to tell us. He asked us if we wanted to listen. We agreed."

"You mean," I asked, "you found someone on the mountain who taught you?"

"Yes, the Masters."

"Non-entities?"

"I wouldn't call them that, no. The Masters are not entities, yet they are quite able to descend from their realm into ours and they do it all the time."

"If I had been with you, would I have been able to see and talk to these men?"

"Yes, because over the years I took thirty-three who can testify to what I saw and heard. I went up on Mt. Shasta for ten years, every year at the beginning of June. They taught me many things.

Over the years there were twelve different Masters in all. I even met the one that the Bible speaks so often of, the one it calls Jesus."

"You met Jesus? On Mt. Shasta?"

"Yes, and he gave us lessons and instructions. We took everything down in shorthand, because we didn't have recorders in that time. This began in 1930 and went on until 1940. Sometimes we stayed a full month, sometimes a little longer."

Remembering other stories I'd heard, I asked, "Could it be that these men were from flying saucers?"

"Absolutely not. They were from the Fifth Realm and they took on the bodies of earth life to be able to work with us. When they spoke to us it was in English. While in our presence they spoke to each other in English as well.

"They could appear and disappear at will. They didn't seem to have worldly attachments. They were fully dressed in long robes. They ate but I never saw them drink. I don't know if they slept. They said they lived on the mountain itself but at other times they said they were in their 'own realm.' Unfortunately we never had a camera with us. I don't know whether we could have captured their likeness on film.

"Today many people go up there and try to find them, but the altitude is high and the terrain is rough. Besides, everything has a season and the season for them to be on that mountain was from 1930 to 1940. When the war broke out, which they told us was coming and told us how it would end, they didn't come anymore. In fact after that the government wouldn't let anyone on the mountain. They said it was a defense measure."

"Did they ask you to found the Radiant School and send out lessons?"

"No. They only asked me to teach the truth, and teach it freely. I tried for a while but when my husband died I had no one and couldn't manage it alone. In 1961 (at seventy-four years of age) I decided to move from San Jose to Mt. Shasta and here I met people who were willing to help me with this knowledge. The school operates only through the mail. There are no resident students. There are twenty-four lessons that take two years to study. That's the trouble. Everyone wants everything all at once and we don't teach that way. We will lead a student and walk beside him, but if he doesn't realize he is unfolding then there is nothing we can do about it. We have a little more than eighty students right now."

Knowing that many psychic schools charge a whopping initiation fee, plus as much as fifty dollars a month for the "truth," I wondered just how much this lady was raking in. I asked her.

"We'd like to give the lessons for nothing, but we can't carry on the work that way. We did try for several years to carry it ourselves, not even asking for donations but the costs of paper and postage were too much for us. So we ask for two dollars a lesson, just enough money to cover expenses."

"But," I protested, "that's a very insignificant fee, when you consider what others charge for their lessons!"

She smiled. "When you are looking for the truth, the price doesn't have anything to do with it."

Mrs. Van Valer's lessons teach the student how to unfold himself and to search for the truth. They teach him to understand when he has the truth. They are not against any religious group or organization and don't ask that their students withdraw from their own churches. They teach about reincarnation, energy, auras, healing, matter formation and the correct interpretation of the Bible. The School doesn't believe that the Bible is being correctly interpreted today, because countless translations have rendered it almost meaningless.

"The original words talk of Gods and Sons *in the plural,* not the singular as it has come down to us. Unless we know that there is more than one God and more than one Son, then we don't know the truth. The Bible teaches you, correctly, that there was one God who created man but it doesn't talk about the other gods who handle such things as force and power. One God does not control the whole earth, but these various gods do all come from one godhead: Almighty God."

"Why are the Masters interested in us?" I asked.

"When you were born you had a Guardian Angel that has been with you in every life that you've been on this earth. He never leaves you. Then when you are around twenty-eight years old, three Masters come to you. One is there to make sure you don't stray from your life pattern, the second brings you all the literature and opportunities for your development. Your third Master brings you anyone that you have hindered or hurt in your past lives and gives you the opportunity to make good on it. He also gives those who have harmed you a chance to make up for it. The Masters come to you and show you the way through dreams and subconscious suggestions."

"Why this particular age? Why twenty-eight?"

"Because we humans have seven-year periods and until you finish your earth period you don't become serious enough until you are twenty-eight years of age. That's when you are able to understand, change your opinions and accept many new things."

"Why does God or the gods care what happens here on earth?"

"Because they have a plan to carry out the same as you have a plan for living. They are in charge of us. They must see that we follow the great overall plan of the universe. Not just this earth universe, but the galaxies and other universes that God has dominion over. Our brains are too small, our conceptions too minuscule to understand the overall plan."

"Well," I asked, "don't the gods get tired or discouraged when they see some of the things that go on on this earth?"

"I don't believe they know what discouragement is."

"Did they give you a look into the future? Did they say that the world would come to an end in the year two thousand, for example?"

"Don't worry about the year two thousand, you won't be living to see it."

"*I* won't be living?"

"No."

"I don't know whether that's encouraging or discouraging!"

"Well, it's the truth. But it's not just you. We are in the beginning of a holocaust right now. The new Messiah is on his way. He is one of the Masters but this time there will be no need for such folklore as the manger and the Virgin Mary. Many people will be alive to see this new way of living in the year two thousand but not 'many' in terms of the numbers who are populating the world now. The new Messiah will make himself known long before that date. He will have his followers but he'll also have his detractors. Those people will have to be born again."

Over the shock that I was going to die within thirty years, I asked: "But in a world so carefully looked after, where does a man like Hitler fit in?"

"He was the son of the devil. There are devils. They were gods that were thrown out of heaven, if we choose to call it that. Their realm is now inside the earth. Many of them have their realm inside people. That's why I am wary of spiritualism. Because that is their stepping-stone. That's why there are so many people in mental institutions. They shouldn't be there, but because they didn't listen to their Masters they have been taken by the devil."

"Well then, where does Jesus Christ fit into this?" Is He just *one* of the Masters?"

"He was one of the sons of Elohim. That is the family name of the God who created man and whose duty it is to look after man. It was his own son who came to earth but he has many sons. Some are in physical bodies right here among us today. The majority are near us, but we cannot see them. The family lives on the planet Oran."

"The one the astronomers call Orion?"

"Yes. Jesus, the spirit, was born and still lives on Orion. This is the truth. This is what He told me."

The Untrammeled Middle

Middle California, for my own reporting purposes, starts at Hollister in the north and runs down to Jalama in the south. This "middle" boasts of large industrial-agricultural centers such as Salinas, Fresno, Bakersfield and Barstow. It has rugged rock-strewn coastlines and sand-heaped deserts. It has the General Sherman Tree, believed to be the earth's oldest living thing and the long dead, unfriendly Death Valley.

Yet it has very few psychics. There are groups of ladies who get together once a month or so in the larger towns to read the latest occult books. There are a few gypsies reading palms and a number of Mexican *curanderos*. But the fight to make the land produce keeps the majority of "middle" Californians with their faces turned toward the reality of the Earth rather than the unknown beyond the stars.

The little town of Lemoore was shocked in September of 1970 when a local Protestant minister complained to the police that a member of his congregation was using witchcraft against his church. The minister, who claims he never had any trouble before the man started using black magic on him, fell four feet off a ladder and broke his arm.

Down in Palmdale, Mrs. Daniel Baker reported to *Fate* magazine that when she visited the dentist and he administered an anesthetic called "sweet air," all sorts of interesting things happened. "I went downward into a vortex and then felt a terrible pulling sensation. When this stopped I was no longer in the chair but sitting atop the bank building across the street looking down and through the dentist's window. I watched with interest but without concern as the dentist worked on the figure in the chair. Probably I remained like this only a few minutes before I was back in the chair, awake and terribly frightened."

And in Porterville a citizen gave a quarter to a tramp on the street who thanked him, smiled and promptly vanished.

The most powerful medium in "middle" California has been imported. He is Reverend Harold G. Plume and he comes from England. The reverend is noted for one amazing ability: he heals by sticking his fingers straight into his patient's physical body.

I went to see him after a woman in San Francisco told me how he had cured her. She said she had a growth on the inside of her rib cage and the only way the doctors could remove it was to saw through the ribs. That, she didn't want. So she went to Monterey to see Reverend Plume. After a few seconds at passing his hands over her, she said, he placed a piece of facial tissue on her rib cage and peering into the tissue he straightened his fingers and pressed against the paper. She glanced down in time to see the fingers, paper and all, disappear into her body. After a few seconds the paper and the fingers reappeared and even though the tissue was bloodless she was told the operation had been a success. On returning to her San Francisco doctor she was X-rayed. The growth was gone.

Reverend Plume is short, white-haired and filled with energy. He speaks with what might almost be Cockney. He laughs a great deal, smiles and buzzes between Monterey and Redwood City on healing missions twice a month. His church is a converted storefront around the corner from the post office in Monterey. It is called St. John's First Chapel of Healing. When he is in town there are services every day at 1:30 and 7:30 P.M.

It is a church in the strictest sense of the word. The man is an ordained minister, given his credentials years ago by the Church of The Good Shepherd of England. The services are hymns, prayers and a sermon. His equally energetic and friendly wife Bertha plays the piano and sings along with the congregation. The altar is a simple affair draped with a white cloth. There is a cross. There is also a vase of fresh flowers and a Bible. The walls are decorated with drawings—of the various spirits who come through Rev. Plume. He believes that his power to heal, through the guidance of a long-dead Chinese physician named Hoo-Fang is a God-given gift. Therefore he charges nothing for his talents. As in any other church there is a collection plate. Give if you want to. Don't if you don't.

He told me that his psychic abilities went all the way back to when he was three years old. "When I would go to bed all the senses that I had used during the day would relax and the other senses would come into play. I used to see people in my room and they would be crying and trying to tell me things which I didn't understand. My mother thought I was just frightened of the dark. There was nothing I could do to convince her that I really saw those people. Sometimes during the day someone would appear to me and whenever my mother heard me talking to them she would get most upset. If she had visitors she would blush and say: 'Oh, look at Harold, he's talking with his imaginary friends again.' Finally, when I was fourteen, my mother took me to the doctor. He was a German who knew more than he cared to divulge to her. He suggested that I get away from the house for a while to a place where I could rest and think about the things that were happening." His mother knew the very place, the cottage of her married brother in a small isolated town.

Nothing could have suited young Harold more, because he was especially fond of this particular aunt. He roamed around the village and thought of the apparitions and the visitors he had seen. He hoped that nothing would happen while he was there, because he didn't want to upset his aunt and have to be sent back to his mother.

One afternoon he was upstairs washing his hands for tea and could hear his aunt and her mother setting the table. When they called him he descended and stopped short, unable to move. "What's the matter, Harold?" his aunt asked.

The young boy blushed in dread, then finally stammered: "There's a man sitting in my chair."

If this had been at his own home, Reverend Plume remarks to-day, his mother would have furiously cut the conversation short and probably sent him out of the room, but his aunt was different. "What's he look like?" she asked.

Encouraged for the first time in his life, he described the stranger sitting at the table. Then he gave the man's first name. Then he added: "And he says he's your father!"

The ladies remained silent until his uncle rose and left the house. "Then my aunt and her mother grabbed me and pulled me upstairs. They said I had given a perfect description of her father. They pulled down the mattress on one of the beds and there were the first psychic books I'd ever seen in my life."

His aunt then wrote his mother telling her what had happened. Harold asked her not to write, saying: "There'll be a telegram." There was a telegram and it ordered Harold to come home immediately.

So his mother took him to the vicar. The old man pulled out book after book and quoted long passages at the young boy. Finally he said: "You know, Harold, this is evil."

And Harold said: "If that's the case, do you believe in the law of attraction?" He knows he was being controlled by an unseen force, because he himself had never heard of the law of attraction. "If that's the case then I must be evil, because only if I am evil will I attract evil."

The vicar answered that the boy was not evil. "Then God will never allow evil to come to me," he replied.

"I have no answer for what's happening to you," the cleric finally said. "I'll pray for you."

Harold thanked him and left with his mother. A few weeks later he left home and went to discover himself in London.

He got odd jobs in stores, fooled around at being a professional boxer and devoured all the literature he could find about Spiritualism. He sat with mediums, attended lectures, sought out fortune-tellers and psychics. Then he met Bertha, chased her for a year until she finally agreed to marry him, and settled down in a middle-class neighborhood determined to be a good husband and father.

But a man moved in next door who was to change his life. His name was Tommy Atkins and he was considered one of the strongest Spiritualist mediums in England. Before long he was teaching Harold everything he knew about apports, healings, trances, clairvoyance, etc. Finally he judged that the young man was ready for professional mediumship.

But Harold thought otherwise. "I'd been able to go into trance and tell people things about their health or their mother on the other side and all that, but I knew most of these people from the neighborhood. I didn't think it was the spirits that were giving the answers but my own subconscious mind. So one day into the séance room walks the whole bloomin' fire department of a nearby town. One by one Tommy Atkins presented me to them, asking me, 'Did you ever see this bloke before?' and of course I had to say no. I'd never seen any of them before. So I went into trance and gave them all messages and advice. They were quite impressed. So was I." Soon after, he began his professional ministerial work and still hasn't stopped.

His first healing was done for his wife. Bertha was pregnant with their second daughter (they have six daughters now) and developed a serious kidney infection. Doctors wanted to remove the diseased organ, saying that it would harm the baby and possibly kill his wife. Reverend Plume considered it for a while, then Hoo-Fang made himself known. He said he was a Chinese physician who had lived 2,500 years ago. He asked Reverend Plume to trust him and allow him to work through his physical body. That afternoon Harold touched Bertha's body where her ailing kidney was and watched in fascination as Hoo-Fang placed his hand over Harold's and told him to push. The human energy from Harold with the spiritual energy of the long-dead doctor caused his fingers to dematerialize and enter Bertha's body. There was no blood, because her flesh was also dematerializing under his touch. He felt the fingers caress the diseased kidney and was told that Hoo-Fang was destroying the dead cells and recharging the energy in the living cells. Then Hoo-Fang asked that the hand be removed. Harold saw his fingers slowly withdraw from the body. There was no scar. There was no pain. And more importantly, there was no more diseased tissue on Bertha's kidney.

His fame grew and soon he was booked months in advance. The war years came and he helped the British Army in special ways that only a clairvoyant could. (In the United States Army he would have been branded a psycho case and not even admitted.) When peace returned he returned to his church. His daughters grew up and married. Two of them came to the United States. One of them moved to Illinois and became so homesick for her parents that her husband wrote pleading with them to come over. Anxious over the health of this daughter and sure he could make a living as a minister in the States, they sold everything they owned in England and flew across the Atlantic. Their struggle to survive in this unbelieving and at times inhospitable land is an epic in itself. But they made it to California, where he set up a church in Los Angeles and then finally, in Monterey, where he intends to stay.

He has been written up in several magazine and newspaper articles as well as in a couple of sensational "spirit exposé" type books. But it is the hundreds of letters in his file that tell the real story.

A woman in Toronto, Canada, was swollen and filled with gangrene. Doctors said she was dying and they prepared to operate on a "tumor in her stomach." Then she heard of Reverend Plume. She walked out of the hospital and took the first plane to San Francisco, where he was holding a special session. Reverend Plume operated on her for a few minutes, his fingers going into her abdomen. The next day she was back on the plane to Canada. In flight she had the urge to go to the bathroom. There she passed a huge black piece of flesh. Putting it into a bag she arrived home and took it to her doctors. They identified it as a five-month-old foetus. Her letter of gratitude tells the story: "Where do I start to thank you? God bless you and your wonderful family. I shall send you a picture of the growth that I passed and which two medical doctors say I couldn't have (1) without unbearable pain and (2) the particular way the growth was secured. It was supposed to be impossible, at least in these times they say and (3) without bleeding to death after. How could I add to their disbelief by telling that that I carried my heavy luggage out of the airport two hours later? But these are the facts and to add a little humor, I had to declare the growth at customs and you can imagine the ramifications."

The star football player at San Jose State College injured his back so badly he was unable to participate in the games. Seven different doctors looked but did nothing. Finally the coach brought him to Reverend Plume. His back was put into place immediately. When the young man happened to mention that he had an appointment to be fitted for special contact lenses that he would wear while playing, Reverend Plume cured his eyesight.

While his batting average is quite high there are some illnesses that he has been unable to cure and some he absolutely refuses to cure. One woman wanted her breasts enlarged. She was refused. A sixty-five-year-old man wanted his sex organs rejuvenated. When Reverend Plume balked, the man said: "I heard you have a Chinese doctor and back in the old days the Chinese used to take a brown powder for their sex organs. Would you ask your doctor what they took?"

"I told this old coot I would never bring my Chinese friend from his high spiritual level for something so low! I won't do this kind of thing in God's house. It's tawdry! It affects my helpers and it upsets the vibrations I need for serious healing. I almost threw the old man out of here, I did."

Naturally, I was anxious to watch the reverend at work and the next Sunday evening I showed up for a service. Bertha played the piano and the twenty-some members in the congregation sang from hymn books. Then Reverend Plume went to a chair by the side of the altar and began to meditate. His head nodded. Bertha played the piano and kept looking backward to see how her husband was doing. He started to stir, then seemed to awaken and walked to the front of the congregation with his eyes closed. Then he started to speak. The odd voice that came out identified itself as a long-dead Anglican minister. He gave a brief message, then went back to the chair in the corner. This happened four times, the last entity to come through being a highly irreverent young Cockney factory worker who talked about sick old ladies doing the "hoochie-coochie." The females in the audience laughed, most of the males looked shocked. After all, this was a house of God. Then he went back and slowly came out of his trance. His face was flushed and his eyes were puffed. It took him a few seconds to co-ordinate his arms and legs. His smile was almost one of embarrassment and he jokingly apologized for "falling asleep in church."

Then the healing service started. They brought in a seven-year-old boy who was fussing and making noises deep in his throat. His father, a man in mid-twenties, carried him like a sack of grain in his arms and placed him on a sheet on the floor in front of the altar. The boy, rosy and chubby, moved his hands and feebly kicked his feet. His bright eyes shone pleadingly like eyes behind a mask. Like they were trying to break free of this prison.

His attractive young mother explained to me that her son had been born normal and had acted like a normal child until he was two years old. Then he started losing control of his muscles. Little by little he forgot how to walk, how to use his fingers and how to talk. It finally got to the point that he forgot how to move his bowels and chew food. They had to take him to the hospital daily so he could be fed by sticking a tube down his throat. The doctors had no name for the disease and no cure. They gave the child two years "to continue to exist as a vegetable." That was when the parents heard of Reverend Plume. "After the very first session," the mother recalls, "he regained his memory to eat and swallow. We've been coming here for two years and the changes have been wonderful."

Indeed, for a child that was supposed to have been long dead, a child who couldn't move a single muscle, the boy looked healthy and strong to me. He had grown considerably, his parents said, was able to follow them with his eyes and register emotions. I watched closely as Reverend Plume massaged the boy's legs and saw the child push back at the pressure on his chubby foot. He smiled at Mrs. Plume and raised his arms toward his father. The parents are more than pleased with the progress, yet Reverend Plume is not. He considers this as one of the most baffling cases he's ever had. "I don't understand why he just doesn't get up and walk out of here," he says. "I've seen so many other immediate cures for people who don't really deserve them, and this little fellow has to be healed almost inch by inch. I'd give my life to make him well. And I will make him whole again. I *will!*"

After the boy had been lifted into his father's arms, a young woman came forward. She sat in a chair wearing a blue knit suit. Under California law Reverend Plume is not allowed to diagnose (or prescribe even an aspirin for a headache), so the patient had to tell him she had a growth in her uterus. She said doctors told her it would have to be cut out. Reverend Plume took a piece of facial tissue and placed it on her abdomen. Then he put his face so close to the paper that his nose almost touched it. "That's quite a scar you have there," he said. The woman answered that she had been operated on in that area when she was a child. Mrs. Plume told me: "Harold's got X-ray eyes. He can see right into the body. It always surprises people when he sees old scars and the like."

Then he placed his fingertips on the woman's abdomen. I was standing a respectful distance away. He turned and looked at me. "David, would you like to see this?" he asked. I came over immediately and, crouching down, had my face about a foot from his hand. He began to push and wiggle his hand as if he were trying to force his way into her abdomen.

Then his fingers slid straight into her body, taking the piece of Kleenex along with them. Both fingers and tissue had vanished. I peered under his hand. There was only the palm to be seen pressed up against the blue knit dress!

Slowly the fingers slid from the body, pulling the facial tissue along with them. There was no blood on the paper. There was no opening in the dress or the body. There was nothing but a gasp from my throat as his hand completely reappeared. The young woman said she felt as if a great pressure had been removed. I felt perplexed and unsure of my own eyesight. I had seen the late Brazilian psychic healer Jose Arigó stick knives in people's eyes and cut growths off arms and legs with no anesthetic. It was a shock then. It was a shock now.

I left the chapel after thanking the reverend and his wife for their courtesy toward me and sought out the nearest bar. I downed two bourbons as I recalled what I'd seen. I'm sure the waitress thought I was nuts as she watched me trying to stick my fingers into my own body and into the back of the booth. I *must* have seen what I thought I saw. Too many people had seen it before me. Too many people have reportedly been cured by what I had seen. The man has a solid reputation on both sides of the Atlantic. Only when the third bourbon arrived did I start to relax.

The town of Carmel prides itself as being an "escape" kind of place. It has grown up over the last thirty years or so and one time was *the* bohemian place of the West Coast. Inhabitants built little homes along the ocean and near the ruins of one of Padre Serra's missions. Artists, writers and pre-World War II hippies did their thing and were happy about it. Then an earthquake hit Monterey and dozens of "straight" families moved into town. Soldiers stationed at Fort Ord returned to settle in Carmel after the war. Today the wealthy and the jet set have invaded the town and the main street is dotted with "arte shoppes," "boutiques" and "salons." Tourists love the place for a day or so but find little to do there. It doesn't swing, they say.

Tarquin (that's the only name he uses and few know his real name) was the original "nature boy" of Carmel years ago. He arrived disillusioned with the world and determined to evaluate himself and calculate the direction in which he had to go. He had no money (his father had been a real estate baron in Berkeley but lost most of it to taxes after the Depression), so he found a piece of land on the other side of a deep stream and built a ramshackle hut of scraps and packing crates. Having no neighbors he ran around naked putting on a pair of shorts only when he had to wade the stream and go shopping in town.

Because of his Tarot classes (every Wednesday night) and the demand for readings (donations are accepted), he moved from his shack into two rooms on the end of an old house that has seen better days. His rooms, bath and kitchen are furnished with a series of dressers, tables and stands that have the "Goodwill" look about them. They serve to display and store the hundreds of books, statues, manuscripts, posters, charts and drawings that he has amassed over the years. The walls of these rooms are covered with lithographs of Indian deities, Buddhas, astrology charts, Egyptian temples, and paintings where the sun is either rising or setting. There is an altar with two white columns that displays a shiny bronze T square. Tarquin claims this was the sign of the lost continent of Mu. He was a high priest on Mu. He shares these quarters with a beautiful black Siamese cat named Pharaoh. This feline, with blue eyes and a profile that looks as if it was taken from the Egyptian symbol for "cat" just moved in one day. They understand each other completely. When Tarquin goes out, Pharaoh gets ready too. Tarquin puts on a green pointed hat and a shirt with a large pointed collar and donning a sport jacket and a pair of cotton trousers he looks like a white-haired Robin Hood. He wears several seed necklaces and sticks a jeweled-eye bat on his hat for decoration. Somehow it all fits perfectly. Somehow it's not a "put-on." Somehow, with him, it all seems perfectly natural.

When Tarquin speaks to explain the Tarot his vocabulary is rich and formal. He thinks nothing of using such phrases as "particularly enamored," "on absolute authority" and "uniqueness of design." You can almost see certain words underlined as he speaks.

"When I am reading the Tarot I am *aware* of the *presence* of the *guide*. We think of guides and other supernatural beings as being far away. And heaven being a state of mind also seems far away. But *being* a state of mind it is within us and that which is within us also has the power to reflect any light, any knowledge, any vibration which is there for the sake of presenting his or her or *its* awareness. In other words, that which we do in this life through Tarot or any other means of divination to help others is not nearly so important as the *reason* we do it. What we have accomplished or not accomplished in the past lives is much more important rather than the place where we are on this earth. The *reason* for coming, the *reason* for the deeds and the *reason* for the leaving is much more important."

We were sitting at his Tarot table and he had just placed the brass mortar that he uses as a "bell" alongside the black wand with brass tips and a forty-eight-star American flag inside that the famed magician Harry Blackstone gave him. He took the wand and struck the mortar three times. It rang with clarity and perfect tone. "It's in the key of B flat," he informed me. "Usually I strike it with a special pendant which gives it a slightly different tone. But I don't want my guide to appear now. Now, where were we? Oh yes, the reason we do things. Have you ever trained a kitten or a puppy and watched that small and frequently beautiful creature try as best he can to obey his master? He has intellect and intelligence but he does not have the knowledge built in him nor the ability to show that he *can* accomplish what the impatient master wishes. The little animal *knows,* but not too much, that he is limited, but he will *not* recognize his limitations. Therefore his trying to express himself for his master, who is often his god, is to me one of the most beautiful things here on this earth."

"Do you think we don't get any farther than we do," I asked, "because we recognize our limitations or put a mental barrier that sometimes doesn't even exist to our capabilities?"

"You have *just* described the Veil of Isis! Eye-sis, which can be pronounced differently, is a combination of numbers when it is written in cryptographic form and it represents the veil with which we surround ourselves. It is a covering we were born with, which we do not shed until we rid ourselves of the I Am This feeling or the I Am That feeling. Not in the spiritual, but in the physical connotation."

"But why are we born with this veil? Is it to protect us in our formative years?"

"It is the veil of *conceit!*"

"But as human beings don't we have to have some kind of conceit? As a kind of identification?"

"It is an identification," he answered, "but an identification that is the feelings of the last *meal.* The last *lifetime.* This particular time, this strata, this third dimension in which we are now living is a veil of illusion. You do not *have* to be trapped in this level, this time layer. By learning to control your vibrations you can slow down your speed and go into the past or speed up your vibrations and see into the future. Let me elucidate. There are many different realms of time for an entity living at the rate of vibrations in one realm to find, to learn of, to seek out and to communicate *with* a being in a different type of dimension. He can accomplish this by his finding himself being a cog in a wheel to another cog. This is the inner meaning of the two of pentacles in the Tarot; light reflects into light according to the light it can receive and for that which it is ready. This is, therefore, significant of our mental and spiritual capacities. Do you understand?"

"I think so," I replied rather vaguely. "Are there many people who are able to speed up their vibrations and look into the future?"

"Oh yes. They've been trained to do this. It has been going on for centuries. I can do it, but remember, I am only a vehicle. I merely receive vibrations from my guide and translate this into information for the person who is having his cards read."

"What happens to you physically and mentally when these vibrations are speeded up?"

"I do not go into a subconscious state. I remain perfectly lucid of what is going on. There have have been times when I've gone into trance. I have many times spoken in tongues. Sometimes I see the spiritual visitors coming into the room to hear what is going on and they are always visitors from other dimensions in time. Often people will look up and say, 'Who is your Egyptian friend or who is your Indian friend?' Once in a while I will see them myself—but not always. But I always *do* see a person's aura and I always see a person's light behind him. Frequently I'm given the view of lights, colors and sounds to indicate that I'm on the right track when I'm reading for a client."

"Does reincarnation have anything to do with the answers the Tarot gives?"

"Most *definitely!* The most *difficult* lesson we have to learn individually is that we are *always* in the right place at the right time. We should not complain, but rather listen to our guardian angel, who will tell us: 'Don't you remember this was programmed into that little thing you held with you just before you decided to go back into where you were? This is the continuation of that lesson you failed to complete. You must continue it!'"

"You say, ask your guardian angel, as if it were as easy as picking up the telephone. How do you contact your guardian angel?"

"First, you must learn to depend upon this guardian angel. You must be able to recognize him or her perhaps through a tap on the shoulder, the feeling of air down your back, perhaps a knocking somewhere, many ways."

"But how do you make that first contact?" I insisted. "By lighting candles? Incense? Prayer?"

"You should do whatever it is that comes to your mind that brings you tranquillity. That tells you *this* is the way. You must first have no doubts and if there are no doubts that means the windshield of your purpose is clear, and the road to your direction is in front of you. Find *that* and you'll know you are being guided."

"But it's not that easy, is it, Tarquin? To find *that?* To clean your windshield?"

"It depends on the size of the windshield, how dirty it is and what you're using for a cleaner." I sighed and frowned. He continued. "I'm sorry if the answer is vague but I cannot give a set reply. It depends on the person, his mental attitude and his knowledge. We must all seek the same thing from our individual levels. But there is no height to which we cannot reach, depending upon what our reason is for reaching it." He smiled and I felt my question *had* been answered.

Tarquin was born in Berkeley, California, in 1911. It's difficult to imagine that he is that old, for his years of outdoor living, yoga exercises and healthy dieting have given him the body of a man of thirty and an even younger mind. Only his white hair and a few facial lines hint at his real "earthly" age. His "cosmic" age is incalculable.

He had his first psychic experience when he was eleven. He was in his family's home high in the Berkeley Hills and in the music room. From there, there was a view that went all the way over to San Francisco and to the Golden Gate. He had been playing the organ and got up to look out the window.

"I had just finished playing an orange, and . . ."

"An *orange?*" (He now had *me* underlining words.)

"Yes, I never played sheet music. Instead, I would put an object on the music rack in front of me and play the emanations I received from it. It could be an object, a picture, a piece of glass, a flower or a lovely candle. Anyway, I rose from the organ that particular evening, so moved by the music that I had played and gazed out at the setting sun right in the center of the Golden Gate. Then I heard a deep beautiful tone that seemed to vibrate all through my being. It was as if this beautiful Earth herself was breathing and beckoning. I was in the middle of the Earth's heartbeat and she was in the middle of mine. I felt like a rose and then I began to unfold. And all that was light became dark and that which had been dark became light. I was aware of myself presenting a negative against all which I saw in the positive and suddenly the positive became the negative and the negative became the positive. If you've ever placed the negative of a photograph against the print of the photograph and suddenly jerked it to the left or to the right you'll have a most *amazing* feeling, because one or the other will seem to move. This is exactly what happened. One or the other *did* move and I saw the world in the *positive*. Every single line, every single form became a chain of lighted colors and I saw vibrating around everything the prismatic colors shining as jewels and *then* I heard the result of the heartbeat. A regular rhythm, a *gorgeously tantalizing jangle* as used in ancient Egyptian rites! The singing must surely have been called at one time "of the gods." And from the vicinity of what is now considered South San Francisco I saw emerging from a mile above the earth to many miles above, gloriously radiant humanlike figures marching in a steady procession from northwest to southeast. These figures were walking, dancing, wearing chains of gold and silver and diamonds and flowers. Their eyes were brilliant. Their beings were almost transparent in many lovely, lovely colors. They were not just a few. There were hundreds of them and as they came marching toward me they became larger in size. They had caissons and caparisoned horses and wagons of all kinds. I could see small animals like rabbits and deer and birds and doves and all in love and harmony and beauty. I stood transfixed. It lasted perhaps fifteen or twenty minutes. I don't know. As they finally departed I could hear them singing in the distance and the beautiful rhythm of Mother Earth eventually stopped and the positive once more turned back into the negative and I could hear my own heartbeat as belonging to me only. Who were these people? From whence did they come? Well, the answer was later given to me."

"Did you tell your family about this?"

"Heavens no! I was ashamed of the vision, because I was sure I was going mad. Then one afternoon, two years later, the vision happened again and has happened several times since. But now I know who these people were."

He paused. I waited. Finally I asked. "Who?"

"They were the characters and representations of the Tarot. These people were attributes of the Tarot. I see them every time I lay the cards. They were grouped together and almost transparent because that is the way I eventually came to read the Tarot. I don't read just one card at a time but usually three at once, as though one were atop the other, as if the *cards* were transparent. Therefore, when I read, it's as if there was one *huge scroll* in front of me."

"Who taught you to lay out the cards this way?"

"My guide. I've laid them out in every possible, conceivable position and I've even used two decks at once. I practiced for about thirteen years to make sure that I wasn't making a complete fool of myself before I read for the public. As a youngster I demanded that people be complete strangers to me. I didn't want to read for relatives or anyone that I knew. I wanted to be tested."

"How many people have you read for?" I asked.

"I've tried to figure this out but get bogged down in the mathematics of it. My first reading was in nineteen thirty-three and, let's see, it's almost nineteen seventy-three so *that* is forty years and let's say there was at *least* one reading every day, but there were really more and . . . well, that's quite a few readings."

"Have you ever given what you or your client considers a 'bad' reading?"

"Oh yes, several times. Recently I was giving a reading and the cards turned into pasteboard before my eyes and there was no response from my guide. I couldn't get anything from them. After he left, my guide explained to me that this particular client was not to know anything about what he was asking. This was a no-no."

"Speaking of no-no's, many mediums refuse to tell a client if they see death for them. What about you?"

"Never! It would be terribly presumptuous on my part to tell them they were going to die and I don't want to be karmicly hooked to anyone. Once a lady came to me just before her mother was to arrive and said: 'Do me a favor and remove the Death card from the deck before you read for my mother. She's highly suspicious.' So I said, 'What Death card?' 'Well,' she said, 'you're a Tarot reader aren't you?' 'Yes,' I replied, 'but there's no Death card in the deck. There is one that is *marked* Death. There are cards which placed together in a certain position do definitely mean a passing on into another *dimension,* but when you can tell me what death *is,* then I'll show you the Death card.'"

"Would you tell me how you've helped someone through the cards?"

He thought for a moment, then let out a loud ha-hah! "Yes indeed. There is a *lovely* story I can tell. There was a gentleman who came to see me who was of the George Raft characterization. He was very nervous and he wanted to know chiefly about a certain business venture he was about to embark upon and particularly about his partner. Could his partner be trusted? When he turned over the first card the information given to me was, yes, his partner could be trusted but did he know his partner had a *friend* interested in this venture? No, he didn't know about his partner's friend. I said, well, don't watch out for your partner, watch out for his friend. He's the one who's not to be trusted. The four of you will not succeed. But, he said, there's only three of us! I insisted there were four. When the reading was over, he left, still shaking nervously, and the very next day there were headlines in the newspaper. It seems there had been a bank robbery and this gentleman had been right in the center of it. In fact, he was the gunman. His friend attending to carrying out the 'swag' had arranged for someone else to arrive in a second getaway car and not use the car or driver originally planned upon. He suddenly discerned that he had been cheated and that they were going to leave him there holding his gun in his hand. When he saw this fourth, and unexpected, character arriving, he quickly raised his foot into the air and tripped the man who was carrying the 'loot,' which gave the local constabulary just enough time to capture all four of them. Funny, but I've not heard from any of them since."

Clint D. Nix lives in Carmel, hails from Oklahoma and came to California because "the Navy brought me." He is tall, used to be a clothes model and wears his hair and sideburns *a la* Engelbert Humperdinck. At twenty-five he is one of the youngest practicing psychics around. He says he is not a hippie but a "free soul." He reads the Tarot cards, sometimes uses the crystal ball but prefers palmistry.

"The other day I was in the local coffeeshop and there was a guy sitting beside me at the counter and we started to talk. I glanced at his hand and said, 'You've been married a couple of times and have two kids. Right?' It just freaked the guy out and he made me tell him other things I saw in his palm. He walked out all shook up but he paid my check. The counterman was amazed. Seems this guy is known for being one of the stingiest cats in town."

He always considered himself a "normal" human being, because he was able on meeting a person for the first time to know a great deal about them and be able to tell them where they were going in the near future. The shock came when he discovered that everyone didn't do this. That he was "different" somehow. He started doing readings by having people sit down with him and concentrating on the cards or the crystal ball. "When they were concentrating I was able to pick up their thoughts and vibrations. I was able to tune myself into them and tell them things they thought were hidden. It's funny but people always know what I tell them. They always know their bad points and what they should do to correct them, yet they never seem to do anything about them. It's as if they just wait for someone else to discover their weaknesses and *tell* them to correct them. A medium is a lot like a Catholic priest in a confessional except that he has to tune in on the sins before he can expiate them."

His first love is palmistry and he is constantly reading new books on it. "It's intriguing because every palm is different. Each new hand is a new challenge, but I can't stand skeptical people, whether it's in palmistry, Tarot or astrology. Anybody who is skeptical scatters his forces so much that he never attains anything in life. A skeptical person's heart lines across the top of the palm will be scattered. You can see it in faces too. If a person is really skeptical he has lots of wrinkles. Even his mind powers are scattered. It's really odd."

Clint, like most psychics, doesn't like reading for close friends. "It's too hard," he admits, "because it's difficult to distinguish from what you know and what's really there. If you see it differently than what they appear then you'll stop and hesitate and you'll not be sure of your reading at all. You won't know how much is you and how much is the message."

It surprised me that he doesn't believe in reincarnation. "I think it's a cop-out," he said. "People have a tendency to say, 'Oh, wow. She is treating me horribly in this life because I treated her horribly in the past life. There's nothing I can do about it. I've got to pay now.' I don't believe it. I do believe in incarnations but not back to this planet all the time. There are other places where souls can be reborn, other galaxies. All you have to do is look up into the sky at night to see them. And what's to be gained by coming back again and again? I met a chick who claims she was a princess in the last life. She's nobody in this one! What's the advantage of it?"

"What about making contact with the dead?" I asked.

"Oh, sure. Spirits are definitely there. You have a child that's born dead, well, it's just because the spirit doesn't enter the body. And if a person dies, they're just lying there without the spirit. They are physically fine. There is no reason for death. We call it old age when the spirit decides to leave."

"Do you meditate?"

"Yes, but that can be misleading. I wish that all the kids who are turning on to Transcendental Meditation would really study it and seriously see where they are going. So many of them grasp the elementals and then go around in a dream world of what they *think* they are getting from their meditation. That's the big problem with psychics too. Most of them live in a dream world and are never sure of what they are getting or from where. I've been studying and have a long way to go yet. I've got youth on my side. How many mediums do you know that are in their early twenties?"

I had to admit that there were very few genuine psychics, mediums or clairvoyants who were not at least in their mid-thirties. In fact, most of the ones I had met were in their forties and some into their eighties. It seems that the older they get and the longer they practice using their gifts the better they become. That's really what interested me in Clint, his youth.

I asked him what his family thought about him, and if they were happy calling him "My son the medium."

"Well," he said shyly, "whenever I phone home my mother will ask, 'Have you read the cards for me lately? Is anything good going to happen?' And my father, he goes, 'I don't believe a damn thing about it.' But every time I see him I tell him things that are going to happen and they always do. But he still looks at me and says, 'Sure . . .'"

The Stonehouse is the nicest guest lodge in Carmel. It's noted for its tradition, good food and charm. It's also noted as being the place that John and Margaret Pawley own and as a center for those interested in the psychic and the occult. John is English, Margaret is American. Both are very much aware that there is "something else" around us. That there are "other reasons" to be living.

Margaret used to call Philadelphia her home. There she worked as a professional psychotherapist for sixteen years. Her method was to "mother" a schizophrenic back to his childhood in order to have him release his earliest tensions. She would hold them, feed them, sing to them and tell them stories. For many, it worked, but for her it was a long-drawn-out and exhaustive process.

Then one evening she was invited to attend a lecture by Kay Ortmans, a well-known therapist from London who was presiding over a relaxation retreat in the forests of Ben Lomond, California. Miss Ortmans used a theory that she herself developed of massaging a person to music. It was her idea that our muscles retained memories and past-life experiences and the only way to free the body (and therefore the mind) of these frustrating past events was to massage the experiences away. Margaret listened to her lecture and then seemed to fly out of her body. She visited the top of a tall mountain and saw trees and fresh green grass. She admits she missed much of the lecture, but she left the auditorium positive that what she had been looking for was in California. "I had searched the East Coast for a way to help my patients," she recalls, "but there were few answers available. Even the explanation for schizophrenia wasn't there. So as soon as I heard that Miss Ortmans was giving a teachers' course I flew out to California. This was in November of 1967. The program is one of muscle movements through rhythm, then relaxation under heavy blankets, massage and then expressing yourself in some way through painting, writing, dancing, etc. It's a wonderful way to get to know yourself better. And in a very short time."

On the second day Miss Ortmans asked for a volunteer to demonstrate the massage technique and Margaret came forward. She stretched out on a table and "as she began to massage me I was suddenly lying in a battlefield in France and there were horses pounding over me! Then she began to work the backs of my legs, where I was never aware of having any discomfort. Yet suddenly there was great pain and I found myself looking at what seemed like a prison cell. It was black with water running down the walls and in the corner, hanging upside down, was a decomposing, blackened corpse."

"Had you ever dreamed or imagined this scene before?" I asked.

"No. The whole thing was an absolute shock! I reacted with terrific shivering and crying and she stopped the massage because I was in such an emotional stage. They wrapped me in a blanket and gave me something hot to drink. I stayed awake all that night trying to figure out what had happened to me. The next day, after the 'relax and rebound session,' I found myself molding a man's head from clay. And I couldn't shake the feeling of being in that cell. The next day I felt compelled to give the head a body— it was almost as if I was trying to put that corpse together in my own mind—and I made the figure of a monk. A lady there who was an ex-nun said it was a Benedictine monk because of the cowl and the sandals. So we figured that possibly this memory that had been released was that I had been a Benedictine monk and had been imprisoned for doing or saying something that the authorities didn't approve. Over the next year I flew to California four times and each time when I had a massage and Miss Ortmans would touch the back of my legs these same pictures would appear. When she did my upper back I saw myself as a cardinal in France, wearing a long red robe and being carted off to be hanged. And when she did my legs I was always a monk in a cell."

"No wonder you're not a Catholic in this lifetime!"

"My one desire was to get this corpse out of that cell and see him buried. Then on the eighth massage the wall suddenly fell down and sunlight streamed into the dark area. Then six men came in carrying a wooden coffin. As I waited the body fell from its position on the wall and into the box. Then they carried it away and buried it. And that was the last time I ever had the vision. After that Kay would massage my legs and nothing would appear at all."

"Did you believe in reincarnation before you had these experiences?"

"I don't know. I never gave it much thought; after all, I was a doctor. I believed in the body and the mind. Now I'm sure reincarnation is a reality."

So taken was Margaret with Kay Ortmans' work that she moved to California accompanied by a young patient named Ken. He was a schizophrenic in his twenties whom she had been treating for years. He had all of the problems of a true neurotic: lack of parental love, hatred of violence, a fear of life itself. There would be days when he would be perfectly normal, then he would go berserk, screaming and crying and physically beating both Margaret and John. They had to confine him to mental hospitals and more than once helped to strap him into a strait-jacket. Margaret placed him in the Agnew Mental Hospital in San Jose but took him out every weekend. She drove him to Kay Ortmans' Well-Springs retreat, but she never told the hospital doctors.

"I'm convinced that Ken is acting out these traumas from his past lives. This is what one of the psychics says he is doing, that he is living out pieces of about six different lives and that he's almost through it. The psychic Dorothy Smith said that he had been a highly evolved young priest in Atlantis but had gotten under the influence of some older priests who indoctrinated him into black magic. In this life he was always talking about magic. He would remove books about magic from the shelves and leave them around where I would find them. He would talk about mysterious black stones. One time we were on a trip and visited a friend who put on an amateur magic show and Ken went absolutely wild. He hated it! He couldn't control his anger. I could never understand what magic had to do with his problem until the psychic said he had been a black magician.

"The other thing I could never explain was that he was always saying: 'I killed my mother.' No interpretation having to do with the death of his mother in this life had any effect. He would get terribly disturbed every time there was a murder or a rape in the newspapers. Then he would have these spells where his mouth would fly open as if he was choking to death or drowning. These would last from fifteen minutes to hours. We would rush him to hospitals and emergency wards and doctors would give him oxygen. He would fight all the time and he's a strong man, six feet tall. He would become terribly frightened by these attacks and they were coming at the rate of two a week. Once when he had this spell he shouted: 'I couldn't have killed my mother!' and it was the first time that I recognized a connection between these attacks and the idea he had killed his mother."

Many psychics have told Margaret that she and Ken have been together often in past lives. They have been priests in temples together, mother and son and brother and sister. That's why she feels so differently about him and has worked more for him than any other patient.

Then one afternoon at Well-Springs everything fell into place. "Ken was being massaged by Kay and I was in a smaller room right off the massage parlor. Suddenly a picture flashed into my mind. As it got stronger I could see it was Ken and me. I was going across a desert, riding on a little burro and Ken was walking beside me. He seemed to be about nine years old. I thought it was in Persia, for we were wearing heavy off-white garments. We continued across the desert until we came to a place where there were trees and a shaded cave with a well in the back. Apparently we lived there. Then the picture changed and I saw that Ken was about nineteen years old. We were still near this cave and still in the same kind of clothes. Then a band of brigands came across the desert on horses. There were seven men and they had long spears. Two of the men held Ken and forced him to look.

"Now in all the years I've known him he had this terrible problem about peeping toms. Once he suddenly developed an eye ulcer and all night long went around with his eyes tightly closed and his hands out in front of him as if he were blind, acting something out. In this picture he was held and forced to look while five of these men raped me. When I told him part of this story he stopped me saying: 'Look, I can tell you part of this myself. I saw them drag you off and rape you.' Now, this agreed with what I had seen. He told this *before* I told him. This seems to explain why he associated sex and violence and was so disturbed by rape. Then these two men castrated him. He has this terrible problem about castration. Just all out of proportion. And then he came over to me and I begged him to kill me. And he choked me to death at my request. Which explains 'I killed my mother.' It also explains why he would sit and stare at his hands for hours and why he can do so little with his hands. And he went over to the well and he drowned himself. He has this terrible fear of water today. I have the feeling that the two men who held him have some connection with his father and brother in this life, because he has unreasoning hatred of both of them. When I told that to him one day he replied: 'Now, that rings a bell. That makes sense.'

"Now, after all this material came up, he's had no more of these spells, with his mouth flying open. He no longer is choking me or drowning in that well. He can read about a murder or a rape in the paper and it doesn't disturb him. These things don't trigger him any more."

"Why does just knowing a problem help you to rid yourself of it?"

"I don't think it does. Just knowing about it doesn't do a scrap of good. You have to get the *feeling* of the emotion out of your system. The problem with most psychiatrists is that they do not show their patients how to *feel*. The problems are often not in the mind but in the *emotions*. There is a wonderful book out now about this very thing. It's called *The Primal Scream* and this man showed how he got people back to the point where they stopped being what *they* wanted to be and started acting out what they thought *others* wanted them to be. This made them neurotic. You have to get the anger out, get the emotion out. You have to empty out the hurts and put something else in."

"Do you feel that Ken has improved because of these psychic massages and sessions? Is he different from the young man you brought out from Philadelphia?"

"Many of the things that were so-called 'psychotic symptoms' have disappeared. Now we are still working on the problem of possession. He no longer is in a mental hospital but living in a boardinghouse nearby. He comes home to see us every weekend. Many psychics have told us that when he has been completely cured he will probably make a great healer because he is an open channel."

"Mrs. Pawley," I asked, "are you of the opinion that the majority of people who are labeled insane or schizophrenic are possessed by entities or are bothered by something in their past lives?"

She looked at me, a serious, level, understanding stare. "I'm not going to make any blanket statements like that, but in Ken's case, which I know and know well, I'm positive he is possessed and acting out traumas from his past lives. The proof of this has been his partial yet remarkable cure."

The Pawleys had told me about Dorie D'Angelo. She had operated on Margaret Pawley's heel and it was cured after two years of pain. She had also removed a mole that had become infected. Tarquin had told me that Dorie D'Angelo had taken the stiffness from a piano player's shoulder and had made a kneecap move again. Petite, brunette and energetic Mrs. D'Angelo admits that she was there when these things happened, but she didn't do it. Her Scottish physician ghost performed the operations.

Dorie, like the majority of psychics in the Psychic State, came from somewhere else. She was born in Canada and worked at psychotherapy in Toronto. There were no spirits involved in her work then, just exercises and routines to reduce tensions and aid relaxation. Then Dorie sat in on a hypnotism session, where she witnessed the "spirit going off someplace and returning, telling what it saw and that it had cured a man in a hospital; well right there, that was for me."

A lady offered to let Dorie work at a healing foundation she was setting up in California and Dorie eagerly accepted the assignment. But Canadian red tape along with American red tape kept her three full months in Toronto. When she finally got her visa and arrived in California the position had been filled. "But at least," she reckoned, "I was in California and it was beautiful."

Dorie set up her own therapy classes in Carmel, content with a few patients and the fair climate. Then disaster struck. It was Christmas Day and her husband, who had been complaining of headaches for weeks, suddenly took a turn for the worse. From his low breathing and his ashen color Dorie knew he was dying. Frantically she called several doctors but none of them was available. It was Christmas, after all. She placed her husband on her massage table and stood caressing his temples with her fingertips.

She looked up. There was a strange man standing beside her. He told her not to be frightened, that he had come to help her. She looked closely at him and saw that he was not made of flesh and blood. He was dressed in a double-breasted suit of the 1900's and wore a pair of glasses on a black ribbon. She knew that he was a ghost. A sense of calmness came over her and she wasn't afraid.

"I am a medical doctor," he told her in an accent heavy with rolling *r*'s from a Scottish burr. "Your husband will die unless we operate. Now, I have not the energy to do this by myself. That's why I must work through you. I will use your forces and vibrations." Then, in a commanding tone he said: "Cut the top of his head off!"

Dorie stared at him and hesitated. "Cut off the top of your husband's head to relieve the pressure!" he repeated.

Dorie felt her finger being pushed in a circle around the crown of her husband's head. It was as if she was using a knife, but it was really only her finger. All of a sudden she could see inside the skull. She could see the brains and the blood and the nerves. The doctor peered inside, then ordered her: "Take your fingers and move these pieces of bone that are pressing on the brain."

Dorie admits to being in a state of shock at this point but somehow she managed to do it. "I could smell that dreadful odor of pus coming out," she recalls. After a half hour she couldn't find any more bone particles and the doctor told her to put the top back on but "not too tight. Leave a quarter inch for pressure and we'll do this again tomorrow."

That night her husband improved noticeably and his fever went down. The next day the doctor showed up as he had promised and together they removed the top of the head and relieved the pressure. "It was incredible. It was as if I was in the middle of some grotesque fairy tale but after a few sessions we had him take an encephalogram and everything was perfect. The symptoms never came back."

Dorie had invited a friend to attend one of these sessions and as she operated on her husband's head the friend saw the doctor's hands moving over Dorie's. She swore the friend to secrecy, afraid of the repercussions in the small town if the story ever got out.

But not long after, the friend fell ill and thought she was dying. She phoned Dorie and asked her to come over and bring her doctor. Dorie went, the doctor appeared and the friend recovered instantly. After that whenever someone was ill the friend would say, "You'd better go to Dorie." And the news spread fast.

Dorie says that in order to summon the doctor she puts out an old-fashioned metronome and starts it ticking. "He told me that as the sounds of the vibrations go out he is able to tune in and use these vibrations as power. He is very real to me now and to many of my patients. Yet he never has told me his name. When I used to ask, in the beginning, he would only smile and say: "Just call me Doctor." She believes that he is a certain Professor Kirk, who wrote a series of medical books in the 1900's in Scotland. She has these books in her library and whenever she doesn't understand the illness or the operation to be performed he tells her what volume and what page to look up. She goes to the bookshelf, opens the volume and there is the medical information.

"Has he ever told you why he has come back this way and why *you* were chosen?" I asked her.

"I've asked him the same question. Poeple think it's very odd that this should be happening to me when I haven't been studying these things. People who are very much aware of the psychic field think it's odd, and so do I. But there it is. But he said that I had had training in hydrotherapy before he came into my life, so I knew what he would be talking about and how to do it. Also I was interested in the natural methods of healing and so is he. We understand each other. He says that I am completely open and he can use the power, the light force, through my hands to move the physical. There is never any blood or pain and you should see him move bones sometimes!"

"Dorie, if just one person out of every million could do what you are doing, this would be a fantastic world."

She laughed. "But that isn't really the most important thing that we do! We give a spiritual healing after each physical healing. *That's* the important thing."

She says that once the operation is performed the doctor tells the patient: "Now you will go to that secret place in your own heart where you look for inspiration and meditation. The physical healing will continue while you go and convalesce in this other place." Then Dorie touches the person and immediately they are transported to the place which the patient feels is his "special, private happy place." Once Dorie found herself with a patient in a magnificent cave filled with water and illuminated by thousands of fireflies. When the man awoke he said that was a place he had visited fifty years ago, in Spain, and had always dreamed of returning. A woman took her along to a place that Dorie is sure is not on this earth but on some other planet, where flowers, stones and waterfalls glisten in the most amazing light.

"They stay about ten minutes in these places," she says, "and when I tell them it's time to go they never want to leave. They all beg me to let them remain just a few minutes longer."

"Doesn't all this debilitate you?"

"On the contrary. Sometimes I make these trips four times a day but I've discovered that what happens to them happens to me also. When they come back from these special places recharged and full of new life, I have also been given the same amount of energy. When I used to work just as a therapist I would be exhausted at the end of a session. Now I'm never tired."

"Have you ever called on the doctor and he's not appeared?"

"Yes. He refuses to cure mental patients or fill teeth. He can heal a cracked tooth but he cannot put in fillings. He says he can only cure the cells of the body, not work with metals and material things."

I had another question all ready. "Dorie, can I ask a heavy one? One that I've been puzzled about?" She nodded. "Okay. *If* our bodies are merely vessels for souls that have been before and souls that will come again, why is the spirit world so concerned about the *physical* well-being of these vessels that eventually are going to deteriorate anyway?"

"I've also wondered about that," she replied, "and I asked my doctor. The answer may surprise you. He said that on the other side there were many things to be learned and to work with and that he was being taught to use light and vibrations and color and that by developing these techniques he would be able to use them."

"In other words he is a student?"

"Yes. He is using on us what they are teaching him. One of the most interesting is a long stream of light, about the thickness of a pencil. If someone has, let's say, a cyst or a diseased wart, he will direct this light onto it and shrink it away to nothingness. He says he is learning to change the cellular structure through the use of light. Then one time he showed me—because I asked to be taken—his medical school. He showed me the inside of it. It was like a great circle and inside the circle were all kinds of things I'd never seen before, things like they have in astronomy. You know, instruments with curves and lenses and light reflectors. He said this was the medicine of the future, and he was learning *now* to use it. Whether that means he is going to come back and use it in another life, I don't know. But he wants to practice."

"When he gives you orders does he do it brusquely or pleasantly?"

"When he is operating he treats me just like a doctor treats a nurse in the surgery room. He's quite definitely in command. That's one of the reasons he says it's so easy to work through me. I'm always willing to take orders."

Dr. Peter Mutke lives and practices in Carmel. He is a surgeon, a psychotherapist and a hypnotist. His specialty? Controlling the mind to make women's breasts grow. And he has dozens of satisfied clients.

Dr. Mutke is a German in his forties, a graduate of Heidelberg School of Medicine and became a surgeon following residencies in American hospitals.

His case history files are fascinating. One woman's breasts grew so fast she discontinued the treatment to avoid becoming too big. Three others, whose small breasts had been insensitive to pleasure, had orgasms only by a man's fondling their new, enlarged-size breasts.

Dr. Mutke treats private patients at fifty-five dollars an hour. Ages usually range from twenty to thirty-seven and results can be expected by the end of ten weeks. He claims it is not necessary for the women to go into trance but that his system works best when they can answer his questions by moving a "yes" finger or a "no" finger. He says this treatment occurred to him when he realized "it is relatively easy to get other people's glands going by suggestions."

Small breasts can be the result of traumas, the most common of which is being teased about breast size. He finds his women patients suffering from "mental disuse atrophy" and that certain eccentric ideas had altered some of their organic processes. "The rationale for the treatment was that some inhibition happened to sensitize such a person so that she was afraid to show her breasts. Frequently such women walk around hunched over, so that the breast profile is hidden."

While under hypnosis he asks his patients to produce a "goal image." He shows them examples of ancient Greek and Roman sculpture, making them realize that in other advanced civilizations women did not have to live up to the sizes displayed in the centerfold of *Playboy* magazine. With their "goal image" in mind he carefully leads them back to the year when their psycho-trauma began. When the basic reason for not having grown larger breasts is discovered and weeded out, then their minds go to work increasing the blood supply bringing nutrients and hormones into the bloodstream. This makes cells grow and multiply.

He asks them to let their husbands and lovers help with the treatment and this masculine fondling has produced "dramatic results." In their last session he gives them a self-hypnosis technique to practice at home.

The worst trauma he ever had to erase was that of a woman who as a girl of eleven saw another girl, of nine, with a fully developed bust. So she decided that "something was wrong with me."

Another client determined subconsciously "not to identify with my buxom Jewish mother!"

Southern California

What can I say about it? That it's sun and beaches and deserts? Or that it's freeways, air-conditioning units and neon? That it's restaurants in the shape of hats, swimming pools in the shape of pianos and trailer courts in the shape of towns? Southern California is heat on the desert, wind in the mountains and the fragrance of flowers. It's ordinary people, painted and bleached people and very friendly people. It's not as terrible as San Franciscans say it is, yet it's not the paradise realtors claim it is either.

What it is, I think, is a warm piece of the United States with too many people who are so busy trying to live the "California life" that they have kicked over the traces of the past and don't have time for the future. They have exchanged plastic for wood and marble. They gulp down preprocessed food at noisy counters rather than savor a full meal in a calm restaurant. They put on sunglasses as naturally as New Yorkers put on neckties. They have exchanged feet for wheels. And the "real" Southern Californians have all been born someplace else.

But one thing stands out above all the others: the gnawing idea that behind the fast living, plastic, asphalt, smog, sunglasses and klieg lights there is something "else." There is something their materialism isn't supplying. That's why they have their churches, mediums, astrologers, psychics, faith healers, gurus, swamis, card readers, palmists, preachers, numerologists and witches. Everybody doesn't "believe," but very few openly scoff.

The Yellow Pages of the Los Angeles telephone book go on for eleven pages listing the various churches and religious groups. Aside from the to be expected Catholic, Jewish and Protestants (so many Baptists!) there are such congregations as the Apostolic Faith Church, El Sendero De La Cruz, Koyasan Buddhist Temple, Christadelphian Ecclessia, Builders of the Adytum Temple, Church of Divine Science, Ethnical Culture Society (with Sun Platform meetings at 11 A.M.), Brighter Day Indian Church, Muhammed Mosque of Watts, Swedenborgian Church of the New Jerusalem, First Temple of Astrology, E.S.P. Laboratory, International Academy of Metaphysics, Science of Living, Seicho-No-Ie Church, Wings of Healing, Foundation of Universal Truth, Church of Advanced Scientology, Central Spiritualist Church, Agasha Temple of Wisdom, Astara Foundation, Institute of Mentalphysics, Tenrikyo Mission and I Am.

In the small midwestern and southern towns where most of the population of L.A. came from they probably only had the Catholic church and two ever battling Protestant churches to choose from. But now that they are Southern Californians they quickly adopt (and fill out) scores of far-out, way-out congregations.

They also patronize their local psychic. Mediums are honored guests at cocktail parties. Astrologers make excellent livings from charts. Tarot readers must be booked in advance. Movies are begun when the stars in the heavens are ready, not when the stars from Beverly Hills are. Shops everywhere sell zodiac charms, zodiac stationery, zodiac drinking glasses and zodiac jewelry. Children and adults play E.S.P. games rather than Monopoly. Witches sell records of their chants and hexes. A shop near the Farmer's Market specializes in bat hearts and black candles. And *everybody* reads the horoscope in the daily paper.

Chief scribe and delineator of these astral guides is venerable, seventyish, charming and wealthy Carroll Righter. His columns appear in 340 newspapers and seven national magazines. He has written four books and been translated into seven languages. He has made almost 150 transcontinental round trips at wealthy clients' requests and shows up unexpectedly in some of the darndest places to give his astrology lecture. He reaches the widest audience of any living astrologer and through public relations, good manners, fantastic parties, has managed to become (to the envy of many others of his profession) the richest of them all. His fees vary with the name and fame of the client but there is a story around that he once collected a thousand dollars from Robert Taylor for drawing up a chart. His jealous enemies say he doesn't write the material himself but employs a staff of underpaid student astrologers to do the dirty work and that he's not really knowledgeable about the movements of the stars and planets. Nevertheless he has been cited as having "the most socially prominent clientele since Nostradamus served the French court" and he is the only astrologer ever to have the dubious honor of gracing the cover of *Time* magazine.

Mr. Righter agreed to see me the very morning I telephoned for the interview. Unlike others in L.A. who leave you hanging for days Mr. Righter is a "now" person. He believes in getting things done and out of the way.

He opened the door to his pink Hollywood Hills mansion himself. It was nine-thirty in the morning, yet he was dressed in a gray suit and wearing a tie and vest. His white hair was neatly combed, his fingernails shining. There was an air of comfort and tradition to the man and his home. As he led me toward the perfectly decorated period living room I got a glimpse of the water in the blue swimming pool on the pink columned patio.

I settled into a chair that bore the crest of his alma mater, the Dickinson School of Law. I asked him where he was born and why he came to California.

He said he was from Philadelphia and was a lawyer. He came to California because he injured his leg.

"You injured your leg?"

"Yes, and I figured out my chart and it said I would be best protected by moving to the Southwest. So I came out here on crutches and a year later I was dancing. This is a marvelous place for my health."

"But what did your family say when you calmly announced

you were breaking off all tradition and your practice and moving to the West Coast because the stars said so?"

"Well, my lawyer friends thought I was a screwball and my mother threw up her hands and said: 'Good heavens, I've hatched a duckling!' "

"When did you start reading the stars? Here in Los Angeles?"

"No, when I was fourteen years old I was introduced to the famed astrologer Evangeline Adams. She told me I had the perfect chart to be an astrologer. I didn't believe there was anything to it at all and actually started studying with her to disprove it all. Here I am a half century later still trying to disprove it!"

His plush home and his expensive ways belie the fact that when Righter showed up in Hollywood he had very little money and no contacts. He began to do charts, slowly, for enough to pay the rent, and, being young and charming, he found himself soon entering the world of Hollywood stars. He cast several charts for the big names but it was Marlene Dietrich who really made his name.

She confided to him one evening that she was going to give up movies. She had gone as far as she could go and it seemed that nobody wanted her any more. He drew a quick chart for her and told her to reconsider, that she was on the verge of a great new career, one that would take her farther than any other star. He also told her she would soon be signed to a new picture. When the picture became a reality she called to tell him, but he had a warning for her: stay away from the studio on a certain day, because the "aspects and angles were disharmonious." Marlene paid no attention and showed up for work on that day. Inside the studio she tripped over a toy fire engine and broke her ankle. The famous Dietrich leg was photographed in a plaster cast and she told newsmen how the whole thing could have been avoided. That did it.

Righter's star hit an all-time high and cinema greats and not-so-greats came to his door. While he doesn't like to give the names of these illustrious clients ("I'm like a doctor or a lawyer: this information is confidential.") a number of them have told the public of their patronage with Righter. The roster reads like the invitation list to the Oscars. There is Clark Gable, Dick Powell, Marlene Dietrich, Adolphe Menjou, Arlene Dahl, Bob Cummings,

Rhonda Fleming, Ronald Reagan, Susan Hayward, Hildegard Knef, Leo Durocher, Marilyn Monroe and Zsa Zsa Gabor. There are probably another fifty Hollywood names who prefer to remain anonymous. "Many times stars will be giving interviews," Righter said, "because they have to have their names in the paper, and if they run out of things to talk about, sometimes they will talk about me."

"I heard that Ronald Reagan asked you to discern the exact time he should be sworn in as governor of California and you chose 12:30 A.M. Is that true?"

"No comment."

"I also heard that you have many people helping you with your charts."

"Well, I'm a very busy man with my columns, books, magazine articles and lectures. I must prepare my daily newspaper columns six months in advance. I do have four secretaries and two mathematicians on my staff, but the final copy is always of my doing."

"Talking about your columns, you must get a lot of people asking how you can draw up a blanket coverage and still expect it to be accurate for different individuals."

"That question comes up all the time. And it's a valid one. What I do is give the position of the sun with the moon, Mars, Mercury, Venus, Jupiter, Saturn, Uranus and Pluto making aspects of it. That's what is known as a 'forecast.' The forecast has to do with the solar sign and all the other planets' positions. Whereas a personal horoscope has to deal with all the planetary positions when you were born. The sun is the strongest planet in our heavens. It can burn you to a crisp on the desert and freeze you to a nub on the arctic."

"Why is it that certain planets thousands and thousands of miles away influence humans back here on earth?" I asked.

"I really don't know *how* the sun or the moon influences us, but the theory of some scientists is that there is a vacuum between the planets until we get into the atmosphere of the earth or some other planet but they say that the distance is a vacuum for the reception of the influences of the other planets. That may be the reason."

"Uh-huh. I think."

"You see, I don't care about the reasons. A lot of doctors will tell people they are interested only in research, but I am interested in giving pills for personality and character. I like to work with people and when I find something that works I don't try to figure out why."

At this point he called out to a movement behind me. "Miss A! Do you suppose we could have a cup of coffee?" A female voice answered in the affirmative. Then he settled back in his easy chair. "I call her Miss A because she's an Aries."

"Well, what are you?"

"I'm a gregarious Aquarius. I love this Aquarian Age. I think it's marvelous. I'm going to Dallas this afternoon for a lecture and I'll be back in twenty-four hours. Isn't that amazing? When I first came to California I took a plane that made seven stops in thirty-two hours. Now it takes just four hours and people complain: 'Aren't we there yet?' "

"When will we be in the Aquarian Age?" I asked.

"We are in it right now! We are in the doorway of this new and wonderful age! It started in 1904 and then in 1962 we had those eight planets in the sign of Aquarius. This new age, to me, means brotherhood. It means each person will be able to be himself. Look how the nations in Africa have been arising to assert their individualities. Look at the minority groups like the Blacks and the Puerto Ricans and the Chicanos. They want to be themselves, and in the Aquarian Age they *will* be themselves. It won't be an easy age, because of the conflicts of so many temperaments. You can't get servants for housework. Why? Because they would rather take a job in a factory and be independent. Before this age is through you'll find a very different society and a different set of values.

"And look at the progress since 1904!" He cleared away a magazine to make room for the silver tray, silver coffee set and two fine porcelain cups and saucers. "We have had more progress since 1904 than we have since the Nativity! At Christ's birth they were using camel caravans and horses and it remained that way right up to the Aquarian Age. Now suddenly we have the motor car and jet propulsion, electricity and moon rockets, television and atomic power. We've made more progress in the last seventy years than we've made in the last seventy thousand years!" He held up a silver tray with some cookies on it. "Have a doggie biscuit."

I took one and then asked: "Many mediums, mystics and some astrologers say that at the great conjunction of planets in 1962 a new Messiah was born. They contend that any child born under those powerful Aquarian influences would have to be a superintelligent, sensitive, psychic individual. What do you think?"

"There's no doubt that there is such a child living today. We think he was born in Peru, probably near Lake Titicaca (which I call Lake Titi-pupu), because the rays were more strongly focused there. When this happened there were eight planets in Aquarius. There was the sun, moon, Mercury, Mars, Jupiter, Saturn, and the south node. The south node isn't a planet but the point where the moon crosses in eclipse to pass the sun. They were opposing the moon and Uranus in Leo, squaring Neptune and Scorpio. The only planet that was not directed was Pluto in the sign of Virgo. Some scientists, if you recall, said this conjunction almost pulled the earth off its orbit. It was followed by terrible weather, earthquakes and floods everywhere.

"In January of 1970 I was invited by the Strasenburgh Planetarium in Rochester, New York, to produce a special show for them," he continued. "They have such a wonderful system that they are able to move the stars into any time of the past or the future and when they asked me what I would like, I said I wanted to see the heavens at the time of the Nativity. They put their gears into motion and there were the five planets of Pisces all converged like the eight planets of Aquarius had been in 1962. But it was not at the time of birth but at the time of *conception!* It does make the birth of Jesus, which is questioned sometimes, around the 25th of December. It was one of the greatest experiences I ever had, to see those planets spinning backward into time."

I finished my coffee and we chatted about President Nixon ("the right man in the right place at the right time") and how one could know if one is fitted to be an astrologer ("look for Uranus in its various aspects, particularly from the sun and Mercury"), and then I rose to go. The man had been most charming. He had agreed to see me even though he was about to dash off for Dallas, and the coffee had been good and hot. I shook his hand as he held open the front door. "I certainly appreciate your courtesy," I said. "After all, you are probably the most famous astrologer in the United States."

"Probably in the whole world," he said, and closed the door after me.

Hollywood-based Sydney Omarr is Carroll Righter's closest competitor for the astrology mass audience. He draws charts for the stars (Jennifer Jones and Kim Novak are only two of them), writes books and runs a syndicated column in some 225 daily newspapers.

Omarr was the only member of the U. S. Armed Forces to be given full-time duty as an astrologer. During World War II, when he was in the Air Corps on Okinawa, he drew up a few charts about important subjects and circulated them around. The information was a sensation. He accurately predicted that Roosevelt would win a fourth term but would die in office. He also gave the date when the war in the Pacific would be over. The Armed Forces Radio put him on their staff immediately and be began doing charts for servicemen scattered around the globe. His show drew more fan mail than any other government production.

Omarr, today, has one of the most respected names in astrology. In fact he's often called "the astrologer's astrologer." He doesn't like the blanket overall daily forecasts appearing in the newspapers and tries to use the position of the moon and other planets rather than just the sun sign. "I cause amusement," he says, "but I don't cause harm. The planets do not have the power to *cause* events nor to cause people to respond in the way they do. But there is a correspondence, a coincidence between the planetary patterns and mundane actions, reactions and events. Jung uses the term synchronicity. There *is* a synchronicity but we don't know why. Yet it happens so often that it is a reliable indicator. The wise man controls his destiny," he smiles. "Astrology points the way."

Southern Californians like to get outdoors and practice spectator sports. Tennis matches and horse races draw large crowds. So do golf tournaments. And baseball packs 'em in.

Capitalizing on this love of baseball, disc jockey Ira Cook teamed up with bearded astrologer D. Modin and convinced the Los Angeles Dodgers they should have their charts done. And that these thumbnail horoscopes should be put into a booklet and sold to the fans. Modin took nothing but the players' names, place and time of birth. He never met any of the players, never saw a single game, yet his sixteen-page *Los Angeles Dodgers Horoscope,* selling at fifty cents a copy, has been one of the most successful stadium sidelines the Dodgers have ever had. Both the San Diego Padres and the Cincinnati Reds have had their charts done and other teams are on the waiting list.

Modin calculates the "birth time" of the Dodgers as April 18, 1958 at 1:30 P.M. That was when they began their first game as the Los Angeles Dodgers instead of the Brooklyn "Bums." "The astrological horoscope at that time," he wrote, "indicated that the team would enjoy great popularity and that the games would be well attended. By the time the team moved to Dodger Stadium to meet the Cincinnati Reds in their opening of the 1962 season, their chart showed an even stronger indication of public approval. Today, it seems, 'everybody loves the Dodgers!' "

The Dodgers team has one each of Pisces, Sagittarius, Virgo, Cancer, Gemini and Leo. Two Scorpios, Aries, Taurus, Aquarius and Libras. But there are five Capricorns. The fans learn that Manager Walter Alston is a Sagittarius. His Mars is in Taurus, which gives him energy and the capacity for steady success. His Mercury controls his thinking and is in Capricorn, giving him the ability to turn chaos into order. His moon in Aries conjuncts the team's sun, which gives him an "exceptionally keen understanding and just the right judgment to guide the Dodgers in 1971." Modin sees "an unusually good year" for Alston with his transiting Uranus conjunct to his Venus indicating "good fortune."

Kiyo is the only name she uses. She is a product of Massachusetts, Japan and the Midwest, yet she is very much Hollywood. She is small, fair-skinned and incredibly sexy. Her voice is low, her laugh and convictions deep.

She lives in a four-level house high in the Hollywood Hills that was built by a movie producer fifty years ago. She is surrounded by odd pieces of furniture, a couple of Alaskan sled dogs and a six-teen-year-old cat, who retains his vitality by having her pick him up and swing him by the tail twice daily.

Kiyo is an astrologer. She says she is not a psychic, yet many of her dreams have been analyzed and even published by experts in the reincarnation field. When you're with her, listening to her steady flow of ideas and watching her self-confidence, it all seems so easy for her. It wasn't that way at all. In fact, she is living proof of her brand of advice to her clients: find your true strength and then go off and be yourself.

"I have a weird background," she says. "Astrologers are weird people." Her father was a Japanese who stowed away on a sailing boat and managed to end up in the U. S. Navy. He attended the College of Dentistry in Boston and started practicing there. He met Kiyo's mother, a prim and proper Bostonian girl, and when Kiyo was only a few months old, returned to Japan. Thus this famed California astrologer is "an American by birth with a Eurasian body but emotionally and psychologically Japanese."

Her childhood was far from happy. She recalls her mother sitting at one end of the dining room table speaking proper Bostonian English while her father sat at the other end giving off Shinto-Buddhist philosophies in Japanese. Her three brothers understood some English but preferred to answer in Japanese. Consequently her mother was cut off from everyone but little Kiyo, who was studying the English language at school.

School was a cross she had to bear. At the Japanese school she first attended the students shunned her because her mother had red hair. In Japan the devil also has red hair, and Kiyo became the daughter of the devil. They refused to play with her and stopped their conversations when she came near. It didn't do her a bit of good to complain to her mother: she only replied with New England platitudes about "being a good girl so that people will like you" and "pray to God for forgiveness."

Finally she was able to convince her mother to enroll her in a school that was staffed by Canadian and British teachers. It was an exclusive academy where the sons and daughters of wealthy foreigners studied. Again, Kiyo was looked upon as an outsider: after all, her father and brothers were Japanese!

"I was perpetually caught in this social no-man's-land, and was under great pain all the time. But it was the pain that drove me on. I questioned the inequities of life and searched for an explanation to my unhappiness. I thought that religion had the answers. My life had been a hodgepodge of religious beliefs. My father was a Shinto-Buddhist, my mother was an Episcopalian, I was sent to a Methodist church but forced to play the organ for the Baptists every Sunday. I remember at the age of nine fervently studying Christian Science. I went through all the books on yoga and Hinduism. At the age of fourteen I devoured a book by Freud from cover to cover. I didn't understand a thing he was talking about but I kept reading it, hoping that 'truth' would be there. Of course it wasn't and this liberal education made me realize that 'truth' was nowhere."

Finally upon her graduation from the exclusive school she won a scholarship to study music. She could choose between Great Britain and the United States. Because she was born in America she came to California. When the money ran out she saw that being a concert pianist didn't pay the rent. "Everyone respected it but nobody wanted to hear it."

Then the war broke out. She was arrested as an alien and everything she owned was confiscated. Because of her American birth she was given a choice: internment camp or relocate in the Midwest. She chose freedom, but "it became the bitterest period of my life. I was young and naïve and I had illusions about Christians and their charity. I still carried the pride of having an American mother and being born in America but all that was soon dashed to the ground when I learned what life was like in these United States. In order to survive I . . . But I don't want to talk about it. It was good in one respect, it increased my search for that 'something' that was not filled with inequities. There was no one I could talk to except God. He became very real to me and I used to thank Him and give Him hell. Finally I went 'underground' in my search, delving into Spiritualism, studying philosophy and psychology, sitting at the feet of Ernest Holmes, the father of modern Divine Wisdom, and I was one of the most devoted students of Manley Palmer

Hall. As I went from lecture to lecture and institution to institution I found the Temple School of Astrology here in Los Angeles. I knew at once that I had come home. That my long, lonely search was over."

Today she has to turn away clients who want charts and counseling. Her specialty is youth and more specifically the young rock musicians and rock stars. "I gave up on older people. They're *hopeless!* You tell them that they've made their own life and they don't believe it. You tell them that it was their own limitations that brought on their sadness and they reject it. Or they may accept it for a few days but then they get despondent again and call me up. 'Kiyo, when is this terrible period going to be over?' What am I going to tell them? *Never?* Because by that kind of belief, that kind of church saturation, they've had it. It's negative thinking. It's really due to Christian negativity. The negative aspects of theological Christianity are what have made Caucasians so morbid. And I'm half Caucasian myself, I'm allowed to complain!

"Most people come to an astrologer," she continued, "and ask, 'How am I going to do in this new business venture?' or, 'Should I marry this guy?' or, 'When will I come out of this bad financial period?' etc. Now, to me all this is pure bullshit, from the standpoint of my astrology. I give people a much more creative approach as to what their true talents are. If they were to harness their true identities and use their natural gifts in the proper direction, they wouldn't be in that state of distress to begin with. So there would never be a problem of 'good' and 'bad' days. It would be more of a problem of how much energy should I put into this venture? It's all up to your own belief about yourself. Man is not a finished product. Okay, so the day he's born he's got a chart, well, he is not stuck with the limitations of that chart for the rest of his life. That's merely the cross section of a moment. It's up to you to take those birth-given abilities and plant them in the proper soil, give them sunlight and the proper nutrition and watch them grow into a massive oak tree."

I asked her what she told the twenty-year-old rock stars that came for advice.

"Well, few of them were 'stars' when they came to me. I'm a king maker. Don't laugh, I really am. They came to me when they were on the verge of hitting it big and I steered them in the right direction. Oh, I don't mean in terms of their music but psychologically and emotionally. I try to make a man *believe in himself.* Somehow he's got to have Mother Earth do it and I try to be as Mother Earthly as possible. And be objective and honest, because they are not going to believe a sugar-coated pill. Kids of today know that life is no bowl of cherries. They don't want panaceas and they don't want the opiates the church hands out. 'Be good and everything will work out.' That's a bunch of bullshit. Be good and you'll be stepped on. Now, don't misunderstand me. I'm not advocating being bad, it's just that that's not the proper hook. The proper hook is finding *who* and *what* you are. What your weaknesses are and what you can do to mend the holes in your nature. The kids trust me because they know I am *not* a product of this culture."

"But," I asked, "can an 'over-thirty person' do this?"

"They could. But they won't."

"But do you show them how?"

"Sure, but it doesn't do any good. I'm not going to live their lives for them and have them depend on me like a crutch. It's not worth the psychic drain. All my clientele in the past were older people and I spent thousands of hours talking to them, reading books for them, drawing up their charts . . . and I doubt that I really did much good at all. I tried to tide them over for the moment but they refuse to take life from a creative standpoint. They're trapped. And this is what young people realize: that society has trapped society on a never ending treadmill. And each person in his own individual way has trapped himself on his own share of the treadmill, that he has imposed it upon himself by accepting it and he can only go on and on and on."

"But if we get off the treadmill we fall, don't we?"

"That depends. If you get off it foolishly without giving any thought to where you will land, then you'll fall. But you must first find out where your true strength is—in yourself! In the belief in your own ability to survive. Actually, it's a belief in life itself." Then she laughed. "This is all very simplified, you understand. Honey, if I were to break this down it would take days to sort out the threads."

"My last question," I promised. "Where does astrology fit into all of this?"

"It fits to help a man find his main stream of consciousness, to help him find out what talents he has, what his aptitudes are. Each human being is never to be duplicated, never. A man must know that he will never meet another man as peculiar or as marvelous as himself. My astrology gives them the courage to go off and be themselves. To go off with greater confidence and conviction to express their own individualities. This is what we all want, isn't it? Freedom!"

If Carroll Righter is the "King" of Californian astrologists, then Doris Chase Doane is certainly the "Queen." Respected by everyone, her books read by thousands, her charts done for some of the state's top actors and politicians, Doris Doane is in a class by herself. Her sharp sense of humor can cut any stuffed astrological shirt down to size and her loud New England laugh has been heard at astrology meetings from coast to coast. Mrs. Doane is on the board of directors of the American Federation of Astrologers (a worldwide organization with headquarters in Washington, D.C.) and is president of Professional Astrologers, Inc., in Los Angeles. She lives in a small apartment in Hollywood crammed with furniture and filing cabinets that once filled the house she shared with her recently deceased husband Edward Doane (author of the excellent *Aquarian Age Philosophy*).

Mrs. Doane allowed me to interview her even though she was far behind in a pile of charts and the book which she is currently writing. Her most recent is a revised *Horoscopes of the U.S. Presidents*. Her best seller is a set of maps and charts titled simply *Time Changes in the U.S.A.* I told her that some people admonished me for including astrologers in a book about psychics and said astrology should not be grouped in with the other divination methods mediums and clairvoyants used.

She disagreed with the critics. "Most people who practice astrology, and are truly sensitive, use the astrological signs as a crystal ball to stimulate their senses. The more one studies and counsels people, the easier it is to tune in on the client. It goes without saying that by doing this the psychic senses develop. As the accomplished astrologer draws up a chart he begins to get a complete picture of the client and as he interprets these symbols, if he is sensitive, ideas and facts about this person begin to form inside the astrologer. He could, if he wished at that point, put down the chart and give the client a reading that would knock his block off. But we go farther than that. We set up the chart, which gives us a scientific index to his basic character. When we get these ESP hunches we look to the chart to *verify* it before we disclose it to him. You know very well that if you are a sensitive, there are certain times when you plug into the negative to be led astray by entities from the inner plane. So if an astrologer has the scientific background to draw up a chart and knows how to interpret his sixth sense, then he has everything going for him."

"Why do you feel that far-out planets affect us way down here on earth?" I asked.

"Oh God! *That* question!" she laughed. "I do not feel that the vibrations from the planets affect us directly. But through the law of 'sympathetic vibratory response' there is a relationship between the heavens and the earth. This has been proven in so many ways. Look at how the moon affects the tides. Ask any policeman about the marked increase in murders and rapes during a full moon. *Why* this happens, I don't know. But it does. For instance, astrologers have shown through the centuries that when Mars is activated by an aspect—a certain angle between Mars and another planet—that vibrations from that aspect hit the earth. And when that aspect comes into a person's chart, the person feels aggressive. We *can* predict, with accuracy, when these different urges will be stimulated but we *cannot* predict with accuracy how the person will react. He will do something Mars but there are many Mars things. A surgeon could perform an almost impossible operation or an athlete could break a world record or a person could have an accident. It's the way a person feels, thinks and acts under the stimulated aggression that attracts it in the environment."

"Well then," I asked, "what's the difference between vibrations and 'sympathetic vibratory attractions'?"

"Maybe I should have used the word 'frequencies' instead. I feel that everything in the universe moves at a certain velocity. The whole kaboodle is energy patterns on any plane: here, the astral, everywhere. It's all a matter of energy and the groupings of types of energy that eventually form into a mass."

"Does this mean, then, that man tunes into the energy of Mars or Uranus in the same way he tunes in a radio set?"

"Yes. The energy that is picked up by the mind really is coming from ten planets, each with their own broadcasting and receiving apparatus. The human tunes in subconsciously and dials the program himself."

"Do we have to tune into Mars at that particular time?"

"Yes, but we do it instinctively. Yet free will must also be mentioned here. Astrology is not fatalistic. The fortune-teller will tell you that it is. The scientific astrologer will not, because he realizes that man has a certain amount of free will. You cannot change a Mars event to a Venus event but you can decide how that Mars energy will express itself through you. 'As a man thinketh, so is he,' said the ancients. So do we astrologers."

"When I tune into Mars, does everyone else also tune into Mars at the same time?" This was getting complicated.

"It can happen but it usually doesn't, because we all have a different makeup."

"Then what's Mars for me is not necessarily Mars for you?"

"Now you've got it! Furthermore the tendency for you to express Mars energy would be entirely different from the next guy's, because every horoscope is different. A horoscope is set up on three factors: the date of birth, the place of birth and the hour of birth. It's impossible for more than one person to be in a situation like that."

"What about hospitals that deliver babies at the same time in the same city?"

"Now, that's what I call the X factor in astrology. It has to do with the parents a child inherits and the environment in which it grows up. Let's take two boy babies born in New York City at the same time and in the same hospital. One's father is a judge and his mother is a schoolteacher. They live in a nice neighborhood and never have to worry about food, clothing or shelter. They send the boy to good schools and give him love and understanding at home. The second little tyke goes back to a slum apartment, where several other brothers and sisters are waiting. His father disappeared and his mother has to go out and work just to get enough money for bread and the rent. There is no guidance, the boy skips many weeks of school and eventually drifts into a street gang. Our first boy graduates from college and sets up an aggressive law business. Our second boy kills a policeman and ends up in prison. Now, both these boys have the same chart but their X factor, *environment,* makes them react to their Mars energy (as well as all the other planets) in completely different ways. So you see, it's not what the stars make you do but what you make of the stars."

"Will a reputable astrologer mention death to a client if he sees it in his chart?"

"No. Never! We can see the *potential* for death. All your life you have aspects to the area in your chart that indicates death but you don't die."

I wondered, "Have you ever done a chart and seen that a person was going to die and then they did die?"

"I have, but I didn't tell them. I tried to wash it right out of my mind, so I wouldn't transfer the thought. I would never plant the seed of death for a susceptible person to brood over and nourish."

Doris was born in Mansfield, Massachusetts, and even though she's been in California since 1942 she still has her New England accent. Her mother was a psychic that used to dowse water for farmers. Doris looked upon her mother's ability as perfectly natural. She and her family were very close to nature and she admits that a number of things happened when she was small that she considered "normal" but in retrospect "were psychic." She says that she has always had the ability to read people's minds. "I thought everybody could do it," she says. "Then when it got to the place where it was crushing me—people saying beautiful things but I could see they meant something completely different—I forced this ability into the background." For many years she heard rappings, witnessed apports, saw auras and entities, but then at "twenty-two years something so moving and terrifying happened to me" that she refuses to talk about it. She admits it had "something to do directly with God."

Doris feels she has gone beyond that early psychic phase and is now concentrating on what she calls "intellectual ESP." This is an awareness in the mind, sudden and without any feeling. "I have to cut the feeling out of it. I still get powerful thought messages from the other plane and I'm sure they are from entities who are interested in my work and are trying to help me. They come in very strong at night, when I turn off the light and am ready for sleep. I don't like to talk about these things, because I don't want to be labeled a 'kook' but they are making me a better channel and helping me in my astrological interpretations."

While she knows and understands what is happening to her, she feels that others with these manifestations might think they were going crazy. She highly recommends the mail-order lessons of The Church of Light (P.O. Box 76862, Sanford Station, Los Angeles 90005). Seekers will find answers here, she claims, because the lessons go into all phases of the occult.

Doris also gets her share of the movie star trade and refuses point-blank to mention any names. She did tell of a "very well-known couple" who came to her for help. The wife came first, saying that they had been married for seven years ("the crucial itching stage") but now the tensions from their work and their domestic squabbles were driving them to divorce. Doris asked for her birth data and that of her husband. She worked on the charts and saw that the tension over the two of them would last for at least eleven more months. Then the female star telephoned her and said that she had given her the wrong information. She had taken several years off her age and a few months off her husband's life. Doris insisted on certified birth certificates before she would go any farther. Finally both came to see her and she explained that these badly aspected influences would last for at least a year. Because of the children she suggested a year's separation. Because of the children the couple agreed. The wife went to Europe to write a book. The husband stayed in Hollywood making movies. "But he flew over three times to see her and beg her to come back to him," Doris remembers, "and each time the wife would call me from Europe and ask me what she should do. I told her to be firm and wait out the year, for those aspects were very heavy. You see, they were really a good couple, with both a physical and mental thing going for them. They were friends as well as lovers. Many couples are not friends and this makes things very difficult in the 'in-between times.' Anyway, she stayed away for almost a year and when she did come back there were a few weeks of friction but after the vibrations passed out of their charts they remained happy and together. They are still together, and they have a better understanding of themselves as well as each other."

"Is there anything to the old adage that there are some days you shouldn't even get out of bed?"

"No. I don't go along with that. If those people who consult the stars for every one of their daily moves have no more control over themselves than that, then they shouldn't even be studying astrology. There is something you can do about everything. The stars impel, they don't compel."

There are a number of reputable mediums in the city of Los Angeles but none of them stand out as do British-born Brenda Rowland Crenshaw and Dutch-born Lotte Von Strahl. Both have years of professional experience behind them. Both have been known to produce amazing messages. Both are tall, cultured and aristocratic. And both are as different in their approaches as the night is to the day.

Brenda Crenshaw lives with her newsman-writer husband James in a house in the eastern end of Hollywood. She holds her sittings there and receives most of her messages there. Except when she's driving down Sunset Boulevard, or in a hospital or speaking from a church platform, that is. Mrs. Crenshaw has many certificates and diplomas to make her the professional she is. She is an ordained Spiritualist minister (her husband cringes when someone calls her Reverend) in California and was on the approved list of mediums of the Spiritualist Association of Great Britain before leaving for the United States. She is a member of the Spiritual Frontiers Fellowship and has lectured and demonstrated for this organization composed of Protestant ministers and laymen. Yet she is very critical of her abilities and what she receives. This due to her desire for complete honesty.

"I know I receive *direct* communication but who is to say where that communication is coming *from?* How do we know that it is coming from the actual person whose name we are receiving from spirit? Suppose I see an entity build up beside you and I get the name John and then there will be some sort of message. But is this really coming from Uncle John? Only you can be the judge. There are so many things about the spirit world and mediumship that we don't know! I've been in this work for years but I still feel as if I'm in kindergarten."

I asked her if in all the messages she's received she has never been able to tie one message in directly with someone who has passed over. She replied that she has received and transmitted hundreds of messages later verified as being from people who have passed over into spirit. "But how do I know if that message has come directly from a particular person named or another authority?"

Her husband tried to clear up the problem. "She constantly gets accurate messages both clairaudiently and clairvoyantly. She will get them as being from so-and-so and she'll repeat them and, as happens with all good mediums, she finds out later that they contained information that could be checked out as being true. Often a complete stranger will come to her and say her name is Mary, for instance. But during the session a spirit will make contact and call that person Louise. Now Brenda doesn't know the sitter and never met the spirit who is supposedly giving the message, but—and this is important—the sitter will agree that this spirit, when alive, always called her by the pet name of Louise."

Once a young man arrived for a sitting. His father had died the day before, but he had kept the appointment anyway. Mrs. Crenshaw had never met the gentleman or his father. Suddenly the dead man's spirit came through her, giving the young man the information that a certain named relative was grieving much too much and giving—correctly—the names of all the pallbearers for the funeral that was to be the next day. The sitter was amazed with this direct communication from his father but when Brenda said that the elder man was happy in the company of Aunt So-and-So, the young man objected. There was no aunt by that name, he insisted. This must be coming from the medium's imagination. Two days later he called to apologize, saying that he had talked with several relatives after the funeral and there definitely was an aunt by that name, who had died years ago before the young man was born.

"When did you first find out you had these powers?" I asked.

"I fancy I was around eleven or twelve and I used to see very beautiful diagrams. They were in color and slightly oriental and they used to come out of nowhere and nestle in the windowpanes of our house. I never mentioned them to my mother or my two brothers, because they were very down-to-earth and practical. My family still doesn't understand me. I had an aunt that was very psychic and possibly I inherited some of it from her. My next step was a kind of knowing, not seeing but knowing, a kind of sensing of things that were about to happen. But I kept very silent about this. In my teens I went through a period of extreme sensitivity. I attended my first séance when I was sixteen. At seventeen I attended a meeting that I shall never forget. It was held by a medium named Lillian Brownfoot. She put us in a circle and went 'round holding our hands and giving us messages. When she came to me, she said: 'You are a medium but you have to work in a practical sense before your mediumship will blossom. You will be to your thirties before you become an active worker in spiritualism. When once you place your hands on the plow you will never let go.' I married at twenty-one and divorced at twenty-four. My first husband's aunt was a marvelous medium in Devonshire. She used to say to me: 'Brennie, one day you're going to do the work I'm doing.' I didn't believe it, yet I was fascinated by it. It seemed perfectly normal to me. There was nothing 'frightening' about it at all.

"Then I opened a small health foods shop in London and was doing rather well when a woman came into the adjoining shop and called me over. She was a psychic who read sand."

"Sand?"

"She read sand! Ordinary, common sand."

"Well, if you say so," I put in. "I've never heard of it, but there's a first time for everything."

"Neither had I!" said her husband.

"Well, it's true and her name was Mrs. Limpenny, a very cultured, very beautiful woman. She asked me to write my name and age on a tiny scrap of paper and push it under a small pile of sand she had in an oriental box. I did this and she took a funny black stick and began to push the sands and gave me a remarkable reading. She said to me: 'You are a born medium and you're wasting your time. Why aren't you doing something about it?' A couple of weeks later she appeared in my shop and wanted to take me to a meeting. She said this man would help me further develop my mediumship. But of course I didn't know if I wanted to do that or not! Good heavens, I was running a shop and there was a war on! But anyway, I did ring him up, went over to see him and after a cup of tea I agreed to attend his classes.

"Now, this was during the war and I used to dash across London while the bombs were falling and go to his sessions. Bombs didn't worry me, because I *knew* I wasn't to be killed. I *knew* I had more work to do on earth and that the bombs would never touch me. While others were running into shelters, I kept up my normal routine. I became a trance medium under his supervision (his name was Arnold Clare) and a nun used to come through me. I also have an oriental guide who works closely with me. Finally I sold my shop and devoted all my time to mediumship."

"But wasn't that a risk?" I asked. "At least the shop gave you a certain amount of financial security."

"No risk. I was told by my nun that if I took up mediumship I would never want for anything, that all my needs would be met. And it's been true. I have never had to worry since then, my necessities have been taken care of. You have to live by the law of the spirit. There is one source and only one source and if you try to live the law the law will look after you. I *know* this is right."

"Tell me about your nun," I asked.

"Her name is Sister Teresa. She is *not* Saint Teresa, even though some people like to say she is. She is a very beautiful soul and works quite quickly through me when I am on a platform. I used to do a tremendous amount of platform work. I don't anymore. I've not done half the public work in this country that I did in England. Before I came here my entire life was dedicated to it. After all, I came here to marry James!"

The story of how they met is typical of the way things happen in the life of Brenda Rowland Crenshaw. He was doing a series of articles on mediums for an American publication and happened to read the front-page story about Brenda in the prestigious British *Psychic News*. He contacted the editor, who introduced him to Brenda. "It was quite an assignment for me, in more ways than one," James Crenshaw remembers today.

The story was that Brenda had been giving a platform (i.e., stage) reading when she went into semi-trance and became controlled by the spirit of a German World War I officer who had died on the battlefield. Brenda could see the blood gushing down her arms and could feel the pain. The spirit gave his name and rank and then pointed to a woman in the audience. He said that that woman had been a nurse and had cradled him in her arms as he lay dying on the battlefield. There was no way Brenda could have known that the woman in question had been a nurse or that as a British nurse she had stopped to minister to a *German* soldier. Then the spirit asked the woman if she still had the crucifix he gave her in his last moments. The woman, visibly shaken by this story, opened her purse and showed everyone the crucifix.

"Brenda," I asked, "why do you think spirits have to come back and communicate? Why did this German officer have to thank this nurse? Why? What compels them not to make a complete break from this vale of tears?"

"For many reasons. Because the person on this side will not learn to release them," she answered after a few moments thought. "I know that it's also the way of the spirit to prove that life does continue after death. The law of the spirit is love. That's the *only* law of the spirit. I *know* you can hold a person here, by love, for a certain period of time. I *know* that when you choose to release them and send out this thought and they in turn choose to release themselves as well they can be free in spirit."

"When you say, 'hold a person here,' do you mean a person who is still . . ."

"Determined to stay on this side of life, and hang onto his physical body for a period of time."

"In other words, an ill person in a bed will remain alive as long as there is someone around him saying 'don't go, we love you.'"

"Yes. I think that's true and yet by the same token it's almost a contradiction, because I feel that there is a time to come into this world and a time to get out of it."

At this her husband cut in. "Excuse me, dear, but I think the time factor can be bent a little bit. In the spirit world one or two years does not make that much difference in their time calculations."

"Of course, you're right," she agreed. "The spirits have a terrible time working with our human time."

Brenda never knows what kind of a sitting she will give a client. She insists that the sitter tell her absolutely nothing except his name. She doesn't want to be influenced in advance by questions and requests. Some persons get very practical help; others, a proof of survival, and still others, a beautiful philosophical discourse relating to them personally. Or they may receive a combination of all these. Brenda plays inspiring music, often hymns, on a stereo record player before each sitting, then seats herself before her client. While the music is playing, she will receive guidelines as to what the sitting will be about. She rarely goes into trance any more, but remains in a state she calls "under control." Of all the levels she is able to reach, the one with the beautiful philosophy pleases her the most. "I think the soul of the person who comes for a sitting is reaching out for an answer and I think the capacity of the reaching is to quite a high level of consciousness and from that level his or her own guide or my guide is capable of filtering that answer through me."

"As the word medium implies," I said. "As a channel or an instrument. Do you hear the words and then repeat them the way other mediums do?"

"No. I only hear my own voice. It just flows through me."

"Are the majority of your sittings higher than the materialistic plane? You know: Will I make a million dollars? Will I buy a new automobile? etc."

"Oh, I won't touch that sort of thing! I wouldn't entertain it. I will *not* drop the level of my work for anybody. I believe I have earned, through past incarnations, the gift of tuning into higher sources of consciousness. Of course this is not true in the case of some other mediums, like the one who fell on his head and became a psychic, for instance. When I was born I fell on *my* head but I don't consider that's the reason I'm psychic. I don't know why I was in such a hurry to get here."

"You mean the doctor dropped you?"

"My *mother* dropped me! She was bending over my brother's cot and I decided at that moment to make my arrival. And I went head first onto the floor."

"Are you serious?"

"Yes, I'm perfectly serious! My mother said she got ahold of me, put me across her knees and cut the cord."

"And that's the way you were *born?*"

"That's the way I was born. At number ten Brenda Road, and that's how I got my name."

Whenever she is close to an accident she gets a warning. The phrase "nearer My God to Thee" comes into her mind. She heard this the day her shop was bombed in London, she heard this once just before her car broke down in the Arizona mountains and she heard it the day her husband crossed the street and was almost killed by a speeding automobile. In the hospital the doctors performed extensive surgery but didn't give him much chance to live. He was eleven days under intensive care. Brenda, because of her nurse's training, worked one of the watching vigils. One night as she was sitting there in his room, she looked up to see two men standing at the head of his bed. One was a monk and the other was an Indian. The Indian spoke in a loud, clear voice, saying, "You will be healed." Then they vanished. Eventually James Crenshaw was up and moving out of the hospital under his own power. The doctors could only call it a miracle.

"Mrs. Crenshaw," I said. "You got all your excellent training in England, but how would you advise an American to develop his sense of mediumship?"

"First of all, the motive would have to be a good one. That is all-important. He would have to keep the goal in front of him and constantly see a line toward that goal. He has to be a person who is somewhat well balanced. Imagination can often be very misleading and a medium is very imaginative. There would have to be a complete withdrawal from other people for periods of time. It cannot be all output. There must be intake.

"A person who wants to become a medium," she continued, "must realize the tremendous responsibility which this places upon him and also realize that there are dangers in it as well. There are spirits on the other side who are willing to come back to a medium and take possession of him. They want to perpetuate their deeds on earth as they did in the past. There are spirits who are impersonators and will come back through a medium and make claims that are not true. And this is a *must:* there would have to be meditation. By meditation I mean a reaching out and a going within. God is manifest in all things, in all creation. But also God is within and this is the source to which the medium should turn, because the soul has come through many, many incarnations and the soul has tremendous wisdom. When the soul reaches to the oversoul, which we call God, then there is the receiving, the seeing, the seeking out but receiving in. The soul reaches out, cries out for a union with the Source.

"A person can be born a psychic," she summed up, "and attuned to many levels of the psychic spheres and not necessarily be a medium. One must seek the spiritual, must seek God. Seeking the psychic alone is not enough."

Lotte Von Strahl is a baroness. Make no mistake about it. You sense her upbringing and family background as soon as you see her. She is over six feet tall, thin, straight as a ramrod, snow white hair and bright blue eyes. She has dined on plates of gold with kings and presidents. She has had to sell her furniture to survive and was once offered a job as a janitress. She has lost a fortune and a devoted husband, yet she has kept her dignity, her sense of humor and her amazing psychic abilities.

Her home is in Beverly Hills. It is an apartment on the ground floor of a pink castlelike building right across the street from the UCLA campus. The small apartment is decorated with the last few items she has been able to hang onto since fleeing Hitler. There is a silver coffee service, two or three magnificent chairs, a couple of paintings of noble ancestors and a few porcelain dishes.

That's about all. She speaks with an accent that is germanic yet terribly British.

She opened the door and led me to a small sofa. I began the interview by getting her upset. "How long have you been a psychic?" I asked.

"Ach. I hate the word 'psychic!' You're going to have that word in the title of your book? That's too bad. I hate it. In England when a person is a psychic you know that he has studied and been studied to give him such a title. But here in the United States into one pot they put the readers, mediums, sensitives, card readers and teacup twirlers. They call them all psychics!

"Another word I hate anymore is ESP! Everything is ESP! Do I have ESP? Of course I do, but so do you and your mother and the man who drives a taxi, etc., etc. Everybody has it. Maybe I have developed mine a little more than most people. Maybe I have been practicing it more, because after all I am in my seventies, but please don't call me an ESPer. I prefer to be called 'a sensitive sixth-sense girl.'"

All right, so I tried it from another angle. "Suppose I came to you and I said, 'Madame, I need your help.' What would you physically do? Would you read cards, get out the crystal ball, or would you . . . ?"

"What?" she exploded. "I don't do that tommyrot! How low are you trying to put me?" Then she laughed when she saw I had been joking. "It's not nice to fool Mother Nature!" And she laughed again. "No, I would just say to you to come in and sit down and tell me your problem. Then I would tune in on you and put my five senses over there and just let my sixth sense go."

"Is this being a clairvoyant?"

"I don't know. Maybe. When you would tell me that you are having problems with your wife, then immediately I would sense your wife, see her and for a few minutes *be* your wife. I would actually be inside your wife!"

She admits that she is never quite sure just how a sitting will go. Once a woman came for a consultation and happened to have her fourteen-year-old son with her. "He was such a nice boy with great big brown eyes. But as I started to tune into the mother, I got him instead. So I said to him: 'You hate your mother, don't you?' And he said 'Yes.' So I said, 'And you are thinking about running away, aren't you?' And he said, 'Yes.' And then I said, 'And also you are on LSD, aren't you?' Well, at this his mother got very upset and demanded that I stop that line of questioning. Of course I didn't. I said, 'And it was your brother-in-law who turned you on, wasn't it?' He agreed that it was. Well! Mother got so excited that I asked her to go and sit in her car while I had a long talk with the boy. Do you know he never took LSD after that?"

"I understand the police have called you in many times," I said.

"As a criminal?" She looked shocked.

"No," I laughed, "to help them with their cases."

"Ah yes. When there is a murder case they bring me a photo of the corpse and I start to psychometrize it. I've been called in to solve many cases for the police."

"How do you psychometrize a photo? I thought you had to have an object that carried the personal vibrations of the person?"

"Oh, no! If you are murdered and they don't have a recent photo of you, they could bring me one of you when you were a child and I could tune in immediately. I have done this in many different countries.

"Once the police came to me with a fancy white dress shirt. It was cut in many places and dry with blood. They told me a man had been stabbed to death as he was leaving his wedding reception. I held that bloody thing and told them that it belonged to a Mexican-American and I described him. They said I was right. Then I told them about the killing and described the murderer. They said that description fit exactly the man they were holding at the jail, but they would have to let him go because there was no evidence he had done it. Then I told them the murderer had a still red scar where he had been operated only four months ago for appendix. They said they didn't know that. I told them to go back to the jail and examine the man for the scar. They did that and there was the scar just where I said it would be. The man was so frightened about my powers that he confessed then and there."

"When you say you 'saw' this scar, just how did you *see* it?"

"In this instance, I felt it. I felt a sharp pain over my own appendix. But in most cases when a person comes to me I see a black spot in their aura and I know this is their weak spot. Many times doctors in Europe would call me in and I would diagnose their patients for them. But in this country? Hah! It is against the law to help a doctor in this country! I don't do anything that is against the law."

"But doesn't feeling all these illnesses and operations take a lot of energy out of you?"

"Of course it does and I have to spend long periods being quiet to regain this energy. After all, I'm not a young woman any more. Young in the head maybe, but in the rest of me, no. I used to get everybody's pains as I walked down the street. And suffer terrible agonies. But no more. I have trained myself to be like an electric light. I switch it on when I want information and I switch it off when I am through. But during that time—oh!—I suffer. Now I have complete control."

"How long have you had these abilities?" I asked.

"I've had it as a child already. After I was married to my first husband the Berlin Medical School of Parapsychology called me and tested me and that was really hell! Fifty of these professor-doctors absolutely bombarded me with questions and tests. It was fantastic! Then when I went to live in London I was tested by their investigators. I passed them all. Then I married my second husband, Otto—he was a baron—and we moved all over the world. I have met and been examined by the greatest names in parapsychology. I speak nine languages, so I can much easier work with the various doctors."

Lotte's first husband was a wealthy Dutch industrialist. She divorced him and married Otto Von Strahl, who was not only a baron but a member of the German Foreign Office. One of her sharpest memories—if not her fondest—occurred when her husband was serving in Norway and had to travel to Berlin to make a report to the new German leader Adolph Hitler.

"This was *before* that little man invaded Norway, I want you to know. Anyway, Otto was to meet him in the monstrous Reichschancellery and I waited out in one of the fancy rooms. Otto was in there for about an hour and I was getting bored looking at all that gilt and scrollwork. Just then two enormous SS men stood over me. Now, I am tall, but these men were giants! 'The Fuehrer wants to see you,' they said. We entered Hitler's private office and it was enormous. About the size of three tennis courts over there at UCLA but without the nets. Come to think of it, he could have used a net! Anyway, there was this little painter fellow standing with outstretched arm and I had to salute him back. Then he asked me to take a chair on the left side of his desk. Otto was on his right side, so in order for me to see my husband I had to look past Hitler. His Highness was perfectly charming and I didn't believe a word of it. As I watched his face I remembered people telling me that when he got angry he would get as red as the Nazi banner, so I, being curious, decided to see for myself. I didn't have long to wait. 'How do you like Norway?' he asked me. I saw my chance. 'I love it and this, Mein Fuehrer, is something that might interest you. The other day I was walking with my dog on the street when suddenly two workmen threw me against the wall and shouted: German Nazi pig!' *Now* you should have seen his face! It turned all shades of red and he shouted and waved his arms and paced around the room and banged his fist on the desk. Otto was sitting there as if he was on a pin instead of a chair, but I loved every minute of it. It was better than going to the theater. Then just as suddenly he simmered down, rose, kissed my hand and walked us to the head of the great staircase. He said he would see us again. I knew he never would."

Her husband was recalled to Berlin and worked there for a year, but then Lotte began to sense where Hitler and the Nazi Party were really heading. She convinced her husband (who respected her psychic powers) to ask for a transfer to the farthest German outpost. He was assigned to South Africa. They took half their furniture and left the other half in Munich. "Unfortunately, because it was all destroyed by the bombs." Then in 1938 the order came that all diplomats must join the Nazi Party. "My husband and I were the only ones in the whole Foreign Office who said no."

Naturally they were fired and recalled to Germany. Prudently they left their household goods in South Africa and after an amazing cloak-and-dagger episode managed to get out of Berlin and back to Pretoria. Three weeks later the war broke out.

They stayed in Africa all during the war, then moved to England and then on to the United States. There was no work for her husband here. He tried everything and so did she. They both answered the want ads and the only thing she was ever offered was a janitress job. She refused.

The jewels and silver and furniture and furs were sold piece by piece to pay the rent on the small Los Angeles apartment. Then Otto contracted cancer and for three years she pawned everything to pay the medical bills. Finally she realized that the only way to survive would be as a professional medium. Her name was already well known in occult circles when her husband died.

Madame Von Strahl has never advertised, the clients come through word of mouth. She has many clients from the screen world and some of them have become her closest friends. The list she reels off is impressive: Glenn Ford ("we are very close"), Goldie Hawn ("Such a little creature. I told her when she first was an unknown that one day she would be a great actress and win a high award for a picture with one of the screen's greatest actresses. And didn't she get an Oscar for her role in *Cactus Flower* with Ingrid Bergman?"), Edmund Purdom ("I told him his private life was ruining his career"), Ann Blythe, Spring Byington, Jayne Meadows, Ann Sothern, Eddie Albert, Efrem Zimbalist ("I adore him!"), Mercedes McCambridge ("a great lady"), Elke Sommer ("I tried to get the ghost out of her house but there was no ghost"), Horst Buchholz, Merle Oberon ("a beauty!") and George Hamilton ("He once crawled in my front window and opened the door when I forgot my key") among many others.

She gets her greatest satisfaction from working with young people. "Their parents don't try to understand them, and chase them into the streets. My God, I can do with these youngsters everything and they listen to me. I just tell them, 'Good heavens, kids, you are just as rebellious as I was but only in another way. And I don't blame them and I don't condemn them. I *do* condemn the ones that use these narcotics. I have taken many of them away from drugs.

"I have the most talented young people who come to me. They compose and they write and they paint. And I have the clean hippies—not the dirty ones—who come here and lie down on the floor and show me all their paintings and I say that I see this and that and this in them. They all say, 'Oh! you are the first adult to see what I wanted to express in this painting!' The poor babies. They have no one to turn to. Not their parents, not their priests and at times not even their own friends."

"Do you work with a spirit guide?" I asked her.

"No. I don't need one. Whenever I must work out a difficult problem I must do it by myself. I usually will say, okay, mind, show me the way, and the door will open and I'll see the right solution. For what do I need an Indian or a Chinese guide standing behind me? God is my guide. He is all I need. Period."

Michael Jackson is the host of a weekly interview show on channel KCOP-TV in Los Angeles. The name of the program is "The Big Question" and Mr. Jackson is calm, suave, respectful and very unflappable. Nothing ever upsets him. Nothing seems to get through that calm English-bred exterior. He is always the perfect host. The perfect gentleman.

Then he decided to do a show on the occult. He interviewed Brother Ananoamoy, a yogi of the Self-Realization Fellowship, and did it beautifully. Then he talked to the Reverend Floyd Humble, pastor of the First United Spiritualist Church of Gardena, California. It was a perfect and cultured job.

Because there are so many mediums and psychics hiding behind the label "Reverend" in California (the law says mediums and fortune-tellers can't operate but churches are free to do anything) some psychics have been forced to *buy* their titles. It is a growing practice and a disreputable one but until the state of California revises its anti-fortune-telling law, it will continue to flourish. Mr.

Jackson, this evening, had as his next guest the Rev. Bishop Kirby J. Hensley of the Universal Life Church, Inc.

The viewers saw the bishop sitting in a chair, his horn-rimmed glasses glinting in the studio lights, his sparse hair sticking up in tufts around his white face and his loud checkered sport jacket unbuttoned. At first glance the bishop looked like a 1930 Dust Bowl refugee or someone hired as an extra for a Lum and Abner movie.

Mr. Jackson, his British tones enunciating clearly, made the introduction: "You could one day be a Doctor of Divinity. You could marry people, open your own church, divorce people, too, if our next guest is true to his word, and there are hundreds of thousands who believe so. Bishop Hensley, how is this possible?"

Hensley [speaking with a high-pitched, twang-filled southern accent]: I want to clarify one little statement. You can't buy a Doctor of Divinity, but you can buy one for an ordained minister. If you become a minister, you can marry people, divorce 'em and so on. We figure that any preacher who can perform a wedding should be able to dissolve it.

JACKSON: In church.

HENSLEY: In church. But it really doesn't have to be in a church. It can be anywhere.

J: How many people have you ordained?

H: Over eight hundred thousand.

J: Why?

H: More than all the other churches put together in America.

J: Did all these people *deserve* ordination?

H: Yes. We keep a record of 'em.

J: I realize that, but respectfully, sir, how do you know that a man has any knowledge at all?

H: Well, the less knowledge he has the better off he is.

J: The less knowledge . . .

H: Oh sure. He's just got a lot of ideals pumped into him from somebody else.

J: But then he's going to take that lack of knowledge and pump it into somebody else!

H: That's the trouble, but if we can help them to all be ministers, they won't go out and listen to nobody else. You see, this is the thing about it, we are trying to relate to people and people want to identify with something. When a man comes up to you and says he's a preacher then you stick your hand out and you say, 'I'm a preacher too.' So you meet him on equal grounds. Then you can communicate with him and stand up to him.

J: Has this conception ever gotten you in trouble?

H: Oh, I stay in trouble! Trouble's my middle name.

J: Well, I'm glad you're in town and out of jail. What I mean is, has this put you behind bars?

H: Oh yes, I've been behind bars several times.

J: Why?

H: Because I sold the Doctor of Divinity in California and they said I broke the educational code and I said I didn't. The Constitution of the United States says that a church can do this and the state says they can't. We've been debating it. We've got about three or four cases going into the Supreme Court now. One of them's pretty well on its way up, so we feel we'll get an answer pretty soon.

J: Bishop, how did you become '*bishop?*'

H: Oh, I took on the name. People just automatically give me the name Bishop. See, the thing we are trying to do is get away from titles. I got twenty-five degrees. You name it and I got it. But that don't make me nothin'.

J: Sir, how many Universal Life churches are there?

H: Over eight hundred thousand churches. Some two and a half million members.

J: Sir, in all respect, but to use your own definition, there are two and a half million *dumb* people?

H: I wouldn't say they's dumb. I don't think anybody's *dumb*.

J: But you did say that. Respectfully, you did say that you could be dumb and become a minister.

H: Oh, I didn't say you must be dumb to become a minister. I said you could become a minister if you *was* dumb. That's a lot different.

J: But you must be a multimillionaire by now.

H: A millionaire? Well . . . hmmm . . . let's just say that I got fifteen cents.

J: What do you eventually hope to achieve through your Universal Life Church?

H: I hope to achieve that everybody relates to each other as human beings, not as somethin' like doctor or lawyer or professional or something like that. We're all human beings. I went before the judges of California a couple of days ago and they come in there with them big long black robes on and they set down and they want you to come up to them and look at them as if they was something different. I relate to 'em as other human beings. If a pretty little girl would have come along in a little mini-skirt they would have felt just like I would, their old hearts would beat just like mine.

J: Yes sir, but why would *I* want to be a minister?

H: Why would you want to be a minister? Because you can do like the rest of 'em do. Just walk on a city bus and do what they do. You watch a priest or a rabbi on a bus, he doesn't put fifteen cents in the little machine. You can just walk in and sit down beside him and if the driver wants you to put money in you say, 'Hey, you're discriminatin' against the ministry. I'm a preacher *too.*'

J: So the world becomes an expense account.

H: Hah! You're saying that, not me.

J: You must have many followers.

H: We have lawyers, we have doctors, we have three senators, we have state representatives, we have all kinds of people. We have movie stars. . . .

J: You corrected me in the beginning that you couldn't buy the Doctor of Divinity here in California, but it is for sale elsewhere?

H: It's not for *sale* anywhere but for a free will offering of twenty dollars you can get it anywhere *but* California.

J: One second, sir. It's not for sale?

H: Nope.

J: There's no cost?

H: Nope.

J: Except twenty dollars.

H: Twenty dollar *offer*.

J: Offering. Which will be accepted.

H: Yeah, you got to say it like that. I can't sell it, then the tax board will be down here jumpin' on my back. They're sittin' out there right now, listenin' to every word I say, don't think they're not.

J: You mean you're tax exempt?

H: Oh yes, we're tax exempt and we're fighting for it. They took ten thousand dollars from me here in Los Angeles. Didn't you hear about that?

J: What happened?

H: Oh, Uncle Sam stuck his big hand in my bank account. But they're going to give it back to us, don't worry.

J: Really? How are you going to get it back?

H: Because we went to court and the church asked for it back. We are a church like any other church, so they have to give it back to us.

J: Sir, this offering—offering—of twenty dollars which will get for you a Doctor of Divinity degree; how many people have 'offered?'

H: Oh, then you'd multiply that by twenty, wouldn't you? Haw! You're tryin' to find out something. Oh, I'd say about . . . well, I'm not too sure . . .

[Long pause]

J: If you were sitting where I was sitting, what would you ask you next?

H: What would you ask me next? Well, I'd probably ask me, What are you going to do next?

J: What are you going to do next?

H: What am I going to do next? I'm going to get political, and we've got the party. It's the Peoples Peace Prosperity Party. The "4-P" party. That's the thing we're working on today, because we believe that it's goin' to be the political future of mankind. We've got many people what's in high places working with us on this.

J: And then you'll ordain everybody a President.

H: Yeah, we'll make 'em presidents then.

J: Sir, I almost kiddingly asked before if you had been behind bars because of all this, but you *have* languished in martyrdom?

H: Oh yes. I've been behind bars. No joke about it. I've won the cases and got out. I've got a year hangin' over my head now. Because I sold a Doctor of Divinity and the state said I couldn't and I said I could. So we went round and round.

J: Surely you have something going for you. The word "divinity" can't be given by the state.

H: I know the state cannot give you a Doctor of Divinity. You can't go to no state school in this country and earn a Doctor of Divinity.

J: You know what's the scary part of this thing, don't you?

H: What?

J: The two and a half million followers! That's only one third the number of alcoholics we have!

H: I wish we had all the alcoholics. Make ministers out of 'em! Get 'em off alcohol. Get 'em off of drugs. Give 'em something to turn 'em on!

J: Well, what do you give them to turn them on? Give them spirituality?

H: What I give 'em spiritually? Oh, I don't believe in the spiritual. I only believe in the natural.

J: Well, what do you give them *naturally?*

H: I give 'em lots of natural things. You can receive a flag, the only Universal flag in the world. It's white and gold. The white represents peace and the gold represents prosperity. Do you know of anybody that doesn't believe in that?

J: No, sir, I haven't met anybody that didn't want a piece of our gold.

H: Well, have you ever met anybody that didn't believe in a party? You know Nixon come along and he said, "We're going to take this government back to the people," but that's wrong. Don't take it back to the people, *give* it *back* to 'em. Don't hold it for control.

J: Right. There is a word that comes to my mind. The word

is *"help!"* May I ask you which great writers, philosophers and thinkers have inspired you in your business?

H: Well, I can't read anything they write, so none of them inspire me.

J: You can't *what,* sir?

H: I don't read nor write!

[Long pause.]

J: At all?

H: No.

J: What did your parents do?

H: What'd my parents do? My parents was farmers back in North Carolina.

J: What would they think of what you now do?

H: They'd probably turn over in their graves. Haw!

J: What do you think is the best thing that you have done?

H: I have wakened people out of the lethargy that they are not livin' no more in this *dream* world. They can relate to a natural world.

J: You mean, what you have taught people is *real?*

H: I'm not interested in this invisible world at all. Something you can't prove. That's why the state don't like me. The state says, "Hensley, if you go out there and preach something that will happen in the future or something in this invisible world, we'll let you alone. Don't be in the material world. It's all right to make them ministers but don't start selling 'em licenses."

J: Have you ever been called [another long pause] a "Weirdo?"

H: Oh, man, I've been called that a lotta times!

J: How does such a word strike you, sir?

H: Just like water on a duck's back.

J: [a still longer pause] How would you describe yourself?

H: As another human being on this earth trying to make life a little better for someone else.

J: I like you. But they say one like me is born every minute.

H: Every minute? Every second! Can I sign you up tonight?

J: [appalled] To what?

H: For your *minister's* license! And I'll even throw in a mar-riage license so you can go out and marry somebody. I'll give you a press card, we have them too. We can make you a member of the press corps.

J: Maybe the Vice-President's right. I'm already married, unless you advocate bigamy.

H: I don't advocate it, no. But it's goin' on in the world quite often.

J: What's the most important word in your whole world?

H: The most important word in my whole world is in-di-vid-u-ality. Being an individual.

J: We have surely just met one! Thank you very much Bishop Hensley. [Staring desperately off camera] I *think* we're going to continue in just a moment . . .

The Los Angeles *Herald-Examiner* used to be the most prestigious paper on the West Coast. Then in 1967 it was rocked with labor troubles. It threw out the union and refused to negotiate with it. There are still pickets at the front door. Now the *Times* is L.A.'s biggest and best.

Wanda Sue Parrott is a staff writer on the *Herald-Examiner*. She came in after the strike had started. She did not take anyone's old job but had a new one created for her. She has been cursed, spat upon and had her car blown into pieces as she drove it down the freeway. Yet she continues unruffled, cheerful and very feminine. Her long auburn hair and her soft voice go well with her lithe curvaceous body and her Hollywood clothes. Yet under this exterior she is brilliant, cultured, witty and quite psychic.

I phoned her, asking if I could interview her. She in turn asked if she could interview me. She arrived at the motel where I was staying with a photographer and a young lady who insists on being called "Felicity." (Her parents would have a fit if they found out she was dabbling in the occult.)

Wanda introduced the girl, saying she was half Filipino and half Scotch-Irish. She lives in a town above Los Angeles. The girl has been having psychic experiences for as long as she can recall. When she was in grade school she used to leave her body, float to the other rooms and "just for fun" look at the teacher through "another student's eyes." She knows when the phone is about to ring and who is on the other end before she picks up the receiver. She refuses to go into a place because she can sense "spirit vibrations." She has done quite an amount of automatic writing, mostly with reporter Wanda Sue Parrott holding the pencil with her. The two of them have picked up many strange messages that have been numbered and filed with the California Institute of Parapsychology. One message came from a famed movie star who supposedly committed suicide. The message came the night of the death, *before* the news was published in the newspapers. The spirit writing said the star had not accidentally taken too many sleeping pills but had been murdered. The name of the killer was given and hinted he worked for a gang who were trying to collect back gambling debts. Felicity refuses to speak of this message. She says she does not intend to get mixed up in any gangland intrigues.

Wanda's psychic history goes back to when she was still a baby in the crib. She remembers leaving her body and floating through the walls of her parent's home "surrounded by golden light and not at all afraid, because I didn't know any better."

She came to Hollywood determined to be a movie star and after a few bit parts (she turned down a hilarious nude movie role) and a stint in nightclubs, she decided to become a journalist. When she tried automatic writing the first time she immediately got a message that a long-lost boyfriend was trying to contact her. It gave a post office address in a small European town. "He was an actor who wanted to get away from me, so he just packed up one day and went off to Europe. He said I would drive him to either jumping off a balcony or joining the Canadian Mounted Police. Anyway, I wrote him and there was no answer. The letter didn't come back either. Then I started dreaming about him. I would see him in strange places and in front of foreign signs and placards. I began writing all these down as soon as I awoke in the morning. One night I had a dream that he was on a bus and waving good-by to his mother. I knew he was on his way back to California. Then I awoke one night to see him standing at the foot of my bed. He was bathed in green light. The next day he appeared at my apartment. He said he had arrived the previous night, had wanted to see me, but decided to wait until morning. His first words were: 'How did you know where to write me?' He had received the letter! Then I showed him what I had written from my dreams and a large percentage of them had actually happened." She paused. "But I didn't marry him. It wasn't that type of a relationship by that time. We both had grown some and sensed we were free of each other at last. I knew he would go on to great things and he has. I can't tell you his name because he's very well known here in Hollywood."

"You too are quite well known around town," I said. "People read your by-line and they have often quoted from your articles, especially the ones dealing with the occult. What do your fellow workers at the newspaper think about your psychic abilities?"

"Oh, they love it. Whenever there is too much bitching and back-stabbing—as happens in all newsroom offices—I walk around and try to dissipate these bad vibrations by sending out love vibrations. If you don't fight evil with love what's the use of being on this earth? And then when my car was bombed they gave me a broom and said I could use that for getting back and forth to the office."

"Do you use your psychic abilities in your newspaper work?"

"All the time, but not as much as I did. I used to write the story in advance, then take it to the interview and ask the person to look it over and verify the facts. I found it was much quicker that way, rather than doing the interview first. But then one day the managing editor called me into his office and gave me hell. He said that a good reporter had the interview *first,* and wrote the story after. He admitted that I had hit the nail on the head the majority of times but he preferred I get the facts first. I couldn't understand what the difference was *when* I got the facts as long as I got them. But I abide by his decisions. After all, he is the boss."

Then she said she had died once in this lifetime. "It was a few years ago and I was in my parents' home and I was in great pain. I was hemorrhaging and the bed linen was soaked in blood. I tried to scream but no sound came out. All I could think of was, 'My God, I've been given this life and I've failed.' Then my muscles quivered, my body went limp and I was gone. It happened so quickly that I didn't have time to be afraid. They say that your life passes before your eyes as you die, well, it's true. Mine did, but it was a summation not of my actions but of my *reactions* to the things that had happened to me. And I saw that all my life I had wanted to run away from responsibilities and the pain that went with them. At the point when I understood this I heard a voice. It wasn't an old voice or a young voice or a male voice or a female voice, it was just a soft voice. It said: 'Now you may go again into the state which man knows himself and you may return to the same body and with the same memories you had when you exited.' So I came back. The hemorrhaging and the pain had stopped. It was then that I knew I had other things to do and that by tending to my responsibilities I could avoid death."

It was at this point that the photographer, who'd been listening to all this and not believing a word, suggested that he take a picture for Wanda's article about me and get out of there. Wanda thought we should pose sitting at a table in my motel kitchen, the three of us holding a pencil and trying to make contact with some entities through automatic writing. We sat around the table, held the pencil and it made a few squiggles. The photographer took his shots and got out, muttering all sorts of things to himself, I'm sure.

No sooner did he leave than the pencil began to make wide swinging arcs across the paper. Then it started going in circles, then in sharp zigzags. Felicity started to tremble and said she wanted to stop. Wanda insisted she go on. Then the words "go away and leave me in peace" appeared quite clearly. I removed my hands from the pencil, leaving Wanda and Felicity to do it themselves. "Where is Jean?" it wrote. "Where is Jean and what happened to it?" Felicity shuddered and closed her eyes. Her brow was speckled with sweat. Wanda removed her fingers, letting the girl take the pencil alone. She wrote across the page and then when she came to the edge of the paper, instead of jumping back to the left-hand margin, the pencil made a slight curve and began writing backward from right to left. Her hand worked just as rapidly in one direction as the other. She filled the page, never opening her eyes, writing regularly in one direction and then backward in the other. She removed her hand and paused. I slipped out the page and read it. It said, "Go away and leave me in peace. I am lost and I must find it. Where has it gone?" Holding the page up to the light and reversing it, I could read *quite plainly* the backward writing. "Must find soon. Must find soon."

Felicity put the pencil back on the paper and I, acting as catalyst, asked this "spirit" what it was looking for. The answer came immediately. "Where is Jean? The place is gone." Then backward again: "Where has it gone? It must be endless."

"Why has Jean gone?" I asked.

"She died," it wrote. "She died for me." Then it wrote ME in large letters and circled the word over and over. "Get out of my place," the message resumed, "there is nobody here. All are dead."

"Who are dead?" I asked.

"All are dead," it repeated.

"But can it be that you are also dead?" I asked. "Look around you and see if there is not a light somewhere and head for that light. It will help you." I had heard a medium in San Jose use this when a confused spirit came into her plane. "Maybe you too are dead and don't know it."

Almost immediately these strong pencil thrusts across the paper calmed down. A few faint circles were made and then the pencil trailed slowly off the edge of the page. It was all over and Felicity looked as if she was about to faint.

That evening I asked the owner of the motel if there had ever been a tragedy in my room or on that site. He didn't know, because he had recently purchased the place but in the few months he had been there nothing unfortunate had happened.

I put it all down as just an interesting experiment, when almost five weeks later the owner came to see me. "Remember you asked me about something happening in your room? Well, today the people that built this motel came over and I asked them. A man died here. Not in your room but in the room directly under yours. He had been traveling and was all alone. It took quite a bit of work to find his family and return the body."

I just gulped and thanked him for the information.

The "Official Witch of Los Angeles" surprised me. And baffled me. It wasn't her beauty that surprised me, even though one always thinks of a witch as being old and ugly and with a wart on the end of her nose. Louise Huebner is no wart-ridden hag: she is a lovely, charming, sex-exuding dark-eyed brunette who knows how to talk, laugh and be serious. What surprised me was her attitude toward her many fans, followers and emulators.

We met at a corner table in a noisy Hollywood Italian restaurant. At times I had to shout above the hissing espresso machine and the loud-talking Mafia-like characters in an opposite corner. She has the unnerving habit of never letting you finish a question. That day she seemed to be reading my mind and finishing the questions for me.

My surprise came with my first question. "If someone came to you and asked you for . . ."

"A curse or a cure? I wouldn't do it. I don't do anything for people."

I was taken aback. "What do you mean?"

"Just what I said. I can't be bothered with people. I don't do any little spells for ordinary run-of-the-mill people. Nothing for the public, just for myself."

I was still startled. "You don't do anything for the public because of the laws against it?"

"No, I just don't want to be bothered. I could not generate enough energy to accomplish a spell for somebody else's project. I just don't operate that way. I have to be emotionally involved to be able to do anything. If I can't do it for a close friend who needs me, I'm certainly not going to do it for Mrs. Joe Blow on Staten Island who sends me five bucks. No, ma'am."

"Would you do it for Mrs. Joe Blow if she sent you five hundred?"

"I don't know. I think it would have to be more than I earn any-place else to turn me on."

"Well, you must have to refuse a great number of people."

"Surely. Constantly. I receive letters from all over the world. My books are translated into other languages and everywhere people ask me to do something. But I don't do any of them. Their problems just don't turn me on. I can get five hundred bucks, just from writing a little article and I don't have to use any of my energies. Every-body's got their price and I think I have too." Here she laughed, her dark eyes flashing. "It's just that no one's met it yet."

But still I insisted. Every medium, psychic and fortune-teller I'd met claimed they used their "God-given talents" to help others. That it was a "sin" not to do so. This fascinating witch was the first person I'd met who kept her abilities for herself. "But for a friend of a friend, and she is . . ."

"No! I hardly ever do anything for a *woman!* I just do not become exhilarated by casting a spell for a woman. Ever since I gained public recognition I've had to turn down doing things for others."

"But isn't that the main idea behind witchcraft? The reason for practicing it?"

"Not for me it isn't."

"Well then, what is your definition of witchcraft? To the public being a witch is working over a cauldron and brewing up a spell for another person."

"The general public has the 'satanic' image as their only clue as to what a witch is. Just because I have these powers, why should I share them with the public? Does every woman who possesses a beautiful voice have to sing in the Metropolitan Opera? I practice my witchcraft for myself. That's enough for me."

"Well then"—hoping to take a different tack—"what have you done for yourself?"

"Do you realize that when I started out there was nothing doing in witchcraft? There was absolutely zero. I was the first psychic-astrologer-whatever to be hired by a large metropolitan radio station to do my thing. This was in October of 1965 here in Los Angeles. That's when the world began hearing about Louise Huebner, the witch. People would call in and I would give them a psychic reading. In fact, I was clocked on WMCA in New York as receiving *sixteen thousand* calls an hour. Of course, I couldn't talk to them all, but sixteen thousand people an hour tried to call me. That's quite a bit of popularity and quite a bit of interest in the occult. And I loved it! I just wish that many people per hour would be buying my books and my record. I'm also the first psychic in the public eye who has mingled on every level and never been considered as being crazy. I've never been handled in the corny, heavy-handed way they handle Jeane Dixon."

I asked her how she got the title the "Official Witch of Los Angeles."

"I was appointed by the chairman of the board of supervisors for the county of Los Angeles. Don't you think *that's* an example of using my powers to help myself? I'm the only one in the world with that title."

"Why did they think they needed an official witch? Wasn't the city getting along all right without one?"

"Because I made them *think* they needed me! I had been working for the city producing shows and festivals and drawing nice crowds. I was giving L.A. a 'human' aspect that is sadly lacking in this mixed-up town. When the county found out what I was doing for the city they said they were going to do something at the Hollywood Bowl and they asked me to work on public relations for them. So I did. The program to kick off the season was on folklore. So when I began to draw up the various acts for the show, I thought: Hey, how about casting the world's largest spell? So I got up there in front of eleven thousand people (that was thrilling!) and we chanted in unison: 'Light the flame. Bright the fire. Red is the color of desire!' I told them we were casting this to increase the sexual potency of the old town. But in order to make it official, the week before I did it I said, 'Gentlemen, it would be nice if I was the official witch at this official thing.' And they said, 'Yeah, that's great.' So they got the chairman of the board of directors out to a cocktail party in front of reporters and with a beautiful scroll that was handed me I became the official witch. Just like that."

The scroll is beautiful and it does say she is the official witch.

This certifies that Louise Huebner has been designated as the Official Witch [in capital letters and fancy printing] of Los Angeles County by virtue of her supernatural powers and is officially assigned to reign over Folk Day at the Hollywood Bowl on July 21, 1968, at which time she may be depended upon to cast a spell over all Los Angeles County.

The seal of the county was affixed and it was signed, "Ernest E. Debs, Supervisor, Third District, County of Los Angeles."

If the county thought it was all just a promotional joke, they didn't figure with the witch they were dealing with. Louise Huebner promptly began signing her newspaper columns as "the official witch of L.A." She was introduced on such coast-to-coast talk shows as Merv Griffin's, Steve Allen's, Virginia Graham's, Johnny Carson's and "What's My Line?" She was written up in *Time, Newsweek* and the New York *Times. Life* ran a three-page spread on her. She drove up to the mayor of Salem, Massachusetts, in a black limousine to "forgive the city" for what they had done to other witches. The mayor gave her a scroll to the city and autographed a broom. She cut a record of chants for Warner Brothers and wrote two books on witchcraft. And of course prominently displayed on the covers were the words "The Official Witch of Los Angeles."

County officials were upset over this unwanted publicity and so on December 29, 1969, she got a letter from the law office of the county counsel. It said, in part: "As you must know, the scroll you received at the Hollywood Bowl, July 21, 1968, was purely ceremonial and intended only to publicize the Sunday Afternoon 'Happenings' at the Bowl, presented by the County Department of Parks and Recreation as a public service.

"We must ask that you immediately discontinue use of the title 'Official Witch of Los Angeles County' or any similar designation creating the erroneous impression that you are affiliated with the Los Angeles County government."

The lawyers should have known that you *don't* pull a double cross on a witch, especially one as determined as Louise Huebner.

Happy New Year [she wrote back]. I would like to clarify my position with the County. It should be understood that the County came to me and asked if they could take advantage of my promotional abilities. They asked that I lend my image and reputation to their activities, rather than as is now being assumed that their activities created my image. It was the Witch who had constant and ample exposure and not the County Department of Parks and Recreation.

Your New Year's Eve greeting to me says I have no authority to use my title: "Official Witch for Los Angeles County." But, I have a signed certificate from Supervisor Debs that certifies that I have been designated as the Official Witch.

You say that something other than what was stated on the

certificate had been intended, but I only know what the language on the certificate states and not what Supervisor Debs claims its intention to be. You say I should know that the certificate was meant only to publicize. I do know this and I have published it.

. . . If the small amount of humor created for Supervisor Debs by his press agents has now failed him, then will he please return the gift I gave him of the Magical Golden Horn that was meant to insure his Romantic Vitality. Certainly he must know that it cannot work now that he has professed a disbelief in goblins, pumpkins, the good tooth fairy and all things that go bump.

> Sincerely,
> Louise Huebner
> Official Witch of Los Angeles County.

Louise held a press conference and read the letters. The newsmen got a big laugh out of it and she got front-page play all over town. She told them that if Supervisor Debs took away her title she was going to take away the sexual vitality she had cast on the county. She would do it one by one and first on the list was Supervisor Debs himself. The county let her keep her title, but after that "Ernie Debs had to go on all the TV shows and tell everybody he was still sexy. It was beautiful!"

This modern witch lives in a "haunted house" with her artist husband Mentor, her son Mentor Frederick and twins Gregory and Jessica. She doesn't have a cat, but she does have a pet beetle. She used to have a pet rat but a *Life* photographer killed it by having it pose balancing on a caldron of smoking dry ice.

Louise is a sixth-generation witch. She has Turkish, Rumanian, Italian, Yugoslavian and American blood in her veins. Her grandmother was a practicing witch in New York City who read cards, palms, searched tea cups and cast spells to keep her family together. Louise feels she owes everything to the woman.

Yet even though grandma did it for a living, Louise is heatedly against professional psychics. She says she has never gotten a good reading from any of them, and "I've been dropping into mediums and fortune-tellers' establishments for the past twenty years."

"Just because a psychic can tune into you and establish a rapport with you doesn't mean she is any great whiz at helping you with your problems. She has no right to make your decisions for you. She has no right to play God and work on your mind. I don't think we should allow ourselves the probings of psycopathic misfits who can't put their own lives in order and then turn around and tell us how to live ours. So what if they can tell me something about myself? So what if they can describe my husband or tell me what color tie he is wearing? Who cares?"

"But don't you consider that *something?*" I asked. "The fact that they can tell you about your husband? Something that only one person in a million can do?"

"Look. When the first creatures started crawling around that actually could see, it must have been very exciting for the creatures that couldn't see. Because their reactions would be so very different. Does it mean because the fly has something similar to one hundred eyes that this fly is any more God-damned brilliant than any other insect? His reactions may be a hundred times more psychotic than something that can't see as well, if he doesn't know what the hell to do with it. And most of these psychics around do *not* know what the hell to do with it! Being sensitive and psychic is an abnormal condition and those who are have a distorted viewpoint. Professional psychics have done more harm to the advancement of psychic research than any other group in the world. Getting advice from a psychic is *not* the thing to do! Having come from a family of psychics, I feel qualified to express my opinion."

"And it's quite an opinion. Does that mean you don't think people should try to develop their psychic abilities?"

"I didn't say that. I think they should! It's exciting. They should learn to do it for themselves, to solve their own problems, to understand who they are. Not to get up on a stage like Peter Hurkos and burn themselves out trying to always come up with the right answer. Not to do it for other people. It's like learning to love and then going to work in a whorehouse. Love is certainly beyond that and I think psychic exploration should take us out of the fortune-telling parlor."

"Let me see if I've gotten this right," I said. "You don't think a person should develop his psychic abilities to help others?"

"You mean for money?"

"No. Just to help other people."

"I don't believe that until you can truly help yourself you are in a position to help others."

"But there are many psychics and mediums who say they can't help themselves at all with their own powers."

"Those are losers who pretend they can't do anything for themselves because of some fantastic spiritual law that says you can only do good for other people. Yet how many of these people *really do* help anybody? How many Edgar Cayces have there been? How many Gandhis? How many Jesus Christs over the thousands of years? If you take the percentage of these men and lay it up against the percentage of psychic fortune-tellers, you'll find out that fortune-tellers are sadly lacking in the ability to help anybody. I don't think we should confuse psychic awareness with spirituality and I think many of the fortune-tellers do."

To change the subject I said: "Most people think of a witch as belonging to a coven, of dancing in the nude and riding a broom, do . . . ?"

"Well, I hate to disappoint them, but I don't do any of these things. I'm not Sybil Leek. The closest I come to doing anything weird is to stare at myself in the mirror. I'll sort of hypnotize myself with a candle and burn some incense to get me in the mood."

"Is this the 'candle power' I've heard so much about?"

"It's not the candle alone. It's me with the candle. The power comes from my psychic self. I'm able to focus all of my creative thoughts by concentrating on the flame of the candle. I use an orangeish-red candle myself, but any color will do. The color doesn't have anything to do with it, it's your subconscious that is doing it. I can do anything in any area with any color."

"How important is it to believe that something will work in order to make it work?"

"It has to be beyond belief," she replied. "It's not just believing. It's having the absolute certainty in your body and blood—not just in your mind—that this thing is going to happen. Your entire body chemistry must *know* this thing will happen. It's very hard to attain but when you do reach that conscious state, you've *become* it. You *become* the recipient of all the marvelous things you want to have happen to you. It's like acting a part in a play and you do it so well that you actually *become* that character. That's the feeling I mean. Not the feeling that it's going to happen, but that you are *it.*"

The waitress in the restaurant was staring at us, wanting to change the tablecloth for the dinner crowd. I asked my last question. "What made you come to California?"

"My mother brought me when I was a middle-aged child. She had a sister living here. Then I married and my husband is an artist who works with the major movie studios and I stayed. I like it here. And let's face it, I could *never* be the Official Witch of New York City!"

Barbara is a witch too. A gray witch. There's a difference. And like Liberace, Twiggy and Snoopy she prefers to use just one name. She has three other last names: her own and that of two husbands but she wants the world to know her simply as "Barbara the Gray Witch."

Like Louise Huebner she doesn't look like a witch. She stands a tiny four-ten, weighs ninety pounds and wears long blond hair. She also wears provocative hot pants and mini-skirts. She is most mysterious about her upbringing (she doesn't want to harm her family back home) but does admit to coming from the mideastern portion of the United States, admits to having a bachelor's degree in art and minoring in sociology and psychology. She had a great-grandmother that was burned at the stake in Germany and an aunt who is still alive (while pushing ninety) who still practices black magic back home. She also is the bane of her father's existence. The last time she visited him she left in a grand flourish. Standing on the steps leading to the airplane she pointed at him and called out: "There shall be rain for forty days and forty nights and your crops will be ruined!" Three weeks later her sister called her long distance, asking her to remove the spell. It had been raining for three weeks and their father's tomato plants were rotting on the ground.

Her aunt (who worked a charm on herself to never grow old and only started to wrinkle when she reached the age of eighty-five) taught young Barbara all she knew about black witchcraft. Then the girl left the group and joined a coven of white witches. She left them too. "I felt they were both too much of the old world," she told me in the air-conditioned studios where they are cutting her record album *Barbara the Gray Witch*. "I don't like rituals and praying. I think it's unnecessary."

"But aren't witches and covens steeped in ritual?" I asked.

"Only the black and white go for rituals. I'm a gray witch."

"Will you explain that please?"

"The black witches and warlocks are fatalistic and worship Satan. All their powers come from Satan. White witches worship God with a lot of magic thrown in and all their powers come from God. Now, the gray worships neither but they use the degrees of energies in their bodies to expand their minds—*not* through drugs—but with meditation and self-awareness. All their powers come from within themselves. When I start someone out in a gray realm, I'll do it, at first, through prayer, because it's easier for them to use as a force to build their inner self. Eventually they won't need to pray. It will become automatic with them to go through *themselves* to get whatever they want. They never pray to God or Satan. That's just a crutch."

"Do you believe in God and Satan?" I asked.

"I believe there is a good force and a bad force but I don't believe in the words 'God' or 'Satan.' They are man-made."

"Well then, where do your powers come from?"

"They come from inside out as well as outside in. It all depends on what you want. To develop your powers you must first learn to control your body. Your inner self."

"Is this a kind of yoga?"

"No, but it sounds like it, doesn't it? Yoga only reaches one certain point. They tell you you can keep building but they never tell you *how*. The gray witchcraft realm takes you one step at a time. It is the only realm that teaches you the secrets of the other two realms. It is the only realm that will instruct you in a proper séance and how to exorcise poltergeists and spirits. I've investigated many hauntings and I can tell you how to remove a hex or how to effect a cure."

"Are you a healer?"

"No. I'm not qualified. When someone comes to me with a cancer or other ailment I send them immediately to a qualified physician. I can tell them what candles to burn but *they* must do it. I won't burn a candle for them."

She explained that the gray realm is the most democratic of all the religious practices. Unlike the white occult, which takes in all organized churches and their rituals, she said, the gray realm has no leaders and no high priests or priestesses. It's based on mutual help and being a free spirit.

Unlike Mrs. Huebner, when someone comes to Barbara, she helps them. Once she worked a spell to make a sixty-five-year-old man to return to his sixty-year-old wife, and they'd been divorced for fifteen years. "But there's a kicker in all of this," she says. "When you use candle power or a love potion, you're going to get your mate back for the rest of your life. You must be really careful what you want him for! If you only want him for a weekend he'll be around forever and no matter how hard you try you'll not be able to get rid of him again!"

I asked her for her definition of candle power.

"Burning the right color candles in the right way for what you want. The white candle is for spiritualism, health and purification. You must put it in a red holder and the candle must be very large. This is used at séances and for calling back someone from the realm of hereafter. The love candle is always red. The money candle is green and a brown candle is used to get rid of the evil eye. These candles must be blessed by dipping them in holy water. The white realm does this by taking them to a Catholic Church. The black prefers to steal the water from a church. The gray realm uses rainwater, or you can boil water, put it in an open jar and set it outside so that the night air purifies it."

"Do you place it so the rays of the moon strike it?"

"No. That's a fable. One of the reasons I decided to go public and speak up is because witchcraft is ridden with fables like that. Of course this is natural, because we've had to remain hidden for fear of persecution from the Christian Church. They are still afraid of us, maybe even more today than a couple centuries ago. The only difference in their attitude today is that they are no longer permitted by law to burn us.

"You know," she continued, "it's awfully funny but Christians claim to be so filled with love and goodness and yet they burn witches. But have you ever heard of witches, supposed to be so full of evil, ever burning a Christian? Have you ever heard of Matthew Hopkins? No? Well he lived in England in the late sixteen hundreds and he murdered seventy thousand people for witchcraft and I'll bet not ten of them were really witches or warlocks. I'm sure he's been reincarnated somewhere in Washington today. Or maybe he was Hitler. Hitler ran his war on the advice of a warlock. Did you know that? And when he put him in a concentration camp he lost the war! Serves him right."

"If I can backtrack a minute," I said, "do you let these candles burn all the way down or do you blow them out?"

"If you are using the white spiritualist candle at a séance, then you blow it out when the séance is over. You may relight it several times. You let your red love candle burn about an inch, then you blow it out and let it rest twenty-four hours before you decide to burn it for that same person or a different person. It must sit in a silver holder, one of those that has a thong in the bottom to secure the candle. You heat the thong and then, concentrating all your power on this thing, push it into the base of the candle. Don't push the candle, push the thong. This sends vibrations into the wax and they are released as the flame burns. Never break a candle or all the blessings will run out of it."

"How do you teach your students to call upon this inner energy?"

"It's a long process that usually takes three years. The most important for my young students between fourteen and nineteen years of age, is to learn to relax. Theirs is a jumpy, action age so they must first learn to calm down. I usually darken the room, have them lie on the floor and tell them to think about each part of their body from their toes to their head. Once they are able to do this and relax they are ready to meditate on each part of their body. This takes time. Meditation is not easy. They must learn to control their breath, their heartbeat, their perspiration, their pulse, etc. Then once they get past this point I start on ESP. Then they go into psychic phenomena. After that, everything comes naturally into them. I don't have to instruct them any more."

Barbara admits that being a witch is a lonely life. She didn't tell her first husband about her talents until they had been married a few years. It took him just a few months to get a divorce. She openly admitted it to her second husband before they married and he just laughed. Then in late 1970 she decided to go public and the local newspaper (in middle-class San Bernardino) ran a long article about her. The publicity put him "up tight." He couldn't take the dozens of telephone calls from cranks and curious, the young people that crowded around her asking for lessons and seeing his neighbors pull their children inside whenever he and Barbara walked down the street. When the townsfolk started burning crosses on their front lawn and hanging dead chickens on their front door he filed for divorce. She now lives in Los Angeles and feels "lighter now that I can do the things I really want to do and not being afraid of hurting people I love."

"Barbara," I asked. "What is your ultimate goal? Where are you heading?"

She paused and crossed her shapely legs. "I want the name of 'witch' to be respectable. I want people to understand that being a witch is not necessarily being evil. I want them to change the dictionaries so that distinction is made between white, black and gray witches. I know if I do this—if I come out publicly and make a stand—then some nine thousand other witches and warlocks in the United States will also come forward and we can become a proud profession, not just a persecuted minority."

In 1965 a thin old man got off a freighter in Boston. He had come all the way from India to America. He was seventy years old, knew no one and had only seven dollars in his pocket. He managed to get to New York City, where he started chanting in a Lower East Side park. Today that man jets around the world, has hundreds of followers, dozens of temples and is considered as being next to God. He is His Divine Grace A. C. Bhaktivedanta Swami Prabhupada and he is the absolute leader of The International Society for Krishna Consciousness.

The last few years have seen adepts all across the United States. They are usually young, white and healthy-looking American kids who wear long saffron robes, shave their heads (the women sometimes pierce their noses) and daub their brows with paint. They stand on street corners beating drums and clanking finger cymbals, chanting:

> Hare Krishna, Hare Krishna
> Krishna Krishna, Hare Hare
> Hare Rama, Hare Rama
> Rama Rama, Hare Hare.

Americans look at them as being quaint, odd or sacrilegious. They don't eat meat of any kind, don't believe in sex unless it's between a married couple for procreation, are against gambling and think all sports are a waste of time. They are also against alcohol, tobacco and drugs. They eat special foods made from grains and milk that are first offered to Lord Krishna. The single ones live in spiritual households called *ashrams*. The married ones are permitted to live by themselves with their children. A married man must work and provide for his family. A single man must work for the Movement. Their funds come from donations, the selling of incense and their beautifully printed books. (Beatle John Lennon gave them $19,000 to publish one book and his Apple Corps Record Company has brought out a long-play of their chants and music.)

And naturally, their World Headquarters is in Los Angeles.

I first saw the Krishna kids in action at the San Francisco International Airport in July 1970. I was there to meet a friend coming from Brazil and before she arrived His Divine Grace came in on a plane from L.A. There were at least five hundred saffron-robed adepts waiting for him. They cheered as he walked from the plane into the main reception room. They beat their drums and banged their cymbals, shouted Hare Krishna and threw armloads of red carnations at his sandaled feet. His skin was a dusky brown, his dark eyes deep set into a lined face. His head was smooth shaven and he had a white streak of paint running from the top of his head to the bridge of his prominent nose.

His blond, blue-eyed healthy American-as-apple-pie followers were deliriously happy. They threw flowers at him, threw them at the newsreel cameramen that were trying to record the event and threw them at the crowd of curious travelers who had stopped to see what was going on.

It was strange, but as many of these button-down-collar executives and their bewigged high-heeled wives watched, the unrestrained happiness of the Krishna kids engulfed them too. Dozens of people were chanting Hare Krishna along with the adepts. Almost everyone was smiling. And a few had tears in their eyes. As the entourage swept out of the airport, they left a floor strewn with flowers and an atmosphere of contentment. For a few seconds perfect strangers smiled at each other as they picked up a carnation for their button-hole or their purse. Men walked around with a briefcase in one hand and a flower in the other. Women fixed them in their hair or hunted for a straight pin to attach them to their blouses. And everywhere people were still singing softly to themselves:

> Hare Krishna, Hare Krishna
> Krishna, Krishna, Hare Hare . . .

I went to interview the man in charge of the Los Angeles Temple. I was met by a young lady with a ring in one nostril and she opened the door to an office that was furnished with just a low table. Behind this table, on pillows on the floor, sat Karandhar, the secretary for the Western Region of the United States. He called for a chair and one was brought for me. As I sat in it someone put a lei of tiny flowers around my neck. Then a heavier garland was added of enormous gardenias and red carnations. It rested on my lap. I said thank you. A young man in a saffron robe replied, "Hare Krishna."

Karandhar's real name was Kelly Smith and he was born in California. He first heard of the movement when he was living the free life in the Haight Ashbury section of San Francisco. His Divine Grace had managed to get across the country to open up a small temple on Frederick Street. Kelly (as he was known then) was fascinated by the dancing and the robes but didn't join immediately. He was searching. He wanted to live a spiritual life and he saw that the much touted life of the "flower children" was leading to drugs, disease and degradation. Then in 1968, at a yoga meeting, he met a member of the Krishna movement. He was invited to see their temple and to attend a service. "It all felt real and warm and understanding and so one week later I moved into the temple as a full-time devotee."

What did his parents have to say about his shaving his head (he has only a long blond "tail" hanging from his shining dome) and his renouncing of worldly goods?

"In the beginning they had no opinion one way or the other, thinking it was just one more of my moods, but when they saw I was serious and intended to make it the rest of my life, they understood."

"Do you intend to make it the rest of your life?"

"Oh yes! There's no question about it."

I asked him if it would be possible for him to put into words just what Krishna Consciousness meant to him and to the others in this new movement.

"Krishna Consciousness simply means to realize who is the Supreme Person, who is God, who am I and what is our relationship with one another. From the Vedas, which are the Scriptures we study, we learn who the Supreme Person is. He is Govinda, Krishna. He actually is a person, he has transcendental form and transcendental qualities. He can actually be described and pictured." He pointed to a series of brightly colored lithographs showing a powerful blue-skinned man in various activities. "Those are all pictures of Krishna. He is the Supreme Lord and the cause of all causes, the ultimate truth of all truths, the perfection for all endeavors of perfection."

"So God is Krishna and Krishna is God," I said.

"Exactly. That's part of Krishna Consciousness, to realize that Krishna is God. Secondly, who am I? I am part of God. God has created everything so I am part of his creation. More specifically, I am an individual spirit. I am part and parcel of Krishna and Krishna is the Supreme Whole; then what is our relationship? What is the relationship between a part and the whole? What is the relationship of the hand to the rest of the body? The hand takes the food and serves it to the mouth, which sends it to the stomach, which sends it to the blood, which nourishes the hand, giving it energy to pick up food and serve it to the mouth. Krishna Consciousness means that I am part of Krishna. That I am a servant and shall always be engaged in serving him. All my activities should be based on the principle of serving Krishna. Pleasing Krishna."

"How do you please Krishna?" I asked.

"Krishna gives direction through the Scriptures, particularly the *Bhagavad-Gita.* In this, our main text, he tells us how to serve him. One cannot serve Krishna simply through his own speculation. Also we must serve the Spiritual Master Swami Prabhupada, who is the living representative of Krishna. He is a pure devotee of the Lord. He knows intimately what Krishna desires. By pleasing the Spiritual Master we know Krishna is pleased."

"Does Christianity have any connection with Krishna Consciousness?"

"The Vedas tell us that religion is one. There is only one religion but it may be manifested and characterized in many different ways, depending on the cultures, climates and societies where it is introduced. Lord Jesus Christ also taught religion. He taught it according to a particular time, people and place. Actually Lord Jesus' teachings are no different, in essence, from Lord Buddha's teachings or Lord Krishna's teachings. When you enter elementary school you are taught that one and one are two. When you get to the university those basic truths still hold but you are taught ideas far beyond those elementary ones. So it is in the teachings of Lord Jesus and Lord Krishna."

"Well then, has Christianity failed? If you, a Westerner, had to turn from Christ's knowledge to Krishna knowledge, then something is wrong with Christianity."

"Krishna's Scriptures are much more all-encompassing and comprehensive than any other Scriptures in the world," he replied.

"That includes the Bible."

"Yes. If you have a small pocket dictionary and a large desk dictionary everything that is in the little book is true, it's just that it's not as comprehensive as the larger one. The Bible stops at the point that God is great. It doesn't say *how* great, what he does or what he looks like. The Vedas describe the Lord's form and his activities. They say not only that Krishna is great but *how* he is great."

"How about reincarnation?"

"It's a natural law. We are not born and we do not die. We are eternal. This material body is simply a temporal covering. The law is that as long as you remain within the illusion that binds you to a material body you are destined to birth and rebirth in the material form. When you were a child you were yourself in another body. When you became a teen-ager you were still *you* but your body had changed, and now that you are a man you have a man's body but inside it there is still the original *you*. Scientists say that the cells in a human body change completely every seven years. They are constantly wearing out and being replaced by different cells, yet the *you* remains inside. So when the body gets too old to function any more you shed it. It is dead but *you* are eternal. It's quite logical really."

I was impressed with just how much Krishna doctrine this young man had picked up in two short years. "But how does Krishna Consciousness help you in your everyday living? How do these ancient ideas help you cope with the modern world?"

"When you have discovered the pure love of Krishna Consciousness and know that your happiness comes through serving Krishna, then success or failure, money or fame is not important. Serving Krishna may or may not make you wealthy, it depends on how Krishna wishes to use you. But no matter what you do, when you do it *for* Krishna it will be perfect. His perfect understanding will make it so. When Krishna is pleased by your devotion you feel that he is pleased and then you are pleased also."

Then I asked a question I had been wanting to ask for a long time. "What is the reason for chanting 'Hare Krishna'?"

He had the answer. "Krishna and his name are absolute. If I look up at the ceiling and call your name, you won't be there, because you and your name are two different things. Krishna has no duality. There is no difference between him and his name.

So by chanting Hare Krishna you are actually associating with Krishna. He is right there."

"Are you calling Krishna to come into your body?"

"You are calling Krishna and Krishna is there and you are showing Krishna that you are calling him and showing him that you know he is there. The chant that we use was brought to this planet five hundred years ago by Lord Caitanya. He was an incarnation of Krishna. (The present Swami Prabhupada is the tenth in the 'supreme chain of disciplic succession' from Caitanya.) Krishna himself came to teach this process. This chant is universal and anyone can chant it. More astounding are the emotions you will feel when you chant it. It is actually a transcendental feeling. It cannot be described."

While there is no set number of times this chant should be said, the adepts do work away all day on a string of large, odd-shaped beads they call the "japa." Working it like a rosary in their left hand they go over it sixteen times a day, saying the Hare Krishna chant sixteen times for each bead. There are 108 beads on the string. You figure it out. "But the pure devotee is chanting every moment," young Karandhar told me, "he never stops, because he never wants to stop being in the Krishna presence."

"Why," I asked, "is it necessary to wear the robes of India? Wouldn't it be detrimental to a man looking for a job to support his family?"

"A man who must work outside the ashram for his family does not have to shave his head or wear the robes. You can worship Krishna without the robes. External things are not that important."

"But," I protested, "it's these very external things that call attention to the movement."

He smiled and shook his head in the affirmative. "That's an important reason for wearing the robes. The whole idea of this movement is that we want to be missionaries for Krishna. Wherever we go we want to arouse interest. If I go down the street in normal clothes and a normal haircut nobody will ask me about the movement. But immediately as I appear in the robes and shaven head they ask: what are you doing? Who is this Krishna?"

He asked me if I wanted to see the temple and we walked from his office across a narrow open corridor to a large white four-columned church. He kept chanting Hare Krishna all the time.

The building used to belong to the Methodists and now instead of pictures of Jesus and a plaque giving the page number of the hymns to be sung, colored lithographs of Krishna line the wall like Stations of the Cross. The altar is in the ordinary position but instead of a cross or a statue of Christ there is a bluish-gray doll dressed in fancy raiments and hung with garlands of flowers. It is, of course, Krishna.

He took me into a back room right behind the altar. I imagine the choir once donned their robes here or it was used as an adult Sunday school classroom. Now the floor was paved with shining marble and the walls were painted saffron yellow, the same color as the robes.

Dominating the room was a magnificent huge chair which sat on a raised dais. They were both covered in plush red velvet and heavy with gold fringe. A red velvet and fringed umbrella hung open over the throne. A young girl sat on the floor in front of this King of Siam stage prop placing vases of fresh flowers on the steps and around the several photos of His Divine Grace A. C. Bhaktivedanta Swami Prabhupada.

"This is his chair," Karandhar/Kelly Smith whispered. "Only he is allowed to sit there. It is sacred to his name."

"Is he in Los Angeles today?" I asked.

"No. Today he is in Ceylon. Next week he will go to Australia and soon to Moscow. At the Russians' invitation," he added.

"Tell me. Just one last question. Is this leader of yours fallible? Even though he is in constant contact with Krishna, does he have human failings like the rest of us?"

Karandhar stared at me and closed the door to the throne room. "His Divine Grace is infallible. The fallible are those human entities who are living apart from Krishna's interests. They are self-motivated. When one is a pure devotee all his actions, all his thoughts, his very breath itself is devoted to Krishna. He has no other interests, no other lusts and therefore he enters into that transcendental nature of infallibility. The Spiritual Master is absolutely infallible.

He is never wrong and there is never any inequity. He is absolutely perfect. Hare Krishna!"

Lest Christians become upset that every young person is turning to Krishna, be advised that Jesus is also getting his share in Los Angeles. They shout his praises, chant old-fashioned Bible Belt hymns and do his missionary work on Hollywood Boulevard. To some people they are an annoyance, stopping you and forcing you to listen to how you must be saved. To other hippie types looking for a place to crash for the night or a free meal they are an easy take. But to most of the non-converted L.A. youth they are members of "The God Squad" or "Jesus Freaks."

Turning kids off drugs and onto Christ is a concern of most ministers in the United States today but to Tony and Susan Alamo, it is more than a concern: it's a command.

Tony (who was born Bernie Lazar Hoffman but changed his name when he came West to get into the record business) was sitting in his office one day in 1964 when he felt this powerful force. "It felt like a warm anointing of oil, and my ears shut off. I could hear this voice cutting through me. It was the voice of God and it told me to go and tell the people about Jesus." It was a shaking experience, especially since Tony was a Jew.

He tried to ignore the message and continue with his normal affairs but one day he got a revelation of Hell. That did it. Drawing on the only Christian source he knew (the film *Elmer Gantry*) he ran around shouting, "Repent! Repent!"

Soon he married a blond actress named Susan who had a fundamentalist religious background and they opened up The Tony and Susan Alamo's Christian Foundation right off Hollywood's notorious and decaying Sunset Strip. Word got around that it was a "right on" place and the lost, broke, drugged and hungry began to stream in. The Alamos gave them friendship, food and Jesus Christ.

The foundation has grown so much that they've had to move out of Los Angeles to the little town of Saugus. (Some of their detractors claim their neighbors on the Strip made them move.) They hold prayer and singing services every night at 8 P.M. and

Sundays at three. There is a free bus that picks up the kids at the corner of Hollywood and Highland.

The Alamos don't keep record of the number of young people who've turned on to Jesus but a careful estimate puts it around a thousand. Maybe more. They've heard harrowing stories about prostitution, robbery and death. They've helped kids kick the habit of mixing dope with cheap wine by giving them the high of Jesus instead.

I was standing on Hollywood Boulevard waiting for a bus one afternoon when one of the "Jesus Freaks" approached me. It was a young girl with a long hippie gown and bare feet. She dragged a small towheaded child with her.

"Accept Jesus as your savior!" she said, and thrust a mimeographed scrap of paper at me. It was the address of the Alamos' church. "Don't you know the end of the world is coming?" she asked.

"I have heard about it," I said, and smiled.

"You have no right to be so smug! If you don't accept Jesus Christ, you'll perish with all the other sinners! Don't you want to know the truth?"

"As a matter of fact," I answered, "I'm looking for the truth all the time."

"The truth is Jesus, man! Either you accept that fact or you don't."

My bus was coming and I edged closer to the curb, hoping she'd take the hint and go away.

"Accept God right now!" she shrilled at me, and several heads turned to look to see what the commotion was all about.

I pointed to my head and, trying to be calm, said: "I have found God. I know where it's at."

"God is not in your head! God is no place where you can really find him!"

More people were staring. "Look," I said, my voice rising. "I think I've found the God that's right for me."

She pushed her face close to mine. I didn't know if she was going to spit or bite. "Look, buddy! You'd better wise up and find God before it's too late! Hell is full of jerks like you!"

Just then the bus came and I stepped aboard. She was still staring, furious with me. I turned and glared at her and stifled the desire to shout "Hare Krishna!" She might have invaded the bus.

Just how strongly these young people have taken to Christ no one knows. How many will stick with Jesus until the next religious fad comes along is also an unknown quantity. But if Tony and Susan Alamo have saved just one lost child from the horrible world of drugs and despair they've done more than all the rest of us complacent onlookers put together.

On September 3, 1969, ten year old Ethan Friedman was riding his bicycle near his Beverly Hills home. Suddenly a truck, driven by Lou T. Watts, came smashing against the child. He was killed instantly. Watts was arrested and a date was set for his hearing.

On April 13, 1970, Watts left the Beverly Hills Police Station and walked to the parking lot where his truck was waiting. At that moment Eugene Friedman, the boy's father, drove into the lot. He stopped his car and went over to Watts. It was an accidental meeting. He tried to talk him into giving up driving lest he kill someone else.

Then suddenly a strange thing happened. There standing beside Watts was the ghost of little Ethan. He was sobbing and begging his father for protection.

Friedman stared at the vision of his only son, then pulled out a revolver. Watts dropped. Dead. Little Ethan smiled and vanished. Friedman offered no resistance when the police grabbed him and booked him for murder.

Judge Adolf Alexander passed judgment in September 1970. "This court is confronted with action of sentencing a most non-violent man for a most violent act," he said. "This was not a knowing use of a gun and the defendant was not conscious at the time he fired. At the time he was arrested he knew nothing of what had transpired." Then the judge gave Friedman three years——probation.

No other event in recent memory stirred up so much shock and resentment in the California occult world as the Charles Manson

murders. The case has been written too much and documented too
thoroughly to go into detail here but astrologers, Tarot readers,
witches and mediums were forced underground for several months.
Forced by public opinion and their own distaste of Manson's claims
to leadership in the occult.

"This Manson thing made us all look evil," an astrologer told
me. "He got high on drugs, said he was Satan and that his female
followers were witches. He didn't frequent any of the psychic circles
that *I* know about and he certainly was no astrologer!"

"His girls were not crafty witches but stupid bitches," a California
warlock said furiously. "What did they know about witchcraft?
Nothing! But reporters need words to sell newspapers and suddenly
there was this hippie LSD freak transformed into a High Priest
of the Black Arts. I suppose he did try a few spells and hexes,
but hell, a lot of other people have too, and they don't go around
killing innocent people and stabbing pregnant women. I never heard
of him before they arrested him but a friend of mine in San
Francisco says he used to visit LaVey's Church of Satan when
it was just getting organized. I don't know if it's true or not, but
I wouldn't be surprised."

The police swooped down on mediums in an attempt to get
more background detail on Manson. Spiritualist ministers were
questioned in their homes and at the station house. Cops, wearing
plain clothes, visited psychics in the guise of clients and then asked
subtle questions about Manson and Sharon Tate.

The police deny it but they consulted many members of the
Los Angeles occult community in an attempt to pin down the
killers. A psychic that prefers to remain anonymous says that three
officers came to her residence and showed her grisly pictures of
Sharon Tate and the others. She said she got the name "Charles
Mason" and told them that he was living in a village that seemed
to have no depth. She couldn't elaborate any on the locale but
it all became clear when Manson was found to have been living
on a ranch that was built around a Western movie set.

Ernesto Montgomery, a Black spiritual consultant in Los Angeles,
says he wrote to several Hollywood personalities on June 16, 1969,
telling them that "five prominent persons will be murdered on

or about the 9th of August 1969 on Cielo Drive in Benedict Canyon." He gave the approximate house number and said that if the entire area could be warned "the tragedy will be averted." The letters were returned to him unopened. Then on October 3, 1969, he says he went into a "transic" state and the name "Charley Mansoon" came to him as the murderer of Sharon Tate. In December Charles Manson was arrested.

Montgomery gives himself claim for many successful predictions, including the assassination of President Kennedy in Dallas. For those who fear for the future of the Psychic State, he claims California will be destroyed by earthquakes and fires on April 22, 1972.

Organizations, institutions and schools that offer to teach the neophyte the secrets of the occult and to help them develop their psychic abilities are few in the United States (or in the rest of the world, for that matter) but four of the nation's most respected are in Los Angeles. (Number one, in size and tradition, is the Rosicrucians, located in San Jose, with two splinter groups in Quakertown, Pennsylvania, and Oceanside, California. None of the three are speaking to each other.) The top Los Angeles four are: Astara, The Church of Light, Builders of the Adytum and the E.S.P. Laboratory. Their methods are unique and completely different one from the other: exactly as you would expect in this confused world of the "unknown."

Astara is the grandest and puts on the biggest professional show. It takes out full-page advertisements in national magazines promising the student he will soon be able to "utilize the power of your higher consciousness." Their motto is: "As Astarian in need never walks alone."

There are two guiding forces behind Astara. Robert Chaney handles the promotion and business side while his wife Earlyne Cantrell Chaney is in charge of the spiritual side. It's one of the few husband-and-wife teams that have worked well in the psychic field. It works all the way to the bank.

Robert Chaney was born in Ohio and worked, for a while, as a printer and advertising man. Then he became interested in occult powers and started lecturing and healing. His talks and the laying of his hands took him from Ohio to Michigan to Indiana and finally, in 1950, to California.

Earlyne was born in Texas, one of four beautiful daughters of a dauntless little woman who was widowed early. She eventually came to Hollywood, where her brunet good looks and her soft voice got her bit parts in some "Boston Blackie" movies, a couple of Westerns with Jimmy Wakeley and speaking parts in *Mr. Winkle Goes to War, Kiss and Tell* and others. She had psychic things happening to her when she was a child and in the movie business she would ask her "guide" for instructions. She worked at the Hollywood Canteen during the war and at Red Cross desks in several L.A. hotels to welcome home servicemen. One day a handsome Air Force captain came up to her desk. They both knew it was love at first sight. The war ended very quickly after that, but he stayed in the service to become a test pilot. Then one day a plane he was piloting crashed. He was killed. This tragedy prompted her to seek out the "reasons" for life and death. She studied for the ministry and had several strange experiences where she was certain her dead lover was contacting her directly. Two years later she attended a Spiritualist camp in Chesterfield, Indiana, and there met Robert. They talked about plans for a church of their own and came back to Los Angeles to get it started.

The original Astara church (the word means "a place of light") was in three rented rooms in a house on South Hobart Boulevard. They discussed occult phenomena, spoke of the spirit world and held classes in psychic development. Soon a regular Sunday congregation began appearing and someone said they thought it would be a good idea to put the lessons in print, as permanent reference material. Robert bought a hand mimeograph machine and turned them out. Letters began coming from all over the United States as these primitive mimeographed lessons were passed from hand to hand. They began inserting small advertisements in magazines stating that the material was available. "Suddenly," recalls Robert Chaney, "this activity far overshadowed our church and classroom activity. A choice had to be made: to continue as we were or go into the publishing field seriously." They made the choice.

The Astara property now is a church building a few blocks from Hollywood Boulevard and two houses right beside it. There are two other buildings a block or so away that house four modern printing presses, a book folder and cutter, a halftone camera, a gathering and stapling machine and several other printing and binding mechanisms. Another building houses a complex mailing and addressing system, where monthly lessons, newsletters, reminders and publicity go out to 12,000 paying students all over the world. Their postage bill alone runs over $40,000 a year.

Astara's lessons are divided into Four Degrees, with twenty-two lessons in each. They are beautifully printed and illustrated and supposedly carry the majority of the wisdom that has been handed down from "centuries so ancient as to have been forgotten even by historians."

All these lessons are written by Mrs. Chaney or "inscribed" by her as they choose to call it. She gets the material through reading what others have written and tuning into her "telephonic inspiration from a Greater Source." Once she has the rough draft, a staff of writers and researchers go over it, pick it apart and suggest new information and ideas. Then she rewrites it until everybody is satisfied.

The Chaneys have become "bigger than humans" (as one lady described her feelings to me) and their names and photos sprinkled liberally throughout their lessons and literature have built a kind of "personality cult" around them. They pose against backgrounds of flickering candles and seated in deep thought; Mrs. Chaney wears a long white gown, grecian style and ornamented with pearls and an ever present pectoral pendant. The student disciples can read all about her life and how she became their high priestess. It'll all there in thirteen illustrated volumes.

It takes money to run an organization like this and it comes from several sources. The students pay a $5.00 fee to join and then $2.00 after that for each lesson. They also have a series of studies written by Dr. Robert that cost $15.00 as well as books, records, posters and meditation tapes that are available for "a suggested donation" of $3.50 each.

An important part of their service for the Astarian is prayer. A member can send in a request (for health, love, business, etc.) and expect the Chaneys to personally pray for it. A donation is appreciated. Other times members can make donations are at Christmas, Easter, birthdays or when they die. Being as Astara is accredited by the U. S. Treasury Department as a non-profit religious organization, donations may be taken as exemptions on U.S. income tax. And being as Astara is a religious organization *it* doesn't have to worry about income tax either.

In 1909 Elbert Benjamine was contacted by the last remnants of something called The Brotherhood of Light. It was an organization that had managed, over the centuries, to retain and hand down information that was taught by the ancients. They supposedly had received it from beings on other planes, other planets or directly from God. Young Benjamine had been studying their lessons secretly for nine years when the call came. He was to travel to a certain place and there he would meet with the Council of Three. When he got there the Three was down to Two. One had passed away and the others feared they would be called soon. They asked him to take the leadership of this organization and, more importantly, prepare a complete system of occult education that would be preserved and taught to the coming children of the Age of Aquarius. It was to be The Religion of the Stars.

He was flattered by this offer, but because of his youth he declined. The next year he was contacted again, but this time by members of the Brotherhood of Light who were on the "inner plane" and they succeeded in doing what the members of the "physical plane" had not been able to do. Benjamine agreed to write twenty-one courses on the twenty-one branches of occult science.

Working through direct guidance from the Brotherhood of the "inner plane" he wrote the books. It took him five years. In 1915 he came to Los Angeles, was contacted by other members of the "physical plane" and began his classes. He called it The Church of Light. World War I was in full swing and the Brotherhood asked him not to open the classes to the general public until the hostilities were ended. His first class, accepting new members, was on Armistice Day, November 11, 1918. And they've been held regularly ever since.

Benjamine did a herculean task in filling so many books with occult, psychic and spiritual lore. The 210 lessons deeply discuss and investigate such diverse subjects as Astrological Signatures, Spiritual Alchemy, Ancient Masonry, Divination and Character Reading, Sacred Tarot, Imponderable Forces, Stellar Healing and Weather Predicting. Modestly he signed the books with a pen name: C. C. Zain.

The Church of Light *is* a church, with religious services the third Sunday of each month at three in the afternoon, where prayers are said and healing is done. Their members who earn a teacher's certificate are considered to be qualified to open their own churches and conduct any ceremony except marriage. The U.S. still has laws about that one. Churches have been set up in other California cities as well as seven other states and nine foreign countries.

It is no secret that The Church of Light makes its money from the sale of books and educational material. Their gross income for 1970 was $114,500, with their hottest item being the course on "The Sacred Tarot." They've sold 42,000 copies of it, along with some 5,000 decks of Tarot cards each year. They are a non-profit organization and so donations are solicited and accepted (although not with the fervor of Astara) and their income tax problem is also a minor one.

While their courses are probably among the best available in any language, several members are beginning to feel restricted by the church's severe limiting list of do's and do nots. Vena S. Naughton is the organizational president and her rule is like her will. Of iron. "We do not believe in human reincarnation. We teach that it is a false and misleading doctrine. We are not a Christian organization. We do not 'worship' Christ, though we do consider him a great teacher and man. We do worship an All-pervading Deity who runs the universe with absolute justice, with no vicarious atonement—every soul responsible for his own 'sins.'" She is against voodoo, sorcery, black magic, astral projection and hypnotism. Surprisingly, even mediumship is frowned upon. "Although people involved with these have contributed much to the knowledge of the occult, they have forfeited control of their own soul."

When you get information from the Builders of the Adytum it looks most unimpressive. The printing is small, on white paper, and no pictures. Then you start to read and you realize that perhaps *here* are the answers.

The Builders (or B.O.T.A. as they like to call themselves) was founded by Dr. Paul Foster Case. A small man with a large forehead and deep piercing eyes, he headed what was then known as "The Order of the Golden Dawn." It was "a previous incarnation of the Qabalistic Way of Return" or in plainer words a direct descendant of the ancient mysteries and knowledge. It was another "brotherhood" that had jealously guarded and handed down the secrets of old.

Back in the 1920's Dr. Case was contacted by the higher spirit forces which control these things and told to prepare new material and to update the old. And (says their brochure) "under specific instruction from Him, Dr. Case formed B.O.T.A. as a non-profit religious organization and as a reincarnation of the Golden Dawn, which had served its purpose for the era just passed."

In 1943 a young woman named Ann Davies was introduced to Dr. Case and immediately became his disciple. The brochure describes what happened. "While this young woman and older man had not previously met in this life, there occurred what can only be termed an explosion of recognition between them. Immediately she knew that at last she had found her way home and what her life work was to be. With humble devotion she performed all the tasks, many laborious and menial, which his care and work required, while absorbing and digesting into her spiritual being the luminous and transcendent teachings which he revealed to her."

In 1954 Dr. Case "was summoned to another state of consciousness" and Ann Davies was given charge of the organization, supposedly continuing a direct chain of command that goes back way before the Egyptians. (The only other person that can make that statement is the Dalai Lama.)

The Builders of the Adytum (from the Greek word meaning Holy of Holies) is a church but more it is a correspondence school. There are five months of basic instruction dealing with "occult psychology" and the "Tarot Keys" and then, if the teachers feel you have mastered the basics, you are allowed to go into the higher studies. They promise to give you "methods and information that have been kept secret for centuries." The curriculum includes "the art of healing and balancing the personality by the use of color and sound, methods of Tarot interpretation that lead to the attainment of higher consciousness, explanation of the ancient diagram called the Tree of Life, which is a Key Symbol to the understanding of the mysteries of man, nature, and the universe . . ."

The base for all this knowledge is the ancient, mysterious, often mentioned but little understood Holy Qabalah. And the Tarot Keys they speak of are not just the cards, but a "complete record in picture form of the secrets of the ancients."

Membership is made after completing a brief questionnaire and sending "dues-contributions" of four dollars a month. Donations are accepted and are tax-deductible. From what others have told me and from their literature (in spite of the florid prose) it is a sincere teaching organization with frills and fancy merchandising eliminated. They promise to answer each student's questions personally and immediately.

The fourth educational academy of the occult in Los Angeles is the E.S.P. Laboratory. There is no talk of Holy Masters and secrets of the cosmic here, but straightforward answers in a college dormitory atmosphere. Their literature is decorated with a rotund little ghost who invites you to come and have "fun and games at the Lab."

Al G. Manning, a former Spiritualist minister, founded the lab in 1966. He had been a psychic for as long as he could remember and had used his psychic abilities and his knowledge of basic metaphysics to erase his migraine headaches, improve his eyesight and remove his ulcers. Doing research for a book he found that he had a great deal of unused material. He knew that if he could get this information into the hands of people in small towns and farms he would be able to reach a bigger audience than he ever had when he was trying to form a regular church congregation. So the E.S.P. Lab was born.

Al Manning is not the ordinary idea of a minister. He peppers his remarks with slang and makes himself the butt of his own jokes. While he admits to being guided by a spirit called Professor Reinhardt (and at times possessed by him) there are no esoteric wanderings about "astral knowledge" and "mantles being passed on." Al Manning knows that today's moderns want to develop their psychic abilities in a modern manner. And that's what he gives them.

His mail-order courses begin with twenty lessons called "A New Light of Help for You." In it he shows how to meditate and use various colors of light for various personal gains, be they spiritual or material. Another course runs twenty-two lessons and deals with "Practical Modern Occultism," taking in how to see your aura, astral projection, séances, yoga and leading the triumphant life. One of his more popular courses is "Practical White Magic and Witchcraft" in twenty-six lessons. In it the student learns everything from how to exorcise to how to make money. He also sells a series of tapes on how to increase income, attract the perfect mate, attract new friends, heal insecurity and eliminate negative conditions. Personally, Al will go into trance and give you a reading on tape for twenty dollars or have Professor Reinhardt possess him and give you a look at your past lives (on tape) for fifty. And of course there are all sorts of things like crosses, incense, perfumed oils, herbs and pendulums that you can also purchase.

While the first year of the school was strictly mail-order, Al opened the second year to classroom studies at his Santa Monica Boulevard offices. The classes were experimental sessions investigating ESP and other phenomena. Now he teaches all the above courses to groups of twenty students and has started classes in Alpha-ray studies and work with the pyramidal form not unlike the experiments currently being done by the Soviets in their laboratories.

Does it work? Well, new students keep signing up and classes are being expanded while letters from satisfied students across the nation ("one problem after another is being resolved in the most beautiful and harmonious way possible"—"every week I see some improvement in myself"—"my savings and checking accounts have increased") keep pouring in. "This is a new age," says Al Manning. "I want to give it meaning."

For high-minded critics who claim that nobody is really *studying* the psychic world from a scientific point of view, let me introduce

Dr. Thelma Moss, a serious and dedicated psychologist and parapsychologist who is teaching and researching the occult at the University of California in Los Angeles. (Her friend and medical doctor Shafica Karagulla is also doing impressive research in this field. Her book *Breakthrough to Creativity* should be on everyone's "must" list.)

Dr. Moss was born in Connecticut in the 1920's and for two decades appeared as an actress in theater, motion pictures and television. She was with Ethel Barrymore in *The Corn Is Green,* with the Lunts in *The Seagull* and with Alec Guinness in *The Detective.* She married producer Paul Moss and they worked together presenting plays and films that she had written.

But in 1954 Paul Moss died and Thelma suffered such deep personal grief that she sought professional therapeutic help. It was during this period that she took a look at her life and decided on a change. She enrolled in UCLA and in 1960 obtained her bachelor degree in psychology and entered the UCLA graduate school of psychology to work toward her doctorate. She was awarded it in 1966 and immediately was asked to join the staff as medical psychologist and assistant professor at the Institute.

Dr. Moss has always been interested in psychic phenomena. Her personal therapy after the death of her husband and her freedom in the university laboratories made her turn to serious investigative work in this field.

In a rare interview granted to *Psychic* magazine (one of the top publications in the occult field, no doubt about it) Dr. Moss told of her life and her experiments. As the questions and answers were the very ones I would like to have obtained, a brief summary of the interview here presented with the permission of *Psychic* follows:

Dr. Moss thinks that psychic phenomena have become popular for two basic reasons—which don't seem to have anything in common. One is the drug culture we are living in. This started about ten years ago when the young people—where new ideas usually come from anyway—became familiar with the psychedelic drugs. They began to learn, from either first-hand or friends' experiences, about isolated, brief incidences of something that might have been telepathy, clairvoyance, traveling out of the body, expanded awareness—something definitely not in the normal range of consciousness.

Apparently this turned them on—these personal psychic experiences they report. The great majority of which have not been checked out and may be just delusionary material. However there is some documented evidence of psychic phenomena during therapeutic psychedelic drug experiences, some very convincing data and she has a strong hunch that psychedelia may be one of the contributing factors that make ESP and parapsychology popular and part of the scene today.

Dr. Moss thinks the other reason, oddly enough, is electronics, which brings in the older generation, embracing those people who started working about twenty-five years ago with computers, transistors and the like. She said some of these scientists have discovered they can get very peculiar phenomena when they are working with certain kinds of advanced equipment. And they are now open to the idea that maybe we can dispense with instrumentation—the elaborate kinds of instrumentation that they use—to get some kinds of communication. In fact, about eight years ago, she reported, two men interested in radio and electronic communications claimed they had discovered in the human muscle, with the electromyograph, frequencies which are used to transmit transatlantic radio messages. Perhaps this has something to do with people getting telepathic messages over long distances, although she doesn't know.

"Anyway," she said, "it may be that the human body has transmitters and receivers of such a delicate nature that can't be detected with the fairly primitive equipment we are now using."

In answering *Psychic's* question about the man-in-the-streets interest, Dr. Moss pointed out that there has been evidence brought forward by doctors and scientists in the laboratory which indicates some form of survival and that the average person may well have had one or two experiences in his life that he couldn't explain logically. She cited the Symposium of E.S.P. held at UCLA in June of 1966 as a good example, which 900 people attended. At the end of the symposium the question was asked: "How many of you have had what you consider a psychic experience?" About three quarters of the people raised their hands. Apparently psychic phenomena are not *that* unusual, yet they are unusual in the sense that in fifty years of living, there may be only one or two experiences that might fit into the category. And if they only occur one or twice, the impact may fade and the incident may be relegated to "coincidence" or "illusion."

When asked if she thought this interest in the occult to be a fad, Dr. Moss said, "For most people, yes I do." She feels that people first find something that looks fascinating and mysterious, so they try to hear what others have to say about it. And often they find themselves a dull lecture about statistics in card guessing or other laboratory experiments. But that is not satisfying. People are romantic, she contends, and they want excitement, adventure. So they gravitate toward more entertaining phenomena—séances, table tapping, Ouija boards, Tarot cards, crystal balls. "That's what's happening, I'm afraid, in the high schools and colleges. Cults are beginning to spring up—and cults are usually short-lived fads," Dr. Moss said.

She also feels these cults can be dangerous and that black magic and witchcraft are very tricky and unpleasant fields to mess around in. Even the Ouija board can be harmful, because most people don't realize that it can lead to a dissociation, and even a serious split in the personality.

Talking about the popularity of the field at the scientific and academic levels, Dr. Moss emphasized if you would have asked her that question five years ago, she would have said "What popularity, question mark, exclamation point." But in the past two years, she contends, the amount of interest academically has rocketed in the sense that it is now accepted at some campuses; at the University of California there are accredited courses offered. She taught a two-unit course in parapsychology one session at the graduate level. The enrollment was closed at 420 students, three weeks *before* the class started.

"Despite this interest, though, you still can't get a degree in parapsychology, which is too bad, because I receive a small but constant stream of letters from people asking where they can get a degree in parapsychology. The answer is: nowhere in the U.S. today," she said.

Dr. Moss thinks more scientists are becoming interested in the field probably for purely practical reasons. The Soviet Union has displayed notable interest in the field and a few of their top scientists, such as I. M. Kogan, who heads the Bio-Communications Institute in Moscow, are doing serious research. Kogan's highly controlled experimental laboratory work explores telepathy over short and long distances.

She pointed out that the Soviet Union is a country dedicated to a materialistic philosophy, which certainly does not encourage religion. So when the Soviets talk in terms of telepathy, it is in terms of another method of communication between people on various parts of the earth—or out in space. They once publicly stated that they were working on telepathy because they hope to train their cosmonauts to keep in contact with the earth in case of an electronic failure during space flight.

So Kogan's work, she thinks, is very good. It is in the area of trying to find out if telepathy can be useful over long distances. He seems to think there is communication, but that it falls off as a result of the distance factor. Karlis Osis at the American Society for Psychical Research has come to the same conclusion with his long-distance experiments. "I guess I'm a lonely voice," she said, "I found in the one successful long-distance study I did between Los Angeles, New York and Sussex, England, that there was no falling off with distance. So telepathy perhaps can be of practical interest. One might envision that form of communications as an eventual substitute for radio or television or the telephone."

When asked what her colleagues and friends think about her interest in psychic phenomena Dr. Moss mused, "At first they thought I was crazy." When she was getting her degree, the head of the psychology department once stopped her and asked incredulously, "You really go for this ESP stuff?" and she answered "Yes, I really do." After that, every time he'd pass her in the halls he'd ask, "Well, how am I today?" Good-natured joshing, then. But now, when the psychology department gets calls pertaining to extrasensory perception, they are kind enough to refer them to her; which is either a compliment or a means of getting the whole thing off their backs—or both.

Currently in her laboratory she does a basic experiment which she designed: a subject in an isolation booth is shown slides that are supposed to have a particular kind of emotional impact—Disneyland, a riot, nude girls, an assassination—each accompanied by appropriate sound effects. One such combination of slides is called an "emotional Episode," to which the subject is asked to give his reactions. He is the "transmitter."

In another room, seventy-five feet away, another person acting as the "receiver" is asked to lie down, relax and report whatever comes to mind. After he's finished talking, he is shown two slides— one of which has been shown the transmitter—and is asked to choose the one which the transmitter has seen. He has a fifty-fifty chance of guessing the correct one, but if his selections continue to be correct, he may eventually score nineteen hits out of twenty-five trials—which is well beyond chance expectation. She has had several people who have accomplished this.

This is baffling to her, since some people give very accurate descriptions of an episode which has *not yet* been shown—or had been shown earlier. She calls that displacement. It happens over and over again, and parapsychologists don't know how to control it. The subjects don't know when they're doing it. When it happens repeatedly, it's very frustrating, because the investigators know that they're getting *something*. Apparently the dimension of time displacement, which is so variable, confuses the experiment.

Dr. Moss thinks she has had encouraging results with ESP experiments. She and others are trying to find out what laws in telepathic communications are at work, and they have discovered a few principles—principles similar to those Dr. Rhine has postulated based on his card guessing experiments.

They have also learned that information received through this process is very condensed, distorted and symbolic. For example, one of the sequences that she shows in her experiment is a series of *Playboy* girls—lightly clad—with background music that's loud, clangy and sexy. But almost never do the receivers report impressions of naked women. Mostly they'll say something symbolic. Her favorite example is what one psychology student reported. He said, "This time, the only thing I get is an open field with a lot of bunnies running around." The distortion there is quite obvious, since *Playboy* girls are often called bunnies.

When asked by *Psychic* what she thought were the philosophic implications of psychic phenomena, she said she thinks that when all the controversies and doubts are laid to rest and people are able to accept it, man is going to have to reconsider our ideas of time and space which means that the mind—whatever the mind is, and she's convinced it isn't just a function of the brain—can probably travel through time in ways that were hinted at by Einstein.

Man will also have to reconsider most seriously the whole realm of religious experience. If the mind does exist apart from the body in the sense that it can travel, then perhaps it can exist after the body ceases to exist, which implies a soul survives death. This then brings man into the whole area, the controversial one few scientists wish to discuss, of survival after death.

"Almost all the great religions postulate the existence of life after death," she added, "and usually those religions evolved from remarkable people who lived in various countries at various times throughout history—independently arriving at the concept of survival.

"This would seem to support Jung's idea of a universal unconscious. Should this collective phenomenon—belief in survival after death—prove to be a delusion, it would mean that a good many persons, at different times in history, suffered the same delusion. Which in itself is a fascinating thing to ponder," she emphasized.

Dr. Moss thinks the great importance of the parapsychological field is the potential it suggests, in terms of other dimensions—rather than studies of successful card guessing. In other words, she doesn't believe we should just concentrate on the scientific, laboratory experiments which many seem to be doing. Certainly science is necessary along the way, but eventually, too, science can only be a means of finding truth.

"And here's another paradox," she concluded in the *Psychic* magazine interview, "apparently truth can only be found within one's Self. After all, Einstein's laboratory was entirely in his head, wasn't it?"

The Movie Stars! God bless 'em. What would Hollywood be without them and where would they be without their astrologers, mediums, Tarot readers and fortune-tellers?

For years the bright names of Hollywood's cinema luminaries have made a nice living for psychics and mystics. Even back in the early days such people as Buster Keaton, Fatty Arbuckle, Wallace Beery and Jean Harlow made regular visits to their mediums. While the rest of the country pooh-poohed it, all the mortal stars checked with the heavenly stars to find out when they should sign a contract, start a picture, take a trip, make a marriage, make a divorce or stay home with the door shut. It is said that Mary Pickford had a vision of what Los Angeles would look like in fifty years, so she started buying up vacant land in what was then the outskirts of town. Today those outskirts are vital commercial areas and Miss Pickford has made a fortune from her vision.

Robert Cummings calls himself an "astrological hypochondriac" and doesn't make an important move until Carroll Righter has figured it out first. When he married his secretary in Las Vegas in March 1971 the ceremony was set for exactly 11:34—the time *two* astrologers assured him would be most propitious. It was a small group with very few friends attending but both astrologers were there.

Beatrice Lillie is certain she has a personal poltergeist who travels with her and plays backstage tricks like sewing up costumes so she can't get into them, hiding props so she has to go on without them and undoing her neatly coiffed stage wigs.

Tough leading man Rod Taylor admitted in an interview that he is sure he has lived many times before. Once when visiting the ruins of Pompeii (with then fiancée Anita Ekberg) *he* pointed out the sights to the *guide*. He'd never been there before but he knew exactly how everything had been. Then when they visited the Forum he gave a brief history of the place and began to cry. "It was the gushy, teary kind. I just knew I had lived there before. Anita stood there laughing."

Raymond Massey lived in a house in New York that was periodically invaded by mice. They would come scurrying from a fine brownstone directly across the street and into his cellar. A few days after it happened for the first time a wealthy woman living in the house committed suicide. When her family moved out, the mice returned. Then they dashed across into the Massey basement again. A few days later the new owner of the house was killed in an airplane accident. As the house remained vacant, the Masseys were nervous when the mice moved out on them. They waited for tragedy to strike. It did. Their furnace blew up.

Lovely Lisa Todd (Miss Sunshine Cornsilk on "Hee Haw") believes in chanting "Namu-Myoho-Renge-Kyo," the sacred liturgy of a Buddhist sect known as Nichiren Shoshu. For at least one hour a day she sits before a scroll known as Gohonzon and chants in Chinese and Sanskrit. "I love chanting because it works," she told *TV Guide*. "I mean you could chant to lose weight. Before I was chanting I was stone broke, in debt up to my ears. Now I make over $1,000 a week and I'm just beginning. I ask myself, why me? There are prettier girls with even better figures all over Hollywood. Chanting is really outa sight!"

Liberace believes that the spirit world saved his life. He was near death, years before he became such a success, and saw and heard things that are difficult to describe. Suddenly he was well and suddenly his playing was better than ever. He believes that his music has some special power that reaches out to those who need it most. Once he was playing in a hospital and a girl in an iron lung was suddenly healed. Once, in concert, a man in a wheelchair rose and moved toward him. Healed, Liberace feels, by his music.

Arlene Dahl went to the hospital to have a baby by Cesarian. She insisted that the doctors wait until the stars were in the exact position to give her child a strong positive astrological chart before they delivered the child.

Glenn Ford submitted to hypnosis and like Bridey Murphy discovered he had lived at least twice before. Once in Scotland and the other time in France. When he regressed to the life in Elgin, Scotland, it was in the early 1800's. He talked of teaching "flibberty gibberty" girls to play the piano and then sat down to play Beethoven and Mozart like an expert. Glenn was amazed when he heard the tape. Not because of the thick brogue but because he can't play a single note on the piano. In the previous life, he spoke fluent Parisian French of the 1600's. (He knows a few phrases of the language but can't speak it in this life.) He was an officer in the elite Versailles cavalry and was forced into a duel because of his affair with a married woman. He was killed by the thrust of a saber.

Glenn adds that where he was pierced by that sword he has a birth-mark today. "This birthmark hurts at certain times. It is the same spot where I was stabbed three hundred years ago."

Karen Black, who was so excellent as the unwanted girl in *Five Easy Pieces,* thinks she was an actress in a former life. She believes in reincarnation, astral travel and ESP.

Diahann Carroll once had an experience at a funeral parlor that she can attribute only to "the spirit world."

Young singer-composer Mike Elly has always known he was psychic and has let his spirit guides guide him on his way to the top. He meditates daily and uses the information he receives in his professional and private life. The very talented young man also has the talents of a healer. A friend of his mother had been in an accident and his fingers would not function. The nerves in his lower arm had been cut and badly sewn together. Consequently this arm was weak and thinner than the other. One evening, as this man was having dinner with the Ellys, Mike heard the words: "You can cure him." Gulping and not wanting to be taken for a fool, Mike told what he had heard. The man asked him to try. After working for about an hour, using the laying of hands technique, the man began to move his fingers. Before the evening was over he could open and close his fist for the first time in years. And over a period of weeks his lower arm fleshed out and became whole again.

Larry Vincent is the host of a popular Saturday night movie program called "Fright Night" (KHJ-TV, Los Angeles). He has had several psychic experiences himself but his real pleasure comes in dressing up as the ghoulish "Seymour" and ad-libbing as he shows 1930–50 horror movies. His audiences are dying to be frightened. "I show many, many films. Bad films on voodoo and black magic, but *why* do film producers grind these things out? Why do they sell? Because people really believe these things! They sit in their front rooms and they go, 'Ha! That's ridiculous. You strangle a doll and everybody drops dead. That could never happen.' Yet deep down inside they're thrilled by the possibility of what the mind can do. This knowledge of the psychic and occult will never be lost. It's in our consciousness and it goes back to the dawn of time."

The list could go on indefinitely of stars who believe in or have had their own personal psychic experiences: Pearl Bailey, Ida Lupino, Elke Sommer, Noel Coward, Jackie Gleason, Dave Garroway, Goldie Hawn, Jimmie Rodgers, Marlon Brando, Lucille Ball, J. P. Morgan, Tony Bennett, Gloria Swanson, Zsa Zsa Gabor, etc., etc. Hollywood reporter Dick Kleiner, who has spent years interviewing stage, screen and TV personalities, says that "seventy-five out of every hundred actors have had psychic experiences."

I was fortunate to be allowed to interview one of the most gracious and charming stars in Hollywood. Not only is she beautiful but she is a psychic. Her name: Ann Miller.

She met me in her large Beverly Hills home and we went into the library. Surrounded by books on the occult, astrology, ESP and mediumship she talked for over an hour. I have always been movie crazy and I'm sure I never missed one of Ann Miller's films. I had just returned to New York after fifteen years in Brazil to see that Ann Miller was playing the lead on Broadway in *Mame*. It was the first Broadway ticket I'd purchased all those years and, undoubtedly, one of the greatest experiences in the theater in years. Critics said she was terrific and the ushers (who had seen them all come and go) said she was the best of all the Mames.

Dressed in a pink blouse and black slacks, she started the conversation by telling me of something that had happened just the night before. She had gone into a restaurant with a man who was directing her for the road company of *Hello Dolly*. She had worked with him often but really didn't know too much about him. As they were seated at the table she heard a voice: "Linda, Linda, Linda." Then: "Ann, this is Linda. Linda. Tell Bill I am here. Tell him. Ask him about me. He was my friend. Ask him. Linda. Linda. Linda."

"Bill," she said, "Linda Darnell is here with us."

"What? What are you saying? Linda Darnell is dead," he replied.

"I know that, in fact I gave her her last blood transfusion. But she is here and she says you were her friend and that you will be very good for me."

He admitted that he had been a friend of Miss Darnell's and had once saved her life. Ann and Linda had also been excellent friends, almost growing up together on the Hollywood studio lots.

"Bill, she tells me that you've got to watch your heart or you're going to die. She says you've gone to a doctor and he's told you to cut down on cigarettes but you haven't done it. Why?"

He gasped and admitted that he'd been to a doctor just a week before to investigate a pain around his heart. The doctor had indeed told him to cut out smoking.

"Today when he came to rehearsals of *Dolly* he didn't smoke at at all. Not once. I guess it really scared the pooh out of him."

"But didn't it scare you too?" I asked.

"Oh no, these things have come to me all my life. I tried to sell Merv Griffin on it, when I did his show, but while he believes, he still doesn't quite *believe,* if you know what I mean. I told him that I can't turn it on the way the professional mediums do, but all of a sudden something will come to me and I just *know, I know.*"

"Has this ability ever warned you about impending disasters?"

"Yes it has. I knew that my mother was going to fall and hurt herself. I was married and living in Dallas then and I'd call my mother here in Hollywood every day. I'd say, 'Mother, be careful. You're going to take a bad fall unless you're careful.' And then she did fall and hurt her leg in six places and the shock brought on a heart attack.

"This ability, as you call it, has been in my family for generations. I believe it can be inherited. My great-grandmother was a powerful medium and so was my grandmother. I was named for that grandmother, Lucille, and she predicted that one of her grandchildren would inherit the forces she had around her. I guess I was that one."

"When did you first sense that you had these abilities?" I asked

"I was four years old and I was playing with my dolls in the center of the living room. I heard a voice call: Lucille. Lucille. I turned around, thinking it was my mother or father but the room was empty. Then I heard it again: Lucille. As I looked to see where the voice was coming from it said: You will hear me often. And it has been with me all my life."

"Do you think that these forces can do evil as well as good?"

"Oh, I know they can! I firmly believe that there is such a thing as the 'evil eye' or whatever you want to call it. Knowledge of it has been around too long to doubt it. It's even mentioned in the Bible. I knew a woman here in Hollywood who was a famous columnist. She'd dead now but that woman practiced witchcraft. I have seen her literally *destroy* lives around her."

"Did she destroy them through witchcraft or by being bitchy in her columns?"

"Oh no, not by being bitchy, that was one thing she never was. She made a big thing out of only writing nice things about people. But I know the woman used power of the mind, what I would call 'the black power.' She turned it on people. She turned it on me. She had a lot to do with the breakup of two of my marriages. One side of her was lovely and beautiful and made a big thing out of going to church. The other side of her was dark and horrible and she was like a witch out to deliberately destroy other people's lives. No one could comprehend that this evil force could possibly be coming from this woman. I can't describe her by calling her two-faced. Maybe it would be better to say she had two souls. Her evil force was stronger than her good force and in the end it destroyed her. She died a lonely, bitter old woman."

"Did you ever face her with this accusation?" I asked. "After destroying two of your marriages did you ever tell her that you knew what she had done?"

"Yes."

"And what did she do?"

"She just laughed."

Years ago when Ann Miller was deeply troubled and needed help she would turn to a Ouija board, but the planchette moved so rapidly that she wasn't able to copy it all down. Finally the board told her to take a newspaper, book or a magazine and place her finger on the page. Then it would move the finger and she would get complete words rather than just letters. She has done this ever since, getting sentences and paragraphs that guide her.

"I use only the sports page of a newspaper now, because it is not filled with evil like murders and wars and rapes. I just don't get the message when I use the front page that's covered with bombings and politics and catastrophes. I converse with this entity and he helps me to help myself. He has asked me not to give his name, but I think I know who he is.

"I never do this unless I really need help. I wouldn't think of doing it as amusement for others or for some simple problem that my own common sense can answer. It has helped me in my career, it's given me strength after the breakups of my marriages (which were like three deaths to me) and it helps me just knowing that I have someone who really cares what happens."

"But, Miss Miller," I said. "Movie stars aren't supposed to have heartaches and problems. They are supposed to lead a marvelous life filled with cocktail parties, photographers and autograph hounds."

She laughed, but it was a sad laugh. "We do have that side and I'm afraid too many stars think that's the only side. But their personal lives can be just as tragic as any bricklayer or housewife or college student. Away from the lights and the publicity smiles we are mortals. Too, too mortal."

Ann Miller would never turn her psychic talents on for money. She believes that when a medium gets too greedy he gradually loses his abilities. Or that a serious illness can diminish the forces. She is also afraid of ending up alone and she is sure that mediums "live lonely lives. They stand alone. They are not like other people and they are quite lonely."

What does she believe in? This beautiful, internationally known actress-dancer-singer? Does she believe in the same things you and I believe in?

"I believe in God. I don't go to church but I have my own private church up here in my mind. I pray to God and to the Virgin Mary and at times to the entity who guides me. I believe in good forces and bad forces and that if you call upon the good forces they will come and help you. I believe in reincarnation. I know for a fact that there is life after death, because I've had departed loved ones come back and talk to me. I don't believe that evil should be praised or used as a base for a religion, as that dangerous Anton LaVey is doing in his San Francisco Church of Satan. I believe he should be stopped. He has already ruined too many lives.

"Maybe if I practiced I could learn to turn this on and get things regularly for people, but I don't want to do it. I don't want to abuse it and then have it leave me. If something comes through to me and it's a message that will help someone, then I'll give them that message. That's the least I can do.

"Oh yes. I believe in love. I believe that men should love one another. I believe that the understanding of love—real love— could solve all our problems. It sounds simple but God made things simple. It's man that has complicated them."

And now, would you believe . . . . . Mae West?

Talk about childhood crushes! And here I was sitting in her apartment waiting for her to make her appearance. The living room is a magnificent setting for a movie straight out of the 1930's. The furniture is French provincial glazed in white and highlighted by gold borders and curlicues. There is a white and gold piano in one corner that is graced by a vase of artificial white flowers and a white plaster nude statue of Miss West. The walls are a soft neutral color, as are the draperies that outline the white curtains that are always closed. An enormous three-sectioned mirror is on one wall and a small white and gold coffee table is covered with photographs of Miss West in all sorts of poses from all sorts of movies. And everywhere, baskets and bowers of artificial flowers.

The Puerto Rican butler told me to sit on the white, soft sofa and that Miss West would sit in a white, soft chair beside the sofa. I sat on the edge, fidgeting with my tie and hoping my hair was combed. I glanced at my watch to make sure I was on time (the appointment was made for 3:00 P.M. sharp) and then down to see if my shoes were still shining from the workout they had received just minutes before entering the lobby of her Hollywood apartment house. I felt like a teen-ager on his first date. I was hoping she would show up but at the same time thinking maybe I should go away. After all, it isn't every day that a man gets to meet Mae West! I made a mental note to tell my grandchildren all about it—if I ever get married and have any.

It seemed like an awfully long time and I remembered the fantastic build-up in *Diamond Lil* where they talk about Mae for at least fifteen minutes before she comes sauntering on stage. I had seen her farewell appearance in this play back in the early fifties in New York. They had reduced the seats for the last week to just seventy-five cents in the upper balcony. It was amazing to see the sidewalk in front of the theater cluttered with Bowery bums cadging coins not for a shot of booze but for a chance to see Mae. They packed the rafters and she played every laugh line to them. She had been wonderful.

And suddenly there she was, sauntering out of a side door and walking in that Mae West Walk toward me. "Well hello there, honey," she said. "Nice t' see ya again!"

I had met her, briefly, a few days before, when I'd been invited to witness her friend and psychic-confident Richard Ireland read billets in the lobby-salon of her apartment building. Ireland is a truly gifted psychic. I had watched him on television as the cameras tried to catch him at some hanky-panky while his eyes were triple blindfolded and stuck down with adhesive tape. Then that night I sat in the third row (about six feet from him) and observed him carefully. There was no way he could have been anything but genuine that night.

Mae had been there that night too, wearing a blue silk gown clear to the floor and a heart-shaped diamond ring studded with smaller diamonds. I introduced myself and told her I'd written asking for an appointment. "Fine," she said (groaned? moaned?), "when I get your letter, I'll call ya!" The call came, thanks to James and Brenda Crenshaw, and now here she was, sitting across from me. Just the two of us. All alone. Except for the butler, who kept peering in from, and walking around in the next room.

She was shorter than I'd expected. Her blond hair hung straight down the way it did in *Myra Breckenridge* and her small eyes were accented by large, false lashes. She was modestly painted, with just a little lipstick and some powder. The lines I had expected to see were just not there.

Even though it was three in the afternoon she was wearing a raspberry negligee that went down to the floor and ended in a big ruffle. She wore a white open-lace wrapper over it that also went to the floor. The low cut of the negligee proved beyond a doubt that the famous Mae West curves were still all there and in the right places.

We talked about me for a while. She was fascinated that I had been in Brazil and had managed to clear myself of the evil eye. She insisted that I tell her how I did it, as she is afraid that people who can do good for her can also turn against her if they choose. Then I got her started talking about herself. Not a very difficult thing to do.

"I have always been psychic," she said. "Ya know, get those little things in my head that other little girls didn't get. I didn't know what they were, didn't know where they came from. For years I managed ta push 'em aside, not use 'em. They had been tryin' ta help me for years, but I wouldn't take advantage of their offer. Then a funny thing happened. It showed me just how much power the mind really has.

"It was in the thirties and I was supposed ta make another picture. I was tired and didn't feel like doin' the whole thing m'self. So I said ta the owner of the studio, 'Look, you got lotsa good writers layin' around here doin' nothin'. Get 'em ta write me a script. They know my personality and my character. I'm too tired ta write another one.' I'd been writin' all my own pictures since I first came ta Hollywood in 1932. Before that I'd been writin' all my own stage plays too. I wrote *Sex* in 1926 and they put me in Welfare Island Prison for ten days. I had a nice rest there—wrote two articles for magazines—and the warden used ta take me out for a ride in his car at night. I got two days off for good behavior.

"Anyway, I was tired and the studio put two of their best guys workin' on a script for me. It was ta be a Gay Nineties thing and took place in Paris. That's in France. The studio had all the sets built and I had all my clothes made. Even though we didn't have a final script I knew what kind of picture I wanted to do.

"So I'm sittin' in my dressin' room one afternoon when in comes these two writers with the producer and the director. They gave me the script and I read it. Then they said: 'What do ya think of it?' I said: 'It's a good script but it ain't for me. This isn't me! There's not a laugh line in here! My audience expects ta laugh when they see me. They don't pay their money for Mae West ta be reminded of all the troubles they got waitin' for 'em at home. I've got ta respect my fans, because my fans respect me!' So the studio owner got very upset and started wringin' his hands and carryin' on, because after all, honey, he'd gone and built those sets and made all those clothes.

"So just then in comes the guy who'd been hired to write the music for the picture. He said he had two songs he wanted me ta hear. Well, the bosses din't want ta hear no songs at that point, but the guy was nice and I didn't want ta hurt his feelings, so I invited him to come on in and play 'em on my piano. Well, the first song was a real drag and the second was okay but it had lyrics like 'Fifi if you are nice to me; then you will see; what Fifi . . .' etc. Ya get the idea, don't ya?

"Well, I couldn't stop ta think about his lyrics, because all I could think about was, my God, I had ta go home and write a complete script in just two weeks! Me who wanted ta take it easy now had ta start hustling my . . . Anyway, rather than have ta talk ta those guys again, I said, 'That last number was kinda cute. Play it again, but don't sing the words. Just let me hear the music.'

"And this is where the funny thing came in. As he started to play I just mentally blanked out. I sat there listenin' but I really didn't hear his music at all. When he was finished, I said ta the producer and the director, who were tearin' at their hair, 'That's a great song. We'll use it in the picture.' The others thought I'd gone nuts. 'What picture? Are you out of your mind?' they shouted at me. 'Relax, boys,' I said. 'I just got your story!' "

In the fifty-four seconds that it took for the musician to play his song, Mae West had received the *entire script* in her mind. It had come in neatly and completely with a beginning, a middle and an end. It took her fifteen minutes to explain the idea to the producer and director and forty-five minutes for her to dictate it to two secretaries. Yet it had taken her only fifty-four seconds to get it. This film was *Every Day's a Holiday* and was "a great hit. My fans loved it."

In 1941 she was at the peak of her career but she still felt "somethin' was missin'." She read books on philosophy and tried several churches. She had gone through Tarot cards and fortune-tellers. "I knew there was somethin' there but I wanted *proof*. I used ta go

ta Sunday school and get headaches. It was always hard for me ta
believe anything, 'cause nothin' could be *proven*."

Then she was introduced to a Spiritualist medium named Reverend
Kelly. She brought in a few friends and had him come up to her
apartment. They put a blindfold on him—"pulled it so tight I thought
it would cut his head in two"—and gave him their questions to be
read. He answered them without even taking them from the sealed
envelopes. Mae asked him about the war and was told: "In three
months we will have a surprise attack in Honolulu by Mr. Jap.
The war will be won by America and England. Roosevelt will run
for a fourth term but he will not live to see it end." And he told
Mae some things of her personal life which she considers "absolutely
astounding."

So it was natural that this strong-willed woman, who had everything but was still searching, would ask Kelly for advice. He told
her she had psychic abilities and should develop them. He gave her
the name of a medium who would teach her what she needed to
know.

"So I called this woman over ta my apartment and told her:
'Look, honey, I want you ta teach me ta develop my psychic
abilities. I'll pay ya X amount of dollars but ya gotta teach me fast.
I ain't got all year, ya know. I got just six weeks until I start workin'
on another picture and when I'm workin' on a picture I ain't got
time for spirits or anythin' else."

The medium protested that she couldn't guarantee results that
quickly, but Mae was persistent. She came to the West apartment
every day.

"We took one of my rooms and put black curtains over the windows. Ya gotta have it dark when ya do these things at first. If not,
your mind starts lookin' around and seein' things like flowers and
things like that. The idea was for me ta make my mind quiet. And
ya know with *my* mind that ain't easy!"

The first few days nothing happened but Mae didn't get discouraged. Then she was able to meditate a full minute, and a few
days later the time was increased to five minutes. Finally she says
that she was able to make her mind a blank for a full fifteen minutes. The medium was delighted. So was Mae.

"Then one morning I wake up and I hear a little voice. It said: 'Good morning, dearie. Good morning, dearie.' It was coming from inside out rather than from outside in, if ya know what I mean. So in spite of the hour I grabbed the phone (it was noon) and called the medium. I told her what had happened. She was happy. She said that the voice belonged to a small spirit called Juliet and that she always came when people were makin' progress.

"A few mornings later I wake up and hear this man's voice comin' out of my belly! It was a rich, beautiful voice and it was talkin' and sayin' things with thees, thems and thous. Things like 'when thy leaves from thou trees' and so on. It went on for fifteen minutes but I don't remember a thing it said, I was so surprised ta hear it. So again I called the medium and told her what had happened. She told *me* that the voice was comin' from my solar plexus. I told her it was from my belly, but later I looked it up and found it was the same thing. She asked me who this voice was and I said I didn't know. So I picked up the dictionary and went ta work." (As long as she can recall, Mae has used a dictionary to solve her problems. She will concentrate on the question, then open the dictionary at random and run her finger down the page. When her finger stops, there is her answer.) "So the finger stopped on the word 'clergyman.' I knew the guy must be an old-fashioned preacher.

"Then a few mornings later I was awakened and there was a man standin' beside my bed! I wanted ta scream but decided to wait awhile and see what he had in mind, when another man appeared. Then another and another until there was a whole bunch of 'em around my bed. They were all wearin' fancy costumes. You know, big hats with plumes in 'em and like that. Then I looked up and there, right over my bed and lookin' down at me was a circle of faces. All men's faces."

"Only men?" I asked.

She drew her lace wrapper across her bosom. "Of *course* there were only men! Whadda ya think? They hung around for about half an hour, making sounds and tryin' ta communicate with me. The next night the same thing and the next night and the next night.

"Finally I had ta put a stop ta it. I said, 'Look, you guys! I 'preciate you hangin' around my bed like this but I gotta get some sleep. I'm workin' on a picture and you guys are disturbin' my rest. It's not that I don't believe in you or trust you, 'cause I do. It's just that all you guys are too much for me every night. Gimmie a break. Go away and let me sleep."

So they went away and never came back. But it doesn't bother Mae that they're gone, for she knows she can bring them back anytime she wishes. Her astrological sign is Taurus and so she had to prove to herself the existence of the spirit world. Once she proved it, she didn't need it any more.

Now she has Richard Ireland to help her with her future. He was introduced to her by the late Reverend Kelly. It was Ireland that took Mae out of semi-retirement when he told her she was going to make two films. In the first one he saw her in a scene where the curtain was going up and down.

"It sounded more like a stage play ta me and I didn't want ta go back on the stage. But he insisted it was a picture. And sure enough there was a set on *Myra Breckenridge* that was exactly like his description!"

And the second film he saw coming up?

"That must be *Diamond Lil*. I'm goin' ta do it again, but this time with music and in color. I also want ta do my homosexual play *The Drag* into a movie. I've got a part in it that would make a *star* out of Rex Reed!"

We talked about other stars and the occult for another hour or so. Her sister Beverly came in and I was told Beverly is also psychic. She can read auras the way some people read minds. She gave up her own career in show business to help sister Mae with hers.

When the interview was over I blew Miss West a kiss and floated out onto the street. As I walked along it felt as if my feet weren't touching the sidewalk. Other people—lesser mortals—passed me and didn't even look at me. What was wrong with them, I wondered. Didn't they realize that *I* had just spent three hours with *Mae West*?

There are other cities in Southern California aside from Los Angeles, although many Angelenos will argue to the contrary. They will claim there are other "groupings of human beings" but no other "city."

On the map something called the Los Angeles District stretches out to engulf dozens of small towns. Years ago (and not too many at that) these were separate communities with their own plans and aspirations. Today these towns have been reduced to nothing more than signs leading off the freeway. Los Angeles District engulfs the ocean front from Malibu to Newport Beach (a distance of fifty-five miles), runs north from Long Beach to San Fernando (another fifty miles) and still another fifty miles from San Fernando to Ontario in the south. Now, these towns all have their own mayors and councils and problems. It's just that they no longer have their own personalities.

They do have their psychics and mystics though. And they also have their kooks and their quirks.

In Anaheim a young couple (who insist on anonymity) live in a haunted house. It looks like all the other suburban tract houses in the neighborhood but there is a difference. Theirs has a ghost. The others haven't.

Mr. X (that's the name he wants used) was sitting in his den one night when he saw a reflection in the window. It was of a swarthy bull-necked man wearing a white T-shirt. Mr. X stared at the reflection as the man walked down the hallway headed for the master bedroom. Then he jumped up and ran after the intruder. There was no one there. He and his wife searched the closets, the basement and under the beds but no stranger was to be found.

Then on reconstructing what he had seen for his wife he realized that it was impossible to get a reflection of the hallway on the den window.

A few days later as Mrs. X was unloading a car full of groceries she saw a young, blond man wearing a white T-shirt standing on her front porch. "I wondered what he wanted," she said later, "and was a little annoyed, sure he was trying to sell something and me with all those groceries to put away." She turned to ask him what he was selling and he was gone.

House and car keys have a way of rising and falling from a kitchen shelf all by themselves and a book about reptiles keeps falling from the bookcase onto the floor. The odd part of this is that one of their friends, who gave them this book, was killed by one of his pet boa constrictors. "He had an exceptionally high IQ," Mrs. X says, "and if anybody could come through from the other world, he could."

Fred Kimball talks to animals. Yes, and they talk back to him. They call him things that he, in turn, tells their owners. If it all sounds strange, just relax. It's all part of the Psychic State.

I first saw Mr. Kimball at a seminar for psychics in San Jose, California. A gentleman came onto the stage with a large black Doberman pinscher. The animal looked at Kimball and Kimball looked at him. Then his mouth began to move quickly (Kimball's, not the dog's) and he asked the owner, "Have you just moved to a smaller home? Your dog says he used to have a lot of room to run and play." The man said they had recently moved from a ranch to a small tract home in a San Jose suburb. "He says he doesn't like your new house, because it's dull and colorless." The owner protested that he had just painted it tan with dark brown trim, then paused and agreed that to a dog it would be "colorless." Kimball also asked the owner why he had stopped serving the dog those delicious meals of meat and cereal. The owner said that since they had moved from the ranch he wasn't able to get fresh meat as cheaply and the supermarkets sold a good dry dog food substitute. "He doesn't think it's so good!" Kimball snorted. "In fact, he's become a very light eater since you moved to the city. He says you took him to a doctor and the man gave him some vitamin shots. He says you wasted your money, because all he really needs is to be put back on his meat diet." The owner, amazed by all this, said that he had taken the dog to a doctor and the dog did get vitamin injections. He also agreed that he had never seen Fred Kimball before.

A lady, stylishly dressed and her hair teased into an elaborate bouffant, came onstage with her Siamese cat. The cat, instead of being nervous (the prerogative of all Siamese), calmed down and stared at Kimball. "She says that there are five children in your house and that she gets more attention from one of them than from all the others. True?" The lady admitted she had five children and the smallest just worshiped the cat. "She also says you have a dog who lives in the back yard and that they are good friends." The woman said this was true. "But there is another dog who comes from a side street who tries to bother your cat every time he sees her. Right?" The woman said she really didn't know. "The cat says you do too know! She says that you chased the dog away only this morning. She says the dog is spotted and limps on his left hind leg!" The woman gasped, admitting that was a perfect description of the dog she'd chased away that morning. Then Kimball looked at her and said, "Your cat likes you but says you are impossible in the morning. She says you come out of the bedroom wearing an old housecoat and your hair in curlers and don't pay any attention to her until you've had a cigarette and at least three cups of coffee. She says the whole household must wait until you've had your coffee before anything gets started." The lady turned beet red. The description was perfectly true. She promised both Kimball and her cat that she would try to be more considerate in the mornings from then on.

This amazing man—who's been proven right almost 100 per cent with his animal conversations—lives in South Gate but works from a mobile home parked in Gardena, California. That's where I interviewed him.

"I've been able to talk to animals since 1944," he said. "It all came about when I was sure I was cracking up and needed the advice of a head shrinker. I was in New York studying psychic phenomena at the same time. I went to the Zoo and there was a lion. So, for some reason, I mentally said to the lion: 'What are you thinking about?' 'Sex!' replied the lion, and looked at me with great annoyance. So I went and asked the keeper why this lion should have sex on his mind. 'He should have!' the man told me, 'the female cat in the next cage is in heat.' So I knew that I could do this. It just came naturally."

Fred Kimball is a psychic's psychic. There is almost nothing he hasn't studied and almost nothing he can't do. Born on a farm near Providence, Rhode Island, he grew up with animals but admits he didn't like them very much. "I didn't communicate with them," he says simply. "Not the way I do today."

He joined the merchant marine and traveled around the globe

for twenty-four years. He used that time to search out yogis in India, voodoo doctors in Rio de Janeiro, a special curative plant in the Amazon, secret teachings in Egypt, Buddhism of North China, Zen in Japan, aboriginal ceremonies in Australia and kahuna witch doctors in the South Seas.

He is a big man in his late sixties with a square chunky face, white hair and blue eyes. His hands make enormous fists and his voice is soft yet gravelly. Maybe it's because he has also been a physical fitness trainer in the Marine Corps, a masseur for athletes and the manager of a string of professional wrestlers. He is also president of several psychic and occult organizations in California as well as being an ordained minister of the Institute of Christian Metaphysics. He has no church and doesn't want one.

The psychic world came crashing in on him in 1943, when he was on a ship stationed in Seattle. He was feeling fine when all of a sudden he fainted. When he came to, he heard a voice telling him to get up and punch one of the men who were trying to help him. Kimball argued with the voice that he didn't have any reason to punch his friend. "Go ahead," repeated the voice, "punch the bastard in the mouth."

That afternoon, in sick bay the voice insisted, "Kill yourself. Jump overboard. No one will miss you. No one will care. Go on! Kill yourself." He admits that he was very naïve in those days, so he got up and went to the police, telling them that someone was trying to kill him. When they heard about the little voice they almost threw him in jail. He went to the psychiatric ward of a local hospital and when he told them about the voice they started glancing at their pile of straitjackets. He even went into a church to talk to a priest but the cleric said there was nothing he could do to save him. He went to the Seattle library, then to the San Francisco library and even to the Los Angeles library looking "for any book that would tell me how to get rid of these voices. To help me rid myself of these hot needles that they were sticking into my body and to make them stop jerking my arms and legs whenever they felt like it." All he could find was one volume on demonology but instead of telling him how doctors freed people from demons it told him how they killed people possessed by demons. Finally he went to New York for treatment. It was there that he started studying the occult with the great Nandor Fodor.

"I have since learned to live with these things and make them work for me," he says now. "It's just like I tell my students. We all have these things that come from our dream mind. If you can bring them into the waking state and function with them, then you're safe. If not, you're psychotic."

Kimball insists that anyone who has ever had a dream has had a clairvoyant picture and anyone who has ever heard a voice in a dream has heard clairaudiently. For him the dream mind is as real and as strong as our conscious mind. "I used to think that this dream mind was a bunch of outsiders. You know, Chinese guides and Hindus and Persians and all that. A bunch of spooks. But it all comes from our own mind and it is a denial of our own soul when we look for some other being to help us out. This is religion. The priests say: 'God does it. Jesus does it. Mary does it. Buddha does it.' It's always somebody *else!* Never do we give ourselves credit for doing it ourselves!"

"But," I interrupted, "the majority of today's mediums still go through this, calling on their guides and believing they are contacting spirits."

"I know they do! And this is childish! This is grammar school knowledge."

"Do you believe in guardian angels and spirits?" I asked.

"Yes, but our guardian angel is nothing more than our own subconscious mind. It is a being that is ever present that extends beyond the self. But we deny it! Religion has told us we are not capable of anything so 'marvelous' as this. So we have to give it a name and it has to put on a disguise. I had all that 'How! Me Big Chief. Big Chief tell you what to do.' I had all that. And I believed it. But now I know better. Who is Big Chief? Me!"

"Most people come to you with . . ." I started to say.

"With every kind of problem that you can have. I had two guys who are actors yesterday. They wanted to work up a program about Black integration and they wanted advice about where to get the money and how to lay out the idea. So I had to dig in and find them answers."

"What do you mean 'dig in'?"

"My consciousness will reach in and hunt into the past, present and future to try to find certain answers."

"Do you go into trance?"

"No. That's shutting the world out too much. That's hundred per cent withdrawal. I just look into their aura." Then he stared at me for a few seconds. "For instance, if you came for a reading, first I'd tell you about the purple light I see around your eye. This means you want to be spiritual on the active side. That you have no desire to be caught in one of these Big Chief things with guides and all that."

I had to admit that was true.

"And I see a small red light, almost iridescent about halfway in. That means your intuition and your insight are about half developed now. If you were an engineer, I'd say you're about halfway to graduation right now." Then he paused and scratched his nose, tilting his head to one side as if listening to someone who was not coming in too clearly. "The purple light of the teacher is *outside* your body. It's almost as if you at one time had been very active imparting information and now you've stopped to gather it and start stockpiling it. The stockpiling . . . of course . . . is because of the book you are researching . . . but . . . why do I get 1962? Why were you imparting more information in the early sixties than you are now?"

I told him that in the 1960's I was working as a newsman in Brazil and it was a daily grind of gathering information and "imparting" it immediately via Telex to New York. It was probably the most hectic "imparting" period of my life. He had hit it right on the head.

"You see what I do?" he asked. "But everybody can do this with the right training. I mean *everybody*. I've only had one failure in the twenty-seven years I've been teaching my technique. I start in with a five-lesson class. No more than that. You don't need any more than that! Why drag it on and on like so many other courses do? It's so simple. Why complicate it? People come to me and ask how they can develop their psychic abilities. Hell, they're already developed. All I can do is teach them how to make them function."

While Fred Kimball does handle all types of human problems, it's the animal clients that have made his name. Hardly a day goes by that someone won't call for an appointment with reference to a dog, cat, horse or even a goldfish. Kimball converses with them all and gives needed information to their owners. He also has a regular radio show where people phone in about their pets. The amazing man wants to know nothing about the animal. All he asks is the name of the owner. Then he goes on to say what kind of an animal it is, the color and the age. "It gives me a headache when it's all over, because I have to tune in on the pet's habits and preferences and find the personality traits that the owner will recognize. I'm seldom wrong. The biggest problem is that animals don't count in human time. For some a winter and a summer are two years. For others only one. It makes things difficult when I have to give accurate time."

"What physically happens to you when you tune in on an animal?" I asked.

"I make an identity. If I get a pain in my leg then I ask about an injury to one of their legs. Maybe my eyes will fill with tears and I know the animal has had a recent sad experience. Then I have to find out what upsets them so. Usually it's the death of another animal or a member of their family. When people separate animals that have been together for a long time they do irreparable harm to both animals. It's like forcibly separating two brothers. People must learn that animals have feelings too. Human beings are not the only ones who mentally suffer."

A few years ago a woman called on Kimball and asked if he would read her pet dog, who had suddenly started going to the bathroom on her living room rug. The dog told the psychic that the woman had just gotten a divorce and had sent the husband away. The dog loved the man and blamed the woman for the whole thing. He told Kimball, "She evacuated him and I am evacuating on the rug." He added that he hated the woman and didn't want to stay with her any longer.

When Kimball questioned the woman she, rather startled, said that she had been divorced and that the dog was really her husband's pet. He advised her to find the dog another home, because he had no intention of changing his behavior.

FOSSU means Foundation of Scientific Spiritual Understanding and is located in Redondo Beach. It's a community on the ocean, under the warm pressure of the wind and sun, which keep it free from the heavy hand of Los Angeles smog. The foundation was founded in 1968 by famed astrologer Doris Chase Doane, her husband, Edward Doane; Mrs. Katalin B. Williams and her husband, Ken. The idea was to provide a vehicle and meeting place for those who were sincere enough to want to study the psychic arts in depth. Or as their prospectus puts it: "to accord them through investigation, research and education the privilege of accepting, evaluating and applying the concepts of Scientific Spiritual Understanding to the betterment of their individual lives and the eternal progression of humanity."

As a non-profit organization it costs you a five-dollar "donation" to join, then another twenty dollars or so to take their courses. Not everyone can be a member. Applicants are screened and those who don't study and progress are simply not permitted to continue to the higher courses. It is one of the few occult instruction centers that diligently supervise each student's progress.

Emphasis is on astrology, so far, with plans for other occult sciences (including astral projection) later on. Each course is seven weeks long and runs from the beginners (where you get "how to do math") to the advanced course III, where "delineation in depth decanates" are analyzed.

There is also a midday daily healing prayer service for anyone who wishes to send in his name and a mid-week meditation seminar. They also get together once a month for a rousing speech-filled and laugh-filled dinner party, where astrological quips and horoscope sallies fly back and forth like balls at a tennis match. Here indeed are astrologers acting like ordinary mortals. It's quite an experience.

President Katalin Williams is an exotic red-haired Hungarian who sounds like one of the Gabor sisters, yet when she speaks you know the lady is not kidding around. "We do not consider astrology merely a predictive art, but a religion as the Ancients practiced it.

A religion in which individuals look with reason and with hope for the cosmic process in immutable universal laws which include Mental Alchemy and Esoteric Logic.

"Astrology is a practical means for solutions for our problems. Everyone has some type of problem to solve, and the process of problem solving keeps the individual alert, alive and seeking for the growth that results in the satisfied feeling of gaining understanding of ourselves in relation to the problem and its solution.

"For the solution of a problem the *individual* must decide how a barrier can be removed, circumvented, reduced or made ineffective, or realize that the barrier is beyond control, such as rain on a picnic day. Such a decision involves the development and implementation of a definite plan of action in accordance with our intelligence and insight as spiritual beings manifesting in and through a material universe."

As I said: only the voice sounds like the Gabors.

Mrs. Gail Hurst, of Lomita, lost a valuable cameo that had been in her family for three generations. Being slightly psychic herself (she has made excellent results with the ESP card test and knows when her faraway sister is physically suffering) she placed an ad in the classified section of the Los Angeles *Times:* "Cameo lost. Authentic Psychometrist Needed. Write Bx. 314, Lomita 90717."

She got answers from across the country. One psychic saw it under the drop of a stage curtain. Another said it was near a red-bound volume of *Mein Kampf* used as a stage prop. A writer from Texas said, "I get the impression of sand palms, the colors red and green. A clock is on a stand like a corner traffic light. Look back from the water for something sticking straight up in the air—but it is silver—a water tower maybe."

Mrs. Hurst lost the cameo while appearing in an amateur play at a building near the beach and next to a large supermarket with a tall sign shaped like a clock and painted silver. But the cameo has yet to be recovered.

He is known as the Sage of Topanga Canyon, that dry and desertlike area just outside the Los Angeles District. He lives in a rather battered house filled with charts, incense, candles, folding chairs and books. His name is Joe Koperski and like all other native Californians he was born somewhere else. Toledo, Ohio, in this case.

Joe is a large man with a soft voice who is somewhere in his late forties. He was in World War II and came to the area in 1951 to get into television. Not as an actor, but as a technician. But he became a medium because several other mediums pointed out his great potential.

"When I started in this field I wanted to be a very good medium and work the various occult arts to help people. Not as a mind reader but as a clairvoyant. The whole pattern has changed so much with me that I am just a channel now.

"I gave up this field three times. The first time I wanted fame and money. This was what I was asking for and I was stopped. Then I got into an emotional pattern with it and had to stop. Then I got into being just a puppet. When that happened, I said, No more, I've had it.

"Then on Easter Sunday, 1968, I was doing a few last astrological charts when Lu Sen came into me. He said he wanted to work through me. I told him if I could be of service that my door would always be open. The following Monday I opened the door and it hasn't closed yet."

"Who is Lu Sen?" I asked.

"My guide, or actually my Master Teacher. He was a Chinese back in the sixth century in his last earthly life. I also have another teacher named Donka who comes through on the healing pattern, but Lu Sen taught me how to heal before Donka was introduced. When either of them come in, I go into trance. The teachings they have brought to me are fused now. Their energy and mine are in a fused condition. I can call on either of them anytime I want them and we are one."

Several high teachers come through Joe Koperski, as several hundred of his clients will attest. All of them have their own names and personalities and each of them vibrates him to their own special frequency. Recently several new and even higher teachers have come through to him.

"They are taking me into a pattern of knowledge that is almost like the beginning of time, like way back in Atlantis. I now have the ability to see auras, not just vertically around your body but horizontally as well. People don't know about this. It's brand new.

"We have twenty-one color bands around us in a horizontal pattern and I can take them to all the steps of your past lives according to your chakra patterns, your psychic centers. Then through the seven chakras I can pick up three color bands which are your positive, negative and neutral aspects. Very often I can read your past lives and see in these horizontal auras when you made your earthly exists and for what purpose. This is all brand new! Nobody has been given this information!"

"And you teach this?" I asked.

"Yes and my students are learning how to do it. I've got about a hundred and forty students who attend four classes a week. Because we do a lot of work with partnerships I like to keep the classes down to about twenty, but sometimes the demand is just too great.

"I teach them to work with the White Energy that comes directly from God and to become in tune with it. As they become in tune they are able to control it and aid and assist others. That's what makes them 'mediums.' In a group of thirty students, I will have fifteen good mediums."

"But can anybody learn to be mediums?" I asked.

"Everyone has psychic ability," he answered. "The degree that you have it depends on circumstances before and while you were being born. The only way to know just how much you have is by practicing and exploring it. But," he warned, "always work with someone who will be true with you. Work with close friends."

The first time anything happened to show him that psychic phenomena existed was back in Toledo in 1947. He was asleep in bed, beside his wife, with his arms crossed over his chest. Suddenly he awoke from the touch of cold, clammy fingers on his hands. He looked into the face of a strange hooded woman who was tugging on his hands trying to make him get out of bed. He says he shook his head violently, telling her he didn't want to go. Then she released her grip and walked slowly toward the door, looking back at him once more before she vanished.

He woke his wife and told her what had happened. He was

sure that his foster mother, living on the other side of town, was dead. It was true. She died just at the time he had been awakened.

He is positive that the hangups we have in this life are a direct result of unresolved problems in past lives. He can look at a person's aura, then go into a different vibratory plane and read everything about them. He takes them back by making the trip himself, unlike Bridey Murphy, who was hypnotized first.

"I travel for them. I become their energy. My master guides and I go back through time and see what these people were. I can't see anybody's energy pattern until I get into my rate of vibration. But once my guides and I get there we can release encased spirits."

"Encased spirits?"

"Yes, entities and negative patterns lying in your past life auras. If you have frustrations and fears about yourself, this releases them. Many times we will find the first negative condition lying right next to the energy pattern. That's the condition we have to release and by releasing it from the negative makes it much more positive and erases the fears and frustrations.

"A woman came to me once who had so many talents she was frustrated by them. She didn't know where to turn, what path to choose, because everything she did was almost perfect. She was more interested in her composing and playing than the others, so I went back into her energy patterns and released this force which made it the strongest of all her abilities. Now she writes her music without ever hearing the music. She just puts the notes down on paper. Then she plays them and hears, for the first time, what she's written. They have made several records from this music already. She is still a little amazed by this ability and would never tell her music teacher how she does it!"

"Then as far as you are concerned," I said, "we are a pattern of all our past lives." He shook his head in agreement. "Well, what is your idea of reincarnation then? Are we here to expiate the sins of our other existences?"

"The Teachers have taught me that you have had many lives, stretching back a million years or better. And every time you make a transition on a death pattern you revert to the spirit plane where there are schools you must attend. After that particular lesson is learned some people may go to the planets for experience and others may move into other earth dimensions for training. You don't have to come back to the earth. You have free choice, you know."

"But we all must clean up our past sins and mistakes."

"Right."

"But every day we commit dozens of injustices against our fellow human beings as well as such things as killing animals and fish for food. Do we have to atone for every one of these little sins and for each animal killed and eaten?"

"We do, and that's why it is such a long process, this business of reincarnation. We are tempted every minute of the day to do wrong. And we do it. And we come back the next time and try to make it up."

"Mr. Koperski," I asked, thinking of the hundreds of times *I* would have to come back, "do you know anybody who has cleaned his life so beautifully that this is the last time around? Is there any man alive who has done this?"

"I feel that way. I know this is my last lifetime. I'm *not* coming back anymore."

Inside the modern Metropolitan State Hospital in Norwalk (in the heart of the Los Angeles District) an aged Indian with an Aztec face wearing a dress shirt and a pair of khaki trousers stands before a young Mexican-American woman. She stares at him as he rubs his hands quickly down her body in short brisk movements as if he were brushing away lint. What he is really brushing away are the evil spirits inside her body. The same spirits that got her committed to the state hospital in the first place.

Apolonio Leon is a *curandero*. That's Spanish for spirit healer or medicine man. In spite of his age (over seventy) he has only been a curandero since 1962. That was when doctors could find no cure for a stomach ailment and he went to a curandero woman in East Los Angeles. She made his stomach well again and told him he also had the power to cure. Since then he has become an important member of the Mexican-American community.

He was invited to work at the state hospital by social worker Ignacio Aguilar, who wanted to give Spanish-speaking patients a better chance inside the institution.

"Not only does the language difficulty make it harder for Spanish-speaking patients to get the most out of their stay," he says, "but different cultural values related to mental illness sometimes make it impossible."

Aguilar explained that Mexicans look upon mental illness in a different light than Americans. They feel it is a form of witchcraft, a possession by evil spirits brought upon by jealous vindictive people who can work the evil eye.

For the Spanish-speaking patient, being hospitalized brings new fears of alienation from his family and friends and only adds to the confusion naturally present in a mentally ill person. Superimposed on this is the fear that evil spirits—over which no human has control—are at the root of all the misfortune.

The hospital is not happy over having the curandero on their staff, even though the old man charges nothing for his services. He says he is merely the intermediary, not the source of the power. After each treatment he thanks the "divine doctor" for having been present. "This is a gift that I have been handed," he says. "I could never charge for its use."

Aguilar calls on his curandero only when the patient seems unreachable by standard hospital techniques. Also he never asks the witch doctor in unless the patient expresses a belief in his powers or has a history of frequenting curandero centers. He says that the treatments have had a beneficial effect on about 80 per cent of the patients treated.

"The curandero's value is in being able to bring the patient to a stage where he feels he has been rid of evil spirits. I don't believe in these spirits," he added, "but what I believe and what the doctors believe is not important. It's what the patient believes that counts."

Another type of spiritual healer got trouble for her work, not praise.

Bertha Kelsey lived in Santa Susana, north of Malibu Beach

in Ventura County. She placed a small advertisement every week in the local paper offering treatment through hypnosis and self-hypnosis on all problems including weight control, smoking, insomnia, emotional and nervous tension. She billed herself as a Ph.D., Hy.D., Metaphysician and Practitioner of the Institute of Applied Metaphysics, Inc.

County officials, prodded by the American Medical Association, decided to investigate, especially when a woman in Canoga Park claimed Dr. Kelsey had cured her of leukemia.

In October 1968 a female special investigator appeared at Dr. Kelsey's residence, saying that doctors had recently diagnosed that she had a serious blood disease, possibly leukemia. She turned on her hidden tape recorder as the practitioner started asking questions.

"I'm not a medical doctor," Mrs. Kelsey said. "I treat with the mind and use hypnosis. The medical profession doesn't have a cure for leukemia. But we have cured leukemia. We have cured cancer, even terminal cancer." Then she outlined the procedure she would use in helping the woman "overcome the disease."

"Loan me your mind to remove the debris and get your mind functioning properly," she said, then went on to claim that the mind must be put into a passive state through hypnosis and cleaned of all the negative "garbage" so positive thoughts could be injected. The mind then purifies the blood and the patient's body functions as it should, she explained.

Then she attempted to put the police woman under hypnosis. The officer faked it. Dr. Kelsey was paid fifteen dollars for the first treatment and she wrote a receipt.

The cops kept their eyes on the healer and in February 1969, they sent another agent, a woman who complained that she suffered from severe headaches, knots in her stomach, etc. Again Dr. Kelsey tried hypnosis (which again didn't work) and was paid fifteen dollars upon giving a receipt. Then the police arrested her.

The case made headlines in Ventura County, because it was the first time in years that a psychic had been hauled into court. Mrs. Kelsey took the stand and declared that she never admitted to being a *medical* doctor but was entitled to call herself Dr. Kelsey because of the degrees she earned while a student at the Institute of Applied Metaphysics in Van Nuys, California. She said she had four degrees: one in Hypnotherapy, one as a Doctor of Metaphysics, a Ph.D. for Doctor of Philosophy-Advanced Metaphysics and one as an ordained minister. She got them all in the same month after studying nights and paying the Van Nuys academy $1,000.

Dr. Kelsey, a dimunitive 110-pound brunette with four divorces to her credit, probably would have gotten off easier than she did if she hadn't tried to pull the wool over the cops' eyes. Two weeks after being arrested she ran her advertisement again and added she was working with the services of Dr. D. M. Camerano. A week later Dr. Camerano was advertising alone but with Dr. Kelsey's address and phone number. Suspicious cops checked it out: Dr. Camerano was Mrs. Kelsey's unmarried sister.

The defendant admitted to making about $6,000 a year from her practice, had bought a car and was paying on a home. She also admitted she didn't know what she would do if she was not allowed to continue her practice, as the only other steady job she'd ever had was as a waitress in the Granada Lanes Coffee Shop.

The deputy probation officer evaluated Mrs. Kelsey in her report: "It appears that strong measures will be needed to stop the defendant from re-offending. It does not appear to be so much self-hypnosis as self-delusion, but it seems that the defendant has convinced herself that she is doing no wrong."

The court sentenced her to twenty days in jail. She served them and vanished from the area, one of the few so-called psychics of the Psychic State ever to serve time for practicing her "talents."

Clara Schuff is birdlike. She can't be over five-two or weigh more than 100 pounds. She survives on a cup of green tea in the morning, another cup with a slice of bread and a piece of cheese for lunch and a piece of fruit or cheese for dinner. Yet she has more energy than a woman half her age. And her age is way up there into the seventies.

Mrs. Schuff lives in San Diego not because she wants to but

because circumstances and her spiritual gurus have placed her there. Her apartment, in an unfashionable end of town, is cluttered with bulky furniture, drawings on huge sheets of white paper and photographs of mystics and oriental psychics. Her white hair is combed into neat little curls that stay close to her head. Her blue eyes sparkle when she is delighted and dim when she becomes sad.

Clara Schuff was born in Munich, Germany, into a family of freethinkers. So free in fact that when she, at seventeen, decided she was going to become a yogi like Gandhi her parents raised no objections. Not even when she suddenly renounced meat, beer and apple strudel.

She began to meditate and read everything she could find about yoga and its philosophies. One memorable day her father walked into the kitchen to find her "making the dishes and chairs dance."

She married a man who, she thought, cared as much about the metaphysical as she did, but when he joined the SS she divorced him. She moved into another house in town and remained there all during the war. Even though she had nothing to do with Hitler or her husband the townspeople attacked her when the war was over and she fled to Switzerland for her life.

There she was able to get a few lecture appearances. Her fame as a psychic had preceded her, for she had been investigated by German, Austrian and Swiss parapsychologists before and during the war. All of them came to the same conclusion: the lady has remarkable gifts.

At one of these lectures she was asked by an American woman for a reading. She told the woman all about her past life and her hopes for the future. She also said that even though she was an American she was living in a tropical country. The woman said it was Panama and asked Clara if she would like to come to America. Clara said yes.

Six weeks later a ticket and a letter arrived from Panama. There were many people anxious to see her and to have readings with her. She left Europe, never to return.

The front pages of the Panama newspapers attest to Clara's powers. At least her powers to amaze the Panamanians. She gave lectures and spoke on the radio through an interpreter and when her seven-month tourist visa expired she went to Brazil.

Brazil was more difficult for her. Few people spoke German and even fewer were interested in a foreign psychic. After all, they had so many of the home-grown variety.

So she managed to go to New York. The first thing she did was to get the Yellow Pages and look under churches. She was able to make enough money to support herself by lecturing and private readings. Then a foundation in Miami asked her to come there. They gave her the necessary credentials for her permanent visa for this country and also gave her a broom and an apron. She was expected to be a psychic as well as cleaning woman and cook.

It was then that a wealthy woman walked into her kitchen and told her she was wasting her time there. She offered to take her to California. Clara accepted and the two women drove across the nation, one speaking English the other trying to speak English. Clara finally chose Santa Barbara, on the coast, and settled down.

But it wasn't for long. The local hippies heard of her and began beating a steady path to her door. They came for classes in meditation and mind control. She respected them and they loved her. One of her prize pupils at that time was the singing star Jimi Hendrix. "He came to me with such a desire to learn but I could see that he had taken the wrong path. I tried to get him off, but it was too late. I was not surprised what finally happened."

Her neighbors became upset with these long-hair types hanging around at all hours and then the telephone calls began. It was always the same woman's voice and she always said the same thing: "I'm going to kill you!"

Clara meditated and tried to send good thoughts to her unknown enemy but the calls continued. Her students would stand guard outside her bedroom door every night. One with a gun and another with a long knife. Finally the Santa Barbara police said they thought it would be a good idea if the little old lady moved away. She chose San Diego.

Interviewing Clara Schuff is quite an experience. She flits from one subject to the other, from one room to the other, always on the move, always chattering in her broken, broken English.

The first thing she did was make me sit down by her desk and place my right hand flat on a piece of white paper. Then she took some colored pencils and traced the outline of the hand and quickly made scribbles, squiggles and whorls in colored leads. Then she told me about my recent past, hitting quite accurately my travels, my health and my hopes. Then she said that my father had trouble with his leg and with his sugar. That's true. Then she said my mother was healthy but had trouble with her heart. That's true. When I asked her about the health of a friend in Brazil she said that he has a small growth on his large intestine that blocks his digestion at times and causes pain and nervousness. She said he should have it operated on. That was also true. (She could have said hc had cancer, a cold, TB or leprosy but no, she picked the *exact* physical illness that has plagued him for years. And he was in Brazil while she diagnosed him from San Diego!)

Then she picked up a copy of my book on Brazilian spiritism, *Drum & Candle,* and, turning to an illustration of a group of Imbanda images, she said: "Ach! But the vibrations are so heavy!" and began to sing and sway to what I recognized as a Brazilian religious song. "I got that from *here,*" she said, hitting her tiny solar plexus. "From here is coming the music, always."

Now she rose and faced the far corner of her living room. "My gurus are with me always. I catch direct the songs from the other places. Now I am going to Tibet," and with that she began to sing a strange melody with absolutely unintelligible words. I sat startled and unsure of just how to continue the interview. I needn't have worried.

"Now in the corner there is China. Ancient China!" And again she broke into an exotic melody with some ching-chow-chung lyrics. "You want hear India? Yes?" And a song came out of the other corner. "Aztec? You like the Aztecs?" And a fourth song came out. They were all different in melody and words, but still unintelligible.

She grabbed a scrapbook that was full of letters and press clippings in several languages. Some of them were yellowing with age. "Look at this!" she pointed. "My enemies say I studied. I never studied these languages! Where you go to study Aztec! Where?"

The letter was on stationery from the University of Vienna. It was signed by a Professor Franz Steyrer. It stated that Mrs. Schuff sang and spoke in what he considered the language of the ancient Motilóns of South America, the language of Kuwait, Tibetan, Chinese dialects and ancient Egyptian. He closed with: "the performance touched me profoundly."

"And look at this!" she exclaimed. "Look at these two photos. They were taken in New York when I spoke on the platform for the Center of Divine Guidance in 1964. You see this one?" She handed me a color photograph of a man standing profile at a lectern. I could see nothing unusual about it. "Now look at this one!" The second photograph was the same scene but this time it was Mrs. Schuff who was standing in profile speaking from the same lectern. But—in the left hand corner a tiny full-length figure of a woman had appeared. She was dressed all in white with a long gown that trailed into nothingness. Her hands were clasped in prayer and it seemed as if she had a crown on her head. She looked exactly like the statues one sees of the Virgin Mary. And superimposed near this image was the face of a man. It was bearded, deep-eyed and many times larger than the Virgin-like figure. I looked back at the first photo. The corner and wall above the male speaker were blank. Nothing there at all. Then back to the photo of Mrs. Schuff. I could make out the same color wall and the junction that formed the corner but there indeed were those two figures.

"When they took these pictures they did not see these guides. They are very big guides. The man sent them to Kodak to develop the film. When he got them returned there he was seeing these two guides. It is amazing, no? The guides are only on this one picture of me. And," she added, "they are on the negative also. Kodak is too busy to make jokes, no?"

One of Mrs. Schuff's specialties are the large drawings in red and blue ink she does on white paper. She started doing them in 1961, when her gurus told her to try it. She sings and works rapidly, making animal faces and strange symbols that are crowded with odd letters and signs that look like hieroglyphics. She claims that they are direct from ancient temples still standing somewhere in the world today. She says they are Chinese, Japanese, Tibetan, Hindu, Inca and Mayan. One of them, a snake emerging from a snail's shell, was taken to a Japanese professor at the Los Angeles Museum of Art, who pronounced it as being an ancient Japanese dialect that was on one of the temple walls of his homeland.

I asked her if we all had psychic ability or if it was a special gift.

"No, not all," she replied with her thick German accent. "The people who have too much eat, too much drink, too much sex and too much money are stopped from these powers. You need meditate and think and these types don't give it time. They too interested in physical to give them to spiritual.

"People think because I medium, I have much money. I have no money. Sometime I have not the money even for my rent. I'm poor. But I don't care. I still young in here!" And she slapped her breast. "When a psychic is rich there is something wrong. A rich psychic is a swindler!"

"And the cat came back . . ." When I heard the story of Miss Edna Rice from San Diego, I remembered that old children's poem about the cat that they just couldn't get rid of.

Miss Rice had a beautiful red Persian cat. Named Ginger. It died and the young lady was grief-stricken. It was the first time anyone close to her had died in years and she mourned the animal as much as if it had been a human being.

One night three months later, she was in bed and, having turned out the light to sleep, there was Ginger! Fully materialized and crouching on her pillow. The lady didn't try to touch her, afraid that the animal would vanish, but she did communicate with her in another way. Thoughts passed back and forth between the ghost and the person. Ginger put three thought messages across: (1) she knew that something had happened to change her condition, (2) she still loved her mistress, and (3) she would be with her as long as her mistress needed her.

The visit lasted about a half hour, until the visitor vanished. Miss Rice started reading psychic literature to understand fully what had happened.

A short while later she was traveling on the train to New York and she felt Ginger riding on her right shoulder all the way. Then nine months later she went for a reading with the well-known medium Caroline Randolph Chapman. Now, Mrs. Chapman had never seen Miss Rice before that day, yet as she walked through the door, the medium exclaimed: "Oh, you have the most beautiful red Persian cat on your shoulder. I seem to get the name Ginger for her!"

And the cat still keeps coming back . . .

And still in San Diego, the Medical School of the University of California has a program to teach students hypnotism. The purpose is "to use the art to permit people to modify their habitual behavior for their own welfare."

The university feels it can train doctors to help people kick such habits as smoking, gaining weight, not being able to sleep and alcoholism by conditioning the mind instead of working on the body.

They demonstrated the ability to control the nervous system by taking two coeds and making them vary the temperatures of their hands by as much as seven degrees just by suggestion.

I traveled from the Pacific Coast straight across the warm desert to El Centro, halfway to Arizona and just a few miles above Mexico. There was a woman there that I had to see. Her name (or at least the one she prefers when she writes) is Lee Baxter. She had been written about in *Fate* and *Chimes* magazines as well as the prestigious *Psychic News* of London.

When I finally reached El Centro, I wondered why anyone would choose to live there. It's hot and dry and with sidewalks that are rolled up every night at eight. I arrived at 10:00 A.M. and the only sound was that of whirring air conditioners behind brick and glass facades. The lady who ran the hotel told me many people came to El Centro for their health. Its dry climate and sea level air make it perfect for sufferers of respiratory ailments.

That's what brought Mrs. Baxter there. Three serious breathing diseases including lung polio.

But you wouldn't know it to look at her. She is average height, a little on the stout side (because of gland trouble) with laughing blue eyes and blond hair. She has been through a great deal, not only on the spiritual side but the physical as well. She told me all about her life and her work as we sat over iced tea at an air-conditioned Grant's Drugstore luncheon counter.

She was born into a poor family of Kentucky farmers. Her father was already an old man when she appeared and her mother, part Cherokee Indian, was never in good health. When Lee was only two years old her mother was struck blind. When she was thirteen the woman became completely paralyzed. "The usual mother-daughter roles were reversed," she said. "Mother became my child—my king-sized infant. Yet her very helplessness and dependence upon me made her even more dear to me."

She married and settled down to what she thought would be a "normal" life. She had three children. Then her husband, who had been a World War II veteran, became mentally ill. Dangerously, psychotically ill. He would beat her and threaten to kill her.

One day, exhausted from her problems with her mother, her husband and caring for three children, she stretched out on the living room sofa. Then her first memorable psychic experience occurred.

"A slow paralysis crept over my body and it seemed that inch by inch I was turning to stone. My legs became so heavy that no act of will on my part could move them. The feeling crept upward until finally I couldn't move my fingers or even bat my eyelashes. I tried desperately to call for help but no sound would come out of my throat.

"Then I felt a whirling sensation in the region of my solar plexus. It was as if the atoms of my body had suddenly started to gyrate at supersonic speed. I wondered if I were dying and for a brief moment experienced a cold fear wondering where they would bury me. The vibrating continued and my consciousness seemed to be thrown up and out of my body. Suddenly I found myself up near the ceiling, looking down upon my paralyzed form.

"I hovered near the ceiling a moment, wondering *how it could be* that my inner self and my physical self could separate. Then, somehow, I snapped back to my body and a few minutes later the heaviness left me and I was able to sit up."

For ten years these experiences came to Mrs. Baxter when she would least expect them. She blames them on her exhausted physical condition. "As the vibrations reached higher and higher levels of speed, I found myself able to go through solid walls and as the fear grew less and less I was able to get farther and farther away from my body.

"At that time," she says with a smile on her light southern accent, "I had never heard of astral projection. Naturally, I thought this strange experience was something that had happened to me alone. As it continued I found I could control it to some degree. I couldn't decide when it would happen, but once it got started I could decide on where it would take me and whom I would see. The controlling factor seemed to be," she emphasized, "an intense yearning to see a loved one.

"But there is no fear of these experiences now. I understand what takes place. I know how the spirit detaches itself from the body. This is what happens at death. It is a sweet feeling to know that death is not any more difficult than that."

Her husband became so unbalanced that her only hope was to confine him in a California hospital for treatment. They went West together. "I was never out of danger, for my husband had twice tried to kill me in fits of violence. But he needed help and I was the only one who cared enough to try to persuade him to have the psychiatric treatments. I left my mother in the care of a close friend. It was the first time we had ever been separated."

But back home the friend was unable to convince the blind and paralyzed older woman why Lee had gone away. The woman was positive she had been abandoned and left to die. This shock put her into a coma. The neighbor thought about phoning Lee and telling her of her mother's condition but decided not to. She had enough problems on her mind without this one, the friend reasoned, and there was nothing Lee could have done about it but worry.

"I was in a bedroom in California and had just turned out the light to try and sleep. I remember glancing at the clock and seeing the time was ten fifty-five. I began to meditate upon my problems when my thoughts were interrupted by my mother's voice calling my name. She called twice.

"I looked around the room and saw her seated on the other end of my bed. I have never seen anything more beautiful. Her face was radiant with happiness and her expression was tender and loving. She was bathed in silver light."

"I have to go now," she said. "I came to tell you good-by." The apparition lifted its arms as a child who wants to be picked up and then, reports Lee, "it seemed that invisible arms lifted her and carried her out the window. Throughout all this I sat in transfixed silence, awed by the beauty of what I saw."

She turned on the light and glanced at the clock. One minute had elapsed. Quickly, so she wouldn't forget any of what had happened, she took a pencil and paper and wrote the entire occurrence. "The scene was one of such beauty that I wanted to remember it always."

Right after this her husband became worse and escaped from the mental hospital. Lee, afraid for her life and the lives of her children, moved seventeen times in the next five years. (Her marriage was later annulled and her husband declared legally dead.)

Her mother died fifteen days after she had seen the vision, still deep in coma. "But in all those moves I had lost the paper on which I'd written the description of her spirit visit. Every time I thought about it, I'd start searching for the paper but it was nowhere to be found."

Then she contracted lung polio at thirty-five years of age and the doctors told her bluntly that she would die. She refused to go to the hospital, determined to stay in her own home as long as possible. Because of her fear that her psychotic husband might turn up at any minute she kept the doors and windows locked. The doors were also chain bolted and the windows nailed shut. No one could get into her Ventura home.

"Even though my astral projections had convinced me that death was easy, I was very much afraid. I prayed, in great anguish, that if the spirit does survive, my mother would return to me and prove the fact.

"When I at last fell into a troubled sleep there was not one thing out of place in my house. The next morning, when I awoke, a folded piece of paper, standing up like a little pup tent, was on the floor beside my bed.

"I reached down and picked it up. It was 'my letter from another world,' proof positive to me that my mother's spirit lives on. That folded piece of paper contained the description I had written, five years earlier, of my mother's astral projection to my room before her death.

"Over the years my searching for it had been in vain, but Mother, who in this world had been unable to see or move, had quickly found the one thing which would prove to me that I had no reason to fear death."

One of Mrs. Baxter's writing assignments in El Centro was a series of promotional articles on the novelist Harold Bell Wright. He lived at Meloland and for a while gained national fame with his books *The Shepherd of the Hills* and *The Winning of Barbara Worth*. El Centro civic leaders thought that his once lovely ranch, now decaying into ruin, would make a tourist attraction if enough people became interested in repairing it.

She made a visit to the estate, overgrown with weeds and sacked by vandals, and felt "an unseen presence. They said the house was haunted and many people were afraid of it. I sensed there was someone there too, but it was a warm, vibrant feeling. Not one to instill fear at all."

When she started to write her series she realized that the material was scant to say the least. There wasn't enough in local archives to make even one good article. "I was desperate until the door opened and an old man asked for me."

"I've got some information that maybe you might like for your files," he told her. "I don't know whether you'll ever be interested in him or not but I was a personal friend of Harold Bell Wright. Somethin' just told me, come and see Mrs. Baxter! He was a novelist. You ever hear of him?"

This old-timer gave her enough material for two full articles.

Then she needed a picture to illustrate the third article on the house as it looked when Wright wrote *Barbara Worth.* She had no idea how to find such a photo or if even the photo existed.

"Then right on schedule," she recalls, "an eighty-year-old man came to see me. He said he was a collector of junk in the area and came across this old postcard. Did I need it, because something kept telling him to bring it to me. I looked at the picture. It was Wright's home as it looked in its heyday. Now, all of these incidents were too perfectly timed to have been mere chance occurrences. I know they were guided by human intelligence and I believe that intelligence was Wright's."

But she still wasn't happy with the series. While she had captured much of what Wright looked like and what his ranch had been like, she still hadn't captured the man himself. "I wanted the heart and mind of Harold Bell Wright and I knew there was only one way to get it. Tell him."

She sat down and meditated. And she called him. "Harold Bell Wright, I know that you have been with me so far in writing this series. I have felt your presence constantly. I've come to love you as a good and wonderful friend as I've learned more and more about you. But I'm not happy that I haven't put your essence on paper, that I still lack the real you. Can't you send someone to me with the missing facts I need, the facts which will tell me why you were *you?*"

The very next day the eighty-year-old "junk collector" made another visit to her office. "I'm old and forgetful," he said apologetically. "When I talked to you before I forgot all about this." He opened a brown paper bag and took out a battered old book. "But last night I suddenly remembered it, so I brought it to you."

Mrs. Baxter looked at the book. It was *My First Thirty Years,* an unlisted and virtually forgotten Wright autobiography. "There will never be any question in my mind," she says, "whether the writing of that series was spirit-directed!"

Mrs. Baxter also dreams, vivid dreams of violence, tragedy and silly things she can't decipher at the time but that usually come true. She has dreamed of fires and earthquakes only to have them happen within two or three days. Once she dreamed of an Indian uprising amid maple leaves and two days later the newspaper carried a story of Indian conflicts in Canada, where the national symbol is the maple leaf.

"Sometimes I feel they are insignificant and I'll forget them until they come back to me in the clear light of reality. I once dreamed that I was sitting down to a fancy dinner that was so hard it was almost ossified. I especially remembered the pumpkin pie. I couldn't cut it with my fork. Naturally, I forgot about this dream. Then a short time later I was invited to a dinner by a local civic organization and they took all the food out of the freezer where it had been for months. The meal was almost inedible but the pumpkin pie . . . it was so hard my fork wouldn't dent it."

I asked her if we should all try to remember our dreams and use them as guides in our waking life.

"I don't think so," she said, "not until a person learns to correctly interpret the symbols in the dreams. Symbols mean different things to different people. I have a friend that when she dreams of pancakes becomes very happy because her father used to show his love for her by making her a big stack of pancakes. But when I was a girl we were so poor that many times there was nothing else to eat but pancakes and I look upon them as sadness and poverty. You see, one must learn what the symbols mean and we must also learn to interpret the *feelings* in our dreams. Especially the feelings we get in our solar plexus."

When Mrs. Baxter goes into her meditation she always keeps a ball-point pen and a stack of paper nearby, for her guides prefer that she receive her messages through automatic writing. They have given her solutions to everyday problems, have helped her face her health and marital crises and have given her a number of predictions.

"I don't know how much of this automatic writing springs from my own subconscious and how much from the spirit world or the Universal Mind. I only know that a great number of personal predictions (which my logical mind *rejected*) have come to pass."

Some of her more startling predictions that may still come to pass: (1) earthquakes in Brazil, a country that almost never has a quake, (2) a microscope to be invented that will prove that cancer is not caused by division of cells but by parasites, (3) a machine to be invented that will enable us to speak with the spirits of the dead, and (4) in or near 1990 flying saucers will make themselves known and they will not be piloted by beings from other planets but instead by discarnate spirits living in other astral planes.

"I believe that sensitivity, be it mediumship, psychism or whatever, is a matter of *attunement,*" she told me. "Attunement is best achieved through *empathy.* The person who has suffered much is *aware* and *concerned.* He *cares* about other people, so he can tune in on their vibrations. Also I believe we evolve more highly through sufferings and sorrow.

"I do not classify myself either as a medium or a psychic— but whatever sensitivity I have comes because I *care* about my fellow beings."

I headed north, up through hot desert country and past the ancient Salton Sea until I reached Indio. There I checked out the story of four-year-old Christina Bowlman. She had been playing near a church in the village of Tamarisk (sixty miles east of Indio) when a sidewinder rattlesnake came from under a woodpile and bit her. She ran to her father to show him the wounds and he, not recognizing the two tiny punctures, brushed the blood away and kissed her, telling her to "Pray to Jesus to take away the hurt."

That afternoon little Christina's hand began to swell and her worried father took her to a local doctor, who immediately rushed her to the hospital in Indio. There, doctors stated they didn't give her a chance but they pumped eleven vials of serum into her hoping they would do the trick.

Back at Tamarisk, congregations of three different churches started continuous prayers for the little girl. They kept it up for six days until the swelling went down and Christina left the hospital "lively as a cricket" one week after having been bitten.

San Bernardino is famous for industry, used car lots, Mexicans, and witches. So prevalent is witchcraft in the area that Dr. Robert Smith, a professor of history at Cal State in San Bernardino has been studying it for twenty years. He feels that "there hasn't been such an interest in witches and warlocks since the days of Salem." He also feels that witchcraft is cyclical, appearing at irregular intervals in history because certain conditions in society give rise to it.

"When the future looks black," he says, "and there is a general loss in confidence for what the future holds, people then attempt to control the environment or other people through witchcraft.

"When the existing system is not responding as you wish it to, you turn to something else. When you are disillusioned with the church you turn to something else. That is exactly what's happening now.

"Magic is a novelty, it's underground and suppressed. Many do it to rebel, to bug other people. There has always been a certain attraction to the bizarre, and this probably accounts for many of our contemporary witches."

It probably accounts for the San Bernardino bunch that includes such people as Jerry (a mod-dressing warlock in his forties), Colleen (a blonde just turned twenty), Jim (a thirtyish neat-appearing businessman) and LaVada (a middle-aged woman who's been a practicing witch since 1956). And the Gray Witch, Barbara, also lived and worked in this little town until she moved to L.A. and the big time.

Reverend Lillian Courtney is against the witches. She is against all forms of black magic, "because I've seen what it can do. We used to study it years ago. It was part of our schooling, but we've dropped it. It's too dangerous."

Reverend Courtney is a Spiritualist minister. She is tall, white-haired and determined. If you are not impressed with her mental abilities (which are formidable!) then you have to be impressed with her energy. The lady was born way back in 1883! At the time I interviewed her, she was eighty-eight years old.

The lady came to the West Coast when she was very young from Cleveland, Ohio. She grew up in a normal Protestant atmosphere but felt much of what she had to listen to every Sunday was "gibberish." She could not believe that a child, not baptized into the church, would suffer eternal damnation. She believed in a just God, a God of love and mercy, not "some long-haired old man sitting on a throne and throwing thunderbolts of fear at the world below."

Then she heard of the Spiritualist Church and started attending the meetings out of curiosity more than anything else. "I went to a circle once a week and heard the voices of many spirits coming through the trumpet. I listened to what the spirits had to say and I was impressed."

But not convinced. It took something stronger than that to make her a member of the church. "I was the friend of a family who had recently moved to Southern California and they had a son. He was a harum-scarum young man who was always doing foolish things. One day, in a fit of pique, he ran away and joined the Marines. Then his mother got a letter from him saying he was in the brig and wanted to come home. So his parents hired a lawyer and had the necessary legal papers drawn up to get his release from the service. Because they needed a character witness, I signed those papers too.

"You must remember," she added, "that was 1922. Getting out of the service was a lot easier in those days. So one night, it was New Year's Eve, I was asleep when I heard a voice. 'Lillian,' it said. 'Lillian!' So I looked around the room but didn't see anyone. I knew it must be spirit. Of course I wasn't frightened, because I'd heard so many at the séances I'd attended.

"It's about Charles, isn't it?" she asked.

The voice said it was and told her the papers she had signed had been pigeonholed and that she must contact Charles's father in the morning. The voice left and she went to sleep.

The next day she told the young man's father and he called their lawyer. Sure enough, the papers had been inadvertently stuffed into a functionary's desk and had stayed there. The papers were worked on and the young man was released.

"If it had been up to me, I'd of let him stew there for a while," she says, "but it served to make me positive that spirits can and do communicate with the living. That they serve a useful purpose and that all we have to do is listen to them and respect them." It was because of that incident that she joined the Spiritualist Church. She was ordained a minister in 1946 and has been an active member for almost fifty years.

She explained to me that the original Spiritualist Church was brought into being "from the spirit world because of the rigid super-stition and the materialism of the orthodox churches. The manifesta-tions of the little Fox Sisters of New York brought about the *fact* that there is life after so-called death. That awakened the thinking people to the realization that there was something besides the old church-ology, that spirit is a fact. From this, many churches were organized and many mediums developed.

"In the early days there was a great deal of *physical* manifestation in order to arouse the excitement and curiosity of the people. The spirits could not reach the minds of people and be recognized but they could cause a great deal of attention through their physical manifestations."

"Seeing is believing, in other words," I said.

"Exactly! When they would see the tables move with no one touching them and see trumpets rise and hit the walls they began to do a great deal of thinking."

"Why is a trumpet necessary?" I asked.

"It magnifies the voice just like the horn they use at football games," she said. "The spirit needs this instrument or else his voice would be just a whisper. Also one of the rules of Spiritualism is that as soon as you hear a voice you must answer it. The spirit uses the vibrations of your voice to come in stronger. Spirits have to use the organism of a medium to manifest. If there is no medium in the room there will be no manifestation."

"Do you do physical manifestations?"

"I used to, but not any more. I still have a trumpet in my closet, but being a physical medium takes too much energy. That's why there are so few good ones around today. A physical medium has a very short life on this plane. Most of them die from cancer."

"From cancer? Is that a medium's occupational disease?"

"I call it cancer. It's a burning up of their energies and their vibrations. A physical medium who lets the public use him more than twice a week is killing himself. Some of them hold séances every night and those are the ones who go the quickest. You cannot burn yourself out like an old bulb. That's why I'm a *mental* medium today."

"Reverend Courtney," I asked, "can you have a group of Spiritualists and not have a medium among them?"

"Of course. Just joining the church doesn't make you a medium. It means that you have accepted the fact of mediumship and the religion of Spiritualism. You have accepted that spirit can make a better person out of you. Our definition of a Spiritualist is one that has accepted spirit and promises to improve his life from the high teachings he receives from spirit."

She made sure I understood that her organization, the National Spiritualist Association of Churches with executive offices in Milwaukee, Wisconsin, is the *true* Spiritualist Church. Unless a church is listed in their directory, unless a medium, minister or missionary is affiliated with them, then they are *not* part of the original Spiritualist organization. She admits that there have been many splinter groups because of the association's rigid laws, but "if they don't want to obey our laws, we prefer that they go elsewhere."

She estimates that there are some six thousand members of the original Spiritualist Church in the United States and an equal number scattered around the world. Once a person has joined the church he can start receiving lessons in mediumship either with the local minister or through a correspondence course. An examination afterward, if passed, makes the student a licentiate minister. Then two years afterward another stiff examination must be taken and, if passed, the student becomes an ordained minister.

"Reverend Courtney, is Spiritualism really a *religion?*"

"Yes, it is," she replied emphatically. "It is because we are striving to know and understand and use the laws of nature which are the laws of God. And that is true religion. We use the Bible on our platform along with our Spiritual Manual. We refer to both books. We pray and we seek the mercy and the wisdom of God. Of course we are a religion!"

"Why are the spirits interested in us? Aren't we awfully corrupt to interest beings on a higher plane?"

She pulled herself up in her chair. "Well, don't you think it's high time they showed us some interest?"

"Well, yes. But *why?*"

"To help us wake up and realize that material things are not the most important things! For instance, Spiritualism tells you that you are spirit and you have a body. You think you have a body and you hope you have a soul. You must reverse your thoughts. You are spirit *first of all* and you have been clothed in a physical body so you can operate on this physical plane. You, the *real* you, nobody can see. It is spirit and a part of the great spirit."

"So it's not that spirits are interested in us as human beings as much as they are interested in helping their spirit friends that are here on earth and clothed as human beings. Right?"

"Right. Now, man goes through many cycles and he is at the end of this one. Look at Atlantis. Look at Lemuria. Look at ancient Greece and ancient Rome. Ancient China had a civilization which far supersedes what we have now in many respects. And we are coming back to it again. But—man can go just so far and he gets materialistic and forgets the laws of religion and he annihilates himself."

"And that's where we're headed?"

"Yes."

"Do you think the Age of Aquarius is going to save us somehow?"

"If we're worthy of it. But I doubt it. Terrible things are going to happen. Avalanches, floods, earthquakes. There is going to be a terrific loss of life without any rule or apparent reason. Those of us needed on the earth will remain. Those not needed will go. They will give up the physical body and go."

"To heaven?"

"There are no twanging harps or streets of pearls or any of that foolishness. Life on the spiritual plane is just like life on this plane. Teachers have come through and told us how busy everyone is there. *I* have been privileged to go into their hospitals and into their homes. I was invited to go into one of their institutions of learning and there was not a word spoken in that hall. You just sit there and absorb the information like you sit here and breathe in the air around you. In their hospitals I saw little babies that were not wanted here. They are taken over there and put into nurseries and many of the women who couldn't have children here are acting as mothers and helpers for these unwanted tots. And there are thousands of them."

"Do these babies grow?" I asked.

"They grow. I have a daughter over there. She was stillborn but she has grown. I've seen her and she's a beautiful child."

"But why are hospitals needed on the spiritual plane? Don't we throw off all our physical afflictions when we pass over?"

"Not right away, no. Most of the deaths of humans are not from old age but from sickness and when that spirit reaches the new plane he must go into a hospital until the *memory* of that sickness has been removed from his soul. Then he will be free to help the others.

"If there is one thing I could tell the young people of today, it would be this: they are children of love. They were *not* born in sin! For generations we have been taught that we were born in sin. That's not true. We were born in love and we are children of God.

"The youth of today can learn to recognize this and govern their lives on that principle. If they do, they will learn to control their lives along the more successful pathways of life. Like attracts like. You send out love and you get back love. You send out hatred and you get back hatred. You send out love and you're not jealous of anyone. Jealousy! Wanting something that someone else has and you haven't earned! If you get it illegally, you lose it. You can never use it.

"But frankly, I don't know where this younger generation is heading. My oldest son is ready to sit down in front of a television set and retire! I can't understand young people. My son is ready to retire and he's only sixty-one!"

The town of Twentynine Palms sits high in the desert between the Joshua Tree National Monument Park and the largest Marine Corps base in the world. It is noted for its clean air, its senior citizens and its flying saucers. Yes, "29" (as they call it) has had more saucer sightings and has more saucer buffs than any other place in the United States.

They claim that there is a hidden saucer station in the almost impassable Joshua Tree Monument. The fantastic rock formations and the hundreds of unpopulated square miles inside the park would make perfect shelter for any shy spacecraft.

A woman from "29" tells of being in San Bernardino and shopping in the dime store when a little lady beside her was having trouble reaching for an item on an upper shelf. She noticed that the lady's fingers were jointed only at the middle and did not move at the tips or at the knuckle with the hand. She was sure the stranger was a space creature.

"Are you visiting California?" she asked.

The stranger replied that she was.

"Where are you staying?"

"Oh, in the desert."

"Near Joshua Tree Monument?" the woman inquired.

"Yes." And the stranger smiled.

"I thought so," said the first woman. "I live in Twentynine Palms."

"I know you do," came the reply, and the little stranger hurried away and was lost in the crowd.

For a long time residents of "29" have seen a light atop a mountain near the marine base. It shows up periodically and just sits there, seeming to spy down on the military activities below. Marine officials have looked right up at it and denied they could see anything. Townspeople knew differently. For them it was a saucer. Then in 1970 the marines put a big star atop the mountain at the very place where they had not seen the light. They illuminate this star from time to time and always on Christmas and New Year's. Now when a civilian sees a light up there he is told by the brass that it is *their* light.

(The marine base also has other troubles, one of them being the mysterious Yucca Valley Monster. He is California's answer to the Abominable Snowman. The Monster has been seen in the area for years. He is over eight feet tall, with enormous feet and broad shoulders. His body is covered with a thick matting of hair and whenever a dog, a cat or chickens disappear it is always the Monster that has eaten them.

In 1970 a guard at one of the lonely outposts on the fringe of this gigantic marine base was brought a sandwich and a glass of milk. He set the food down and went into the shack to wash his hands. When he came out the food was gone. Looking up he saw an enormous shaggy man running rapidly across the desert carrying his sandwich and milk. He yelled for help and then fainted. Several marines came to his aid and fired at the Monster but didn't hit it. The footprints it left in the sand were over a foot long and had but three toes.)

I was invited to spend the weekend in the Twentynine Palms desert home of Mrs. Jan Washburn. She has been living amid the cactus and the stars for almost ten years. She is a respected member of the community and one of the strongest saucer buffs in town.

There was another guest that weekend, a Mrs. Lisa Henderson. Lisa purchased a cabin near Jan's but it's still not habitable. She lives and works in the town of Alhambra and takes the freeway into "29" as often as she can.

It was a lucky weekend. In more ways than one.

Lisa is a medium. I had heard about her from people in Los Angeles but no one could give me her address. She doesn't like to have others know of her talents. "I still have a family to raise," she told me, "and the neighborhood I live in is predominantly Catholic and Mexican. They would pull in their skirts at me if they knew some of the things I have done."

Lisa has many talents, one of them being able to talk to trees. When she lived closer to Los Angeles there was a cluster of eucalyptus trees in her back yard. One day she was out enjoying their shade when one of them started talking to her. "It wasn't that I heard a voice," she stated, "it was the feeling of a distinct personality and a complete thought." The tree identified itself as being the one in the middle. It said it was in great pain because her children had put nails in its trunk. Lisa's boys had decided to make a tree house and got as far as nailing on the steps before they abandoned the project. The tree asked her to take away those steps. She did—at once!

Another time her mother came into the house and told her to go out and see what was wrong with one of the trees nearest the neighbors' place. "It's raining under the tree," her mother said, "and not raining anywhere else."

Lisa went to the tree and sure enough, "large drops of liquid were falling from its leaves. I asked it what the trouble was and it told me there was going to be a tragedy in a few days and it was very upset by it. It said it was going to lose two close friends. Beyond that it wouldn't tell me any more."

Four days later the old house next door caught fire and burned rapidly to the ground. The aged couple living in it managed to escape but two trees right next to Lisa's tree were consumed by the blaze.

She also had an avocado tree that never bore more than two or three pieces of withered fruit. Her mother had been fussing with it for two years, carefully banking it with leaves exactly as she had been told by a tree expert. Lisa asked the tree one day why there was so little fruit. "It's your mother," the tree replied. "She is suffocating me. I can't breathe! Tell her to take those leaves away and give me some air around my base." Lisa and her mother removed the leaves and "the next season the tree was loaded with the most delicious avocados we had ever seen."

Lisa has also written three books, all under assumed names. Her best known is a slim volume called *All That You Are*. It's really a textbook on living and loving from the spirit and spiritual point of view. "I can't say that I wrote it," she admits. "Once a week I was told to go to the typewriter, put in some paper and wait. I did and a chapter would come through my fingertips. The entity that dictated it told me to sign 'Mary' and told me what publisher would print it. I'm pleased that it sold out and has been reprinted and I'm overwhelmed that I had anything to do with it. On my own, I would never have been able to do it. That's not me in the book. It's an entity named Mary and she's a very good and wise person."

Then there was the time she was invited to see a home some friends had purchased in Tujunga, near the national forest at San Fernando. It was an old house and when Lisa walked into the living room "it was suddenly filled with all sorts of creatures in sizes and shapes that I had never seen or heard of before. They were little people, some as small and as thin as a pencil, others with bodies like upside-down teardrops. They were dressed in odd clothes and were running or hopping or flying around the room. One of them told me he was what humans refer to as an elf, but I have no idea what the others were. They were from a dimension that I had no idea existed."

Once, at "29" she was walking around the desert when she looked up and saw "the most perfectly beautiful man I've ever seen in my life. He was naked, his skin was a creamy tan and his hair was tawny white. His eyes were huge, oriental eyes but with a wild look in them. I saw him first and then he saw me. We startled each other. Then he shook his enormous brilliantly colored butterfly wings and vanished.

"So put me away in the funny farm if you wish," she laughed, "but send him along to share my lonely nights!"

Lisa has also had contact with flying saucers. In the early fifties she started fooling around with the Ouija board. Soon messages were coming through that saucer people wanted to prove themselves to her and that she must tell others about them. They made a date, marking the following Friday at five-thirty in the afternoon, and said they would be directly overhead.

When the time arrived Lisa and her husband took the Ouija board and went into the back yard. Immediately a message came that the saucer was over their house. Both looked up but saw nothing but an expanse of blue cloudless sky. Then her husband, who had been in the Navy, used the scanning method he'd been taught. Suddenly he cried out: "There it is! It's up there!"

Lisa saw it, then called her mother and a friend, who also saw it. In order to make sure they weren't watching a weather balloon or something similar Lisa asked it to move to the right. It did. Then she asked it to move to the left. It did. "It told me that it was about fifteen thousand feet up and that the ship was three hundred and sixty feet in diameter. It looked like a giant light bulb in the sky. Then it told me that it had to leave, that it was needed on the East Coast. It made a sharp turn and sped away faster than our eyes could watch. It was a fantastic experience and it took my husband months before his scientific brain would admit that he had really seen a saucer."

I asked her why saucer people must go through this elaborate hide-and-seek with humans. "Why don't they just land on Fifth Avenue and be done with it?"

She had an answer. "My contact told me that humans were frightened of them and they did not want to create a panic. Also they did not want to fall into the hands of the U. S. Air Force. The Air Force was hostile to them even though they were observing the earth with peace and goodwill. He reminded me of the time a saucer hovered for forty-five minutes over Indianapolis and the panic it caused there. They decided after that not to try it again. They said they were from Venus.

"The one thing that has helped me be so lucky in seeing all these phenomena is that I've never had a moment of fear. I've never been up-tight about a talking tree or an elf or making contact with a saucer. I've taken it in my stride. That's why so many beautiful things have happened to me. I'm positive of it."

Jan and her husband, George Washburn, built their home in the desert themselves. It took a long time and a lot of hard work but they were proud of it. George lived in it for only a few short years before he suddenly died.

"My loss was great," recalls the white-haired Mrs. Washburn today, "but I had one consolation: George was never afraid of death. We used to talk about it and he always said that if there was a way he would come back and prove there was life after death.

"One day I decided to take all the tools that we had used on the house and wrap them in oiled rags to keep out the sand and put them in their proper places in the tool shed. I didn't know a whats-a-hammer from a thinga-ma-driver and as I gathered them all up and started putting them away I heard George's voice. 'That goes over there, with the bits and brace,' he ordered. 'You won't need that, you can put it in the deep chest. Take that over there and put it with the saw. You'll need it when you have to repair a broken window.' He gave me complete instructions on how to sort his tools. It was his usual bossy self, the self I loved and I knew he had managed to get back to me."

Another time she was trying to siphon water from their back yard tank but no matter how many times she climbed the ladder and jiggled the hose the liquid refused to flow into the cans she had on the ground. "Finally someone knocked the hose from my hands and as it fell there was a gurgling of water and the siphon system went to work. I never would have learned how to operate that thing if George hadn't come back and knocked it from my hands."

Then there was his birthday present to her—after he had died. "I was driving down the highway toward Joshua Tree when I remembered it was George's birthday. He had been gone for two months and the loneliness suddenly hit me full force. We would have celebrated if he had been alive. But then up from one of those dips in the highway came a tremendous truck. It came roaring right at me and there painted across the front was 'Washburn' in huge letters. As it roared past I saw the name Washburn repeated several times and then the words 'Macon, Georgia.' What better way could George Washburn use than to send this truck just at that moment with the name 'Georgia' and 'Washburn.' Coincidence? I don't know. Yet I never saw a truck like that before and I've never seen another since."

George will return from time to time and carry on a conversation with Jan. This usually happens when Lisa is there to act as the medium. "He will walk between us," says Jan, "and I'll feel a current going up and down my arm and I'll know he's there. Then Lisa will tune in to his vibrations and we'll sit down and chat."

George has told them that he's happy on the spirit plane because there is so much to learn and do. He was afraid that when he died there would be nothing but harp practice on fleecy clouds and he always hated harp music. He told them that he is working with many others on a huge prayer tube that is being used to send good vibrations and good thoughts to the human plane. The thoughts are, hopefully, to counteract the negative thoughts of racial strife, drug abuse and war. "He tells us that the spirits won't interfere with our plans," says Jan, "but they will try to influence us to do the right thing."

"George has changed," adds Lisa. "He's not the same personality he was when he first went over. He is becoming more knowledgeable and more distant. His visits are becoming less frequent. I wouldn't be surprised if one day he graduates to another level and doesn't come back at all."

When he was alive, he and Jan used to sit on their patio and gaze at the clear night sky. The air is so pure and so cloudless at "29" that the sky looks like an illustration in an astronomy book.

One night she noticed two bright stars close together. She called her husband's attention to them and asked him which planets they were. As he was trying to figure their position one of them suddenly moved quickly to the left. The other hung there for a few seconds and sped upward. They knew that they had seen two saucers.

It was just about that time that they saw George Van Tassel being interviewed on a Los Angeles television station. Van Tassel had been an engineer with Lockheed for fifteen years and when he retired he leased a few acres from the government at Landers, California, just north of Twentynine Palms and almost touching the marine base. Part of his agreement was that he was to maintain an emergency landing strip there. And part of the charm of the location was a huge rock, eight stories high, where some "mad scientist" had carved living quarters in the base.

One night Van Tassel and his wife were sleeping in a temporary hut when a man awoke him. He asked him to come with him. Van Tassel, used to helping pull people out of the sand, wasn't surprised by his request. However, when he tried to awaken his wife he was surprised. The stranger told him his wife was in a deep sleep and would not awaken until he returned.

Intrigued, Van Tassel followed him and he was taken to a giant flying saucer that had parked nearby. He was told to take off any metal, such as his watch, his belt and even the tips of his shoelaces. Then he was asked inside. He was given a complete tour and explanation of the working principle of the saucers. Because he had been an engineer he could evaluate the information and feels that is why the saucer people contacted him.

According to what he received, saucers travel inside cone-shaped magnetic fields: pockets of air they have created which neutralize the pull of gravity. These cones are connected to other astral levels and an ordinary airplane flying through one would be immediately switched into another dimension.

Van Tassel was told that the saucer people were from another planet and that they meant no harm to the human race. They were concerned, however, with the way the human race was heading. And, they said, if the earthlings should go to such extremes as to threaten the delicate interplanetary balance they would step in and take control of things.

The saucer people promised him that there would be a demonstration on a specific evening and that he was free to tell as many people about it as he wished. That's why he went on television and was interviewed.

When Jan and George Washburn heard the program they immediately made plans to go to the demonstration. When they arrived there were about 200 people lying on the ground in sleeping bags and staring at the sky. They got out their equipment and did the same.

"I kept my eyes wide open," Jan recalls, "because I didn't want to miss anything. Then all of a sudden, directly over my head there was a funny swirl. It was small at first but then it got bigger and bigger and bigger. I called out and everyone saw it. It grew and grew and seemed to be bathed in swirls of white fire. Then it got down to about ten miles from the earth and just disappeared. Like a gigantic electric light, it just turned itself off.

"Dozens of us had binoculars and cameras but nobody thought to use them. We had all been so startled that we just lay there like frightened little bunnies. It sounds foolish now, but you never know how you're going to react in any situation. That was all we saw and we went home. George and I both content that we had seen a saucer."

The sightings became an annual affair at Big Rock and the spot is now considered *the* flying saucer convention spot in the United States. The Washburns went to many of the reunions but the thirteenth one was the most memorable.

"There were about fifteen thousand people there and I had my tape recorder ready. I was sitting near a friend of ours, a man named Bob Short, who has had all sorts of saucer contact, when suddenly Bob went into trance and the loud voice of Korton came booming out. Korton is his special space advisor. I could not see the cone of light that was being used to communicate with Bob but I could most certainly feel its vibrations!

"Korton said that his particular mission was the mapping of all the earthquake faults and other structural weaknesses. He said they did this by scanning the earth with light.

"Then all of a sudden three huge circles of light came swooping down across the crowd. We all oohed and ahed and watched as they grouped in formation and hovered over the landing strip. They were white light and pulsated almost like a heartbeat. Or maybe it was my heart that was beating so strongly!

"Yet even as Korton was explaining what they were, the scoffers in the crowd began shouting that it was anything but saucer lights. They said it was three spotlights whose reflections had been carried by the wind. Or that they were weather balloons with lights inside them. Or some kind of desert gas. Human beings can be very strange creatures! Here they had come all that distance to see saucer manifestations and then stood there denying what they were seeing!

"In the course of everyone arguing and talking the lights just swooped up into the sky and vanished. They made no noise, they just went. It was quite exciting and I felt they had put on quite a show for us."

The weather in "29" the weekend I was there was nothing but contrast. Friday had been hot and moist. Saturday had been warm and beautiful but Sunday had been impossible.

It started about nine that morning. The wind came out of the north blowing sand and desert debris. It howled like the sound track of *Lawrence of Arabia* and Jan's wooden home shook steadily with the force of the wind and the blasting sand. The fine grains crept in under the doors and around the window panes. It crunched as we walked across the floor and grated against our teeth when we passed our tongues across our lips. It was in our food, in our hair and in our nerves.

Jan was visibly upset by the storm the longer it lasted. She would peer out of the window and not be able to see trees and shubbery only six feet away from the house. We talked about flying saucers and mediumship and tried to pretend we weren't bothered by the storm, but when night came and there had been no letup in the howling wind we all grew concerned.

We were seated at the dinner table conversing about anything just to keep our minds away from the burying winds outside when I felt a strange sensation. It was a vibration like you get when you lie on one of those "relaxing" beds or vibrator lounge chairs. It was subtle but it was there.

Knowing I was with two women who were used to kooky things, I asked them if they also felt it. I thought that possibly it might have some connection with the storm. Maybe a tornado.

Both Jan and Lisa said they felt it. We looked at each other and then I said: "You know, I'll bet there is one of your saucer friends up there and this is his way of contacting us."

Lisa agreed. "This is exactly the feeling I used to get when they would reach me through the Ouija board."

Jan rose from the table. "Let's go see," she said.

"In this sandstorm?" I asked. "We can't see the patio, let alone the stars. It's been blowing all day!"

Then Lisa was on her feet, excitedly. "But don't you hear?" she said quickly, "the wind has stopped. There is no noise at all."

I listened. She was right. The howling that had gone on continuously since midmorning had suddenly ceased. The three of us headed for the front door.

The sky was perfectly clear. There was not a cloud in it, or a grain of sand blowing. There was a calmness and a lucidity that was breathtaking.

I looked up toward the southwest and gasped. A brilliant explosion flashed briefly among the stars, but not so briefly that Jan and Lisa didn't have a chance to see it too.

Then from out of nowhere came a bright orange sphere about the size of a baseball. It traveled straight across the heavens in an absolutely horizontal position and then vanished. We were speechless. Then it appeared again, coming out of nowhere to retrace its first path. Again it vanished.

We stood there staring up at the sky. The stars hung majestically and serene. Then the wind came up again and the sand began to sting our faces. Soon dark clouds covered everything and we dashed inside to get out of the storm. It had resumed with its old intensity.

Lisa looked at me. "You realize where all this talk about saucers led us, don't you? Do you know what you were privileged to see?"

"No," I said slowly, "I'm not sure what I saw."

"Think about it," she said.

And I have been ever since.

Why California?

As I traveled from Mt. Shasta in the far north to El Centro in the far south I kept asking the mediums, mystics, healers and just plain folks *why* California should be singled out as *the* Psychic State of our Union.

The answers were vague and often plain "I don't know's." Those who did have an opinion stated it with hesitation. The majority of them agreed that it was a most psychic state while one said the vibrations were horrible and another just laughed.

Jean Hartman, the San Jose graphologist, thinks it has this reputation "because we are free to do what we want to do here. The climate helps of course but there is also a climate of freedom in cultural things. The entire atmosphere, spiritual, physical and mental is conducive to studying and expanding."

Rita Brown, the numerologist from San Jose, agrees. "Many of the people here are from the Midwest and southern states who grew up having to conform to midwestern and mid-Victorian ideas. Here in California they can do what they want. The vibrations here are such that nobody is looked down upon for *believing* in anything. Being called a kook here doesn't carry the social stigma it does in other places."

Vassily, who reads crystal balls and cards in San Francisco, thinks it has something to do with the geography of the place. "This is the remnant of both Lemuria and Mu and certain factors make California unique. For instance, the Indians here were unlike any Indians anyplace else in the United States. Mystics have proven, in the geophysical sense, that there are certain areas of the world such as Tibet that are known to produce very accurate psychic phenomena. California has long been known for this ability. California does not have the high rate of thunderstorms other states have. The electrical impulses within the atmosphere have a great deal to do with producing of phenomena. Men in a trance state need a certain amount of oxygen in their brains to produce their effects. The psychic climate exists because the right geophysical climate also exists."

Joe Koperski, the Los Angeles medium, thinks that the same strong forces that brought the early pioneers to California are now bringing the pioneers of the occult movement. He sees them coming "this time not for gold but for knowledge. They study here and are exposed to the higher teachings as nowhere else in the United States. Then they leave to set up their own centers, become teachers or live out the rest of their spirit pattern. They come and they are guided out much in the same way that the Atlanteans were guided to the font of knowledge and then out into the world. My teachers told me that."

Sue Handley, the San Francisco astrologer, thinks she has the answer. "Didn't you hear that God picked up the United States right under the East Coast and tilted it into the air? When he did that all the loose nuts rolled down into California."

Louise Huebner, the witch of Los Angeles, doesn't think it is a psychic state. "I'm basing this on my own personal involvement. I think because we are a show-business state we are able to have things happen like being appointed Official Witch and so on but as far as actually being involved in the occult I think the midwestern and the northeastern communities are more involved. Those people out there really believe in it. There's a difference between believing in it and wearing your astrological sign on your car bumper. But being the Psychic State is our reputation. I only know that in California they think I'm an actress who is making believe she's a witch but in New York City they are sure I'm a witch."

Jacob Needleman, in his masterly book *The New Religions* also tried to sum up the state's psychic powers. "One of the things which makes California unique is the degree to which all this is taking place. In all the world there is probably no other place where the 'attainment' of saisfaction occurs on such a scale.

"The thousand strange cults, sects and fads that flourish here may be seen as part of this fever of satisfying the desires and allaying fears. But among these organizations there may be some that are reaching out for something more fundamental than gratification. Of this handful of groups, some may perhaps be channels through which timeless traditions are speaking anew to modern man.

"Sooner or later we are going to have to understand California . . . We are going to have to stop thinking about it simply as a phenomenon of people leaving reality behind. Something is struggling to be born here amid all the obvious absurdity and grotesquery."

But for Macielle Brown, the San Francisco astrologer, California is what it is because the stars made it that way. Taking the chart she drew up from the hour, day and year California was declared a state (September 9, 1850 at 10:15 A.M., 6:21 P.M. Greenwich Time) she reads "the sign of Scorpio rules the ascendant and this is the typical embodiment of a state or a person. The moon, which is your subconscious, is also in the sign of Scorpio. Venus, which gives the ability to relate in an easier smoother manner, is in the sign of Scorpio and these two planets are in the twelfth house, which is considered to be the psychic sign. Virgo, oddly enough, is also a very psychic sign and the sun, which is the very heart of our state, is in Virgo, bringing in additional psychic ability. The planet Uranus, which rules astrology per se and other occult sciences, is in a degree which gives the ability to manifest the ambitions, push and drive. Sometimes it is blinded as to what is happening but still has a tremendous drive in occult directions. The sign of Gemini, which is the mind and also verbal expression, is in the eighth cusp and here you have the state right into another Scorpio influence. Neptune, which is Pisces of itself and Pisces' ruler in the sign of Pisces, is in the fourth house, which is considered to be the end of the matter or the traditions. So the whole state had . . . really . . . no choice. It is a Psychic State. It couldn't help but be!"

And There Are More

There are several practicing psychics, mystics and metaphysicians in the Psychic State who have not been included in the text for one reason or another. Mostly it was due to either a lack of time or a lack of space. I have not interviewed the majority of those listed here but each comes recommended by at least three others whose opinions I trust.

NORTHERN CALIFORNIA:

Mary Vohryzhek, astrologer. San Francisco.
Shirley Dicker, astrologer. San Francisco.
Milo Kovar, astrologer. San Francisco.
Lenora Huett, automatic writing. San Jose.
Gayne Meyers, flying saucers. Auburn.
Gayle Pierce, healer. San Jose.
Jim Jones, healer. Redwood Valley.
Dr. T. M. Collins, hypnotist. Sacramento.
Pat Healey, hypnotist. Petaluma.
Helen Wallace, "Tai-Chi-Chuan." San Francisco.
Kriya Ananda, yogi. Nevada City.
Milan Ryzl, scientific research. San Jose.

SOUTHERN CALIFORNIA:

Fred W. Andrews, reincarnation. Redlands.

Charles Berner, enlightenment. Lucerne Valley.

Reverend William Hornaday, religious science. Los Angeles.

Kathryn Kuhlman, healer. Los Angeles.

Maurice Woodruff, medium. Los Angeles.

George Daisley, medium. Santa Barbara.

Mark Probert Foundation, medium. San Diego.

Damien Simpson, Universal Mind Science. Long Beach.

Hertha Tuntland, ESP. Santa Ana.

Peter Hurkos, medium. Los Angeles.

Douglas Johnson, healer. Los Angeles.

Maya Perez, medium. Los Angeles.

Cassandra Salem, witchcraft. Huntington Beach.

Rita Norling, witchcraft. Los Angeles.

Morloch, witchcraft. Los Angeles.

Manley Palmer Hall, spiritual teacher. Los Angeles.

Bibliography

Ball, Dr. John. *Spirits and the Destruction of San Francisco.* J. Ball Publishers, San Francisco. 1906.

Bari, Valeska. *The Course of Empire.* Coward McCann, Inc., New York. 1931.

Bolen, James. "Interview: Thelma S. Moss." *Psychic* magazine, August 1970. The Bolen Co., San Francisco.

Buckley, Doris Heather. *Spirit Communication for the Millions.* Sherbourne Press Inc., Los Angeles. 1967.

Cerminara, Gina. *Many Lives, Many Loves.* William Sloane Associates, New York. 1963.

Cervé, Wishar S. *Lemuria—The Lost Continent of the Pacific.* Rosicrucian Press, Ltd., San Jose, Cal. 1931.

Craig, Marge. *Can You Learn to Be a Psychic?* Unpublished ms. 1970.

D'Angelo, Dorie. *Instant Energy through Dynamic Rhythmics.* D'Angelo Publishing Corp., Carmel, Cal. 1968.

Doane, Doris Chase. *Astrology. Thirty Years Research.* Professional Astrologers Inc., Los Angeles. 1956.

Doane, Edward. *Aquarian Age Philosophy.* Foundation of Scientific Spiritual Understanding, Redondo Beach, Cal. 1969.

Graves, J. A. *My Seventy Years in California.* Privately printed, Los Angeles. 1927.

Hart, Jerome A. *In Our Second Century.* Pioneer Press, San Francisco. 1931.

Hine, Robert V. *California's Utopian Colonies.* Yale University Press, New Haven, Conn. 1966.

Holdredge, Helen. *Mammy Pleasant.* G. P. Putnam's Sons, New York. 1953.

Huebner, Louise. *Power through Witchcraft.* Nash Publishing Corp., Los Angeles. 1969.

————. *Never Strike a Happy Medium.* Nash Publishing Corp., Los Angeles. 1970.

Jamison, Daisy. *Astrology as Taught by the Lotus Group.* Dorrance & Co., Philadelphia, Pa. 1967.

Jennings, C. Robert. "Swinging on the Stars." *Playboy,* March 1970.

Karagulla, Shafica. *Breakthrough to Creativity.* De Vorss & Co., Los Angeles. 1967.

Kazan, Nick. "The World from the Other Side." *San Francisco Magazine,* April 1970.

Kimball, Fred. *Improve Your Psychic Life.* Private printing, Los Angeles. 1965.

King, Kenneth M. *Mission to Paradise.* Franciscan Herald Press, Chicago, Ill. 1956.

LaVey, Anton Szandor. *The Satanic Bible.* Avon Books, New York. 1969.

Lloyd, B. E. *Lights and Shades in San Francisco.* A. L. Bancroft & Co., San Francisco. 1876.

Mahony, Patrick. *Who's There?* House of Words, Hollywood. 1970.

Mary. *All That You Are.* De Vorss & Co., Los Angeles. 1959.

McClure, Rosemary. "Witch Way Do We Go?" Newspaper series in the *Sun,* San Bernardino, Cal. October 1970.

Needleman, Jacob. *The New Religions.* Doubleday & Co., New York. 1970.

Parsons, George F. *The Life and Adventures of James W. Marshall.* George Fields, San Francisco. 1935.

Patterson, Major Tom. *Spirit Photography.* Regency Press, Ltd., London. 1965.

St. Clair, David. *The Mighty, Mighty Amazon.* Souvenir Press, London. 1968.

St. Clair, David. *Drum & Candle.* Doubleday & Co., Inc., New York. 1971.

Scharlach, Bernice. "Ethnic Museums." *California Living* magazine, San Francisco *Sunday Examiner & Chronicle,* San Francisco. Sept. 27, 1970.

Shaw, Bradley. *Mediums and Their Dupes.* Waldteufil Publishers, San Francisco. 1887.

Tallant, Robert. *Voodoo in New Orleans.* Macmillan Company, New York. 1946.

Walker, Danton. *I Believe in Ghosts.* Taplinger Publishing, New York. 1956.

Plus such newspapers as the San Francisco *Chronicle,* the *Examiner* (San Francisco), Los Angeles *Times,* Los Angeles *Herald-Examiner,* Anaheim *Bulletin* and the *Star Free Press* (Ventura). Also such magazines as *Psychic, Fate, Chimes, Carrier Dove* and the *TV Guide.*

Index